Personalities
on the Plate

Personalities
on the Plate

The Lives and Minds of Animals We Eat

BARBARA J. KING

The University of Chicago Press • Chicago and London

The University of Chicago Press, Chicago 60637
The University of Chicago Press, Ltd., London
Printed in the United States of America

26 25 24 23 22 21 20 19 18 17   1 2 3 4 5

ISBN-13: 978-0-226-19518-6 (cloth)
ISBN-13: 978-0-226-19521-6 (e-book)
DOI: 10.7208/chicago/9780226195216.001.0001

Library of Congress Cataloging-in-Publication Data

Names: King, Barbara J., 1956– author.
Title: Personalities on the plate : the lives and minds of animals we eat / Barbara J. King.
Description: Chicago ; London : The University of Chicago Press, 2017. | Includes
bibliographical references and index.
Identifiers: LCCN 2016034780| ISBN 9780226195186 (cloth : alk. paper) | ISBN
9780226195216 (e-book)
Subjects: LCSH: Food animals—Social aspects. | Animal behavior.
Classification: LCC SF41 .K553 2017 | DDC 636.088/3—dc23 LC record available at
https://lccn.loc.gov/2016034780

♾ This paper meets the requirements of ANSI/NISO Z39.48-1992 (Permanence of Paper).

For Charlie and Sarah
Always

"The meat defiant, the meat insurgent, the meat fighting, Sofia thought. The meat in full cry. . . .

Sitting by his head, she ran her hand along the fine soft fur of his cheek, over and over, while his body cooled and she paid the awful debt of love."

Maria Doria Russell, *Children of God* (sequel to *The Sparrow*)

Contents

Introduction

*We never seem to doubt that an animal acting
hungry feels hungry. What reason is there to disbelieve
that an elephant who seems happy is happy?*

Carl Safina, *Beyond Words: What Animals Think and Feel*

The barbecued meat (*nyama chama* in Swahili) kept coming, carved right at our table. The pork and chicken were familiar enough, the rabbit and venison less so. Ox and zebra? To our eyes, exotic.

It was a cool Nairobi night in 1986, and my mother, Elizabeth; my Aunt Barbara, for whom I am named; one of my dearest college friends, Jim; and I had ventured to Carnivore Restaurant. Upon arrival, our little group was ushered to an outdoor patio. At first I worried that the air might be too chill, but how gloriously inviting it was to dine under open skies! The staff even provided tableside braziers to warm us.

"Waiter after waiter came with meat on huge skewers," my mother wrote that night in her travel diary, a tiny notebook that now, after her death, I cherish along with her other keepsakes. "They removed pieces or cut chunks out of huge pieces of meat, 10 kinds altogether." I'm pretty sure we ate antelope too. Kudu was once served at Carnivore-Nairobi and remains on the menu at Carnivore-Johannesburg in South Africa.

Despite the Kenyan government ban on serving game, ostrich and crocodile are brought to diners' tables even now at Carnivore-Nairobi.

Back in 1986, I was living several hours' drive south of Kenya's capital in Amboseli National Park, near the border with Tanzania. From my backyard, which often hosted wildebeest and zebra and sometimes elephant, the volcanic peaks of Mount Kilimanjaro loomed big and beautiful. At Carnivore, I was enjoying a brief holiday in the midst of a fourteen-month monkey-watching stint. My project focused on how infant baboons learn what fruits, grasses, and tubers to eat as they roam the savannah with family members and group-mates. For a graduate student in anthropology, carrying out this research at Amboseli was a dream come true. Enthralled not just with the primates that the National Science Foundation had funded me to study, but also with the park's elephants, lions, Cape buffalo, ostrich, warthogs, and marabou storks, I animal-watched purely for fun whenever I could steal some time from science. To sit quietly and try to work out who was friends or rivals with whom, or what the animals' sounds and body language meant, was pure joy. On my rare days off, when I wasn't in Nairobi to Xerox and mail data back home (no scanning and emailing in those days!), I would sit outdoors and soak up what the African plains had to teach me.

And yet at Carnivore, sitting outdoors with loved ones who had endured a twenty-two-hour Pan Am flight from New York in order to visit me, that sense of wonder and connection with other animals fell away. I didn't see *animals* on the plates set before us, I saw (and smelled) *meat*—and a chance for an animal-tasting adventure that would yield a good story back home.

An invisible toggle switch had flipped in my brain, one that I wasn't aware of, much less able to reflect upon: Barbara the avid observer of animals became Barbara the voracious eater of animals. That memory makes me uncomfortable now, especially because I enthusiastically consumed individuals of the very same species I so loved to observe running wild in Amboseli.

Of course, the evening at Carnivore wasn't the first, or last, time I did something like that. How many barnyard or ocean animals did I avidly watch or read about, then eat, over the years? That peculiar duality comes easily to our species. When touring Yellowstone, the 2.2-million-acre national park that spills across the borders of Wyoming, Montana, and Idaho, my foremost passion is bison-watching. For hours, my husband and I observe the heavy-shouldered males as with raw power they engage females—or their big bull rivals for those females. The females themselves huddle with their youngsters, who romp away from the moms to play in the meadow. In Yellowstone's Lamar Valley, we once stood pressed against our car as a bison herd of more than a hundred individuals flowed close around us. (To actively approach wild bison is a mistake that people may pay for by being tossed in the air by sharp horns, sometimes fatally; in our once-in-a-lifetime experience, the bison chose to walk calmly past us.) Usually, we watch from inside a car stationed in a snaking length of other wildlife enthusiasts' vehicles. If we break for dinner at a park restaurant, happily sharing our descriptions and photographs of that day's most majestic animals, right there on the menu are the bison's ranched counterparts. We always select the pasta.

On another trip, leaving Everglades National Park in south Florida, we drove roads that cut through the greater Everglades ecosystem. We flashed past signs for roadside family businesses that tout airboat tours: See beautiful alligators in the morning! Enjoy "gator nuggets" at midday! This kind of thing, what I've called our "peculiar duality" in relation to other animals, is ubiquitous. Aquarium-goers admire the tentacle beauty of an octopus, the planet's smartest invertebrate, then order grilled baby octopus at lunch. Parents read their children bedtime stories starring sweet chicks or plucky pigs only hours after having served chicken or pork for dinner.

Psychologist Hal Herzog titled his book about our relationship with other animals *Some We Love, Some We Hate, Some We Eat*, and nails it in a sentence: "Human attitudes toward other species are inevitably paradoxical and inconsistent." We love the dog and eat the pig, or, we love the bison and eat the bison. Who exactly *are* these someones about whom we are so conflicted? The newest science from anthropology, psychology, and zoology can help us tackle that question by showing us how the animals we eat—for some the octopus or the chimpanzee, for many others the chicken and the goat—think, feel, and act as distinct individual beings. *Who are we eating?*

This book isn't an attempt to rank animals according to some abstract standard of what it might mean to be a smart, feeling creature. Nor is it a primer on who to eat and who not to eat. Instead, it's an invitation to see clearly who we eat, and our connections with animals who, in their different ways, experience the world with awareness and intention. These connections are easily obscured in a world where most of us encounter the animals we eat as shrink-wrapped products in a grocery store. "Forgetting, or not knowing in the first place, is what the industrial food chain is all about," writes Michael Pollan in *The Omnivore's Dilemma*. As we will see, though, it's not *only* the industrial food chain. It's good to take a hard look at all the whos we eat, no matter the path by which they arrive at our table.

When I write about animals, some readers of my articles and blog posts assume, and assert, that I have an agenda: Deep down, I want everyone to become vegetarian or, better yet, vegan. Though wrong, this assumption deserves a thoughtful reply.

More plants and less meat. This is advice we hear over and over as a key step toward improving our own health, the health of our planet, and the welfare of the animals all around us. In its Environment Program (UNEP) report of 2010, the United Nation recommends shifting our diet away from animal proteins toward more plant foods "in order to dramatically reduce pressures on the environment." For UNEP, a central concern (along with issues of fossil fuels) is the raising and processing of animals as livestock, because these animals are fed more than half of all the world's crops and require a staggering amount of water. Notably, the UNEP recommends not just that we work to reduce stress on our resources and other negative impacts of agricultural system, but also that each of us acts at the root and embraces a *dietary* shift.

The UN isn't alone. In the United States, the Dietary Guidelines Advisory Committee's 2015 report urges lowered intake of salt, saturated fats, and, especially sugar, then adds a kicker: a vegetarian diet as a shining example of healthy eating. Food activists, global and local, echo these urgings; probably most famous of all is Michael Pollan's streamlined dictum: "Eat food. Not too much. Mostly plants."

I aim to follow Pollan's advice. Of the eight types of animals profiled in this book—insects, octopus, fish, chicken, goats, cows, pigs, and chimpanzees—I eat one: fish. More accurately, in large part owing to a complicated health history that includes a struggle to recover from recent extensive chemotherapy and radiation, I eat certain types of fish now and again. In carrying out research for the chapter on insects, I purposefully sampled crickets and grasshoppers and, like everyone else, have since childhood swallowed scores of insects that unintentionally hitchhike on agricultural products (see chapter 1). Will I sample more insect dishes in the future? I'm not yet sure. At least to my knowledge and memory, I have never eaten octopus, goat, or chimpanzee; when I was offered monkey meat at a restaurant in Gabon, West Africa, I requested chicken instead. That "swap" (refusing a primate like me, but readily consuming a bird less like me) I made in 1984. Chickens, cows, and pigs I haven't eaten for more than five years now.

For reasons ranging from environmental health to animal sentience, I see reduced meat-eating as a superb and necessary goal. Many paths, ranging from veganism and vegetarianism to people's choosing to eat more plants and less meat than they did before, may move us in that direction. (I explore this stance in more detail in the afterword.)

I just used the term "animal sentience." But what does that mean? What do I mean by intelligence, emotion, and personality when writing about nonhuman animals? Animal behaviorists certainly don't speak with a unified voice when they define these terms—a sign, I should underscore, of the vibrant debate that is part of healthy scientific practice, not of any fundamental confusion. Still, the best bet here is to go with plainly understood definitions already in wide currency. Excellent ones are presented by Carl Safina at the start of his book *Beyond Words: What Animals Think and Feel.*

Sentience is the ability to feel sensations like pleasure and pain.

Cognition is the capacity to perceive and acquire knowledge and understanding.

Thought is the process of considering something that's been perceived. As this definition implies, and as science writer Virginia Morell also emphasizes in *Animal Wise: The Thoughts and Emotions of Our Fellow Creatures*, thinking is not dependent on language.

To these Safina added, in an email exchange with me:

Emotion is how we feel about our perceptions.

Safina emphasizes that these dimensions of experience are found on a sliding scale in the animal world. We shouldn't expect octopus sentience to be identical to chimpanzee sentience, or pig intelligence to closely resemble cow intelligence—or any nonhuman animal's intelligence to be identical to our own.

Personality is another key term. It doesn't refer to a chicken's ability to work a room and charm everyone in it—except, as we'll see in chapter 4, when it *does!* Generally, though, personality refers to the stable ways that an individual feels, thinks, and acts in the world in regards to things like extraversion versus introversion or agreeableness versus antagonism.

Some psychologists contrast an animal's biologically rooted temperament with personality, which is seen as more open to modification by what an animal experiences during life. With occasional exceptions, the single term *personality* works well for this book, with the understanding that the relatively stable patterns in question may come about through a mix of life experiences and inborn genetic factors. I add personality to the dimensions I consider because seeing animals as individuals who may be distinct one from the other in their dispositions and behavioral tendencies is another way, in addition to learning how they are smart and how they feel, that we can train ourselves to *see* the complexities of animals' lives.

The need for clear-eyed seeing is the central message I want to bring forth in the pages to come: it takes effort, and it pays off, to *see* the animals we designate as our food. Even as we bring them to our family tables and our restaurants in their anonymous billions, other animals sense, and sometimes suffer; learn, and sometimes love; think, and sometimes reflect. Their lives matter to them, and they should matter to us too.

1. Insects & Arachnids

THE BUGS WE EAT

Fried wild-caught dragon flies and spider rolls featuring rose-haired tarantulas, katydid-and-grilled-cheese sandwiches and tacos stuffed with grasshoppers: The variety of foods laced with insects and spiders available in the United States and Europe today—when you go looking for them—is considerable. The venues in which they may be found are equally varied, ranging from upscale restaurants to streetside food carts and science-museum bug festivals. Entomophagy is on the rise and generating excitement.

I've not been adventuresome enough to try anything like tarantulas for lunch. One spring day in 2014, though, a package showed up for me with a return address in Austin, Texas, and I knew it was time to take an entomophage's baby step: I was about to eat crickets. Or at least, cookies with crickets baked into them.

At the time, I didn't yet know that crickets are "the latest nerd cuisine trend," as Xeni Jardin puts it. I had noticed in the media a small but dedicated band of entomophagy enthusiasts, including scientists, chefs, and writers who sing the praises of insect-eating. These enthusiasts aim not only at the exotic-food eaters among us—those who eagerly seek live octopus or pig uterus—but also adults with more conservative palates, and children who might think it's just that cool to swallow bugs. One insect-cuisine champion, Robert Nathan Allen of Little Herds, an Austin-based nonprofit organization that promotes insect farming, kindly sent me the cookies, which he had baked himself.

I knew that eating the crickets wouldn't count as my first episode of insect ingestion. It's just that all previous instances came about by accident, a by-product of the nature of our food supply. The statistics make insectivores of us all: the FDA deems it perfectly acceptable for peanut butter to host thirty insect fragments per hundred grams, and twice that amount is allowed in a comparable serving of chocolate. Considering how much of these two foods I've downed over the decades, it's clear that insects were no strangers to my digestive tract, even before the cookies' arrival.

Likewise, anyone who regularly eats fresh vegetables ingests an occasional mini-animal-protein-package along with their intended meal. Once, sharing dinner with my mother in a senior-living facility dining room here in Virginia, I moved a leaf of lettuce across my salad plate and was startled to spot a large beetle nestled calmly in the greens. Noting with some relief the intact nature of its body—no ingestion of any bit of this insect had occurred—I planned to quietly ask the serving staff for a replacement salad. This scheme was thwarted when my mother, a confirmed insectophobe of eighty years, caught sight of the beetle and—I'll fall back on the word "ruckus" to convey what happened next.

Deliberate ingestion of insects, however, felt to me wholly different. It's not that the cookies were repulsive in appearance or made me squeamish; they looked like, well, cookies. The crickets were baked into small, round, chocolate-chipped-studded shapes. The ingredients, save one, were entirely unsurprising: potato flour, brown rice flour, tapioca flour, coconut flour, sugar, brown sugar, butter, eggs, vanilla, baking soda, chocolate chips, and salt—plus cricket flour.

The cookies tasted good. I can't say they rivaled the best chocolate chip cookies ever made, because those are baked at Delicious Orchards in Colts Neck, New Jersey. But that's, in a way, exactly the point: Those New Jersey cookies are delicious to me in part because they come from my home state, indeed from Monmouth County where I grew up, and even more specifically, from a market, now on tourists' as well as locals' radar, that offers everything from fresh fruits and vegetables to breads, pies, and cookies. Those chocolate chip cookies were the ones my parents brought to me when I ventured twenty-eight miles northwest to attend Douglass College, and felt homesick for familiar things. Now, four decades later, when I travel from Virginia back home to New Jersey, a visit to Delicious Orchards is a high point for my own family; those still-perfect cookies unlock treasured memories.

The foods each of us loves, and the foods we love to hate, are about so much more than flavor—a theme central to this book. Many of us eat pigs and cows without a second thought but blanch at the idea of consuming chimpanzees—or insects.

For Little Herds to offer insects in familiar cookie shapes, mixed with chocolate chips (which might contain their own insect fragments!), makes good marketing sense. That's the logic as well at a cricket farm in Youngstown, Ohio, established in 2014 as the first in the United States to raise crickets specifically for human consumption. For entomophagy novices, cricket cookies—or, in the case of the Youngstown operation, cricket chips—may be far more palatable than food items that feature recognizable insect parts. It worked for me, anyway. To the extent that I can disentangle all the cultural overlays from the actual taste of the cookies, I would evaluate them as appealing, with a specific flavor I find hard to describe: slightly nutty, maybe, with a granular texture that I am guessing comes from the cricket flour.

Still, I'm sympathetic to the shivery reactions some people may voice to the practice of insect-eating, or even to day-to-day encounters with insects. As disappointing as I find this in myself, I'm less than calm around some of the bigger flying insects or spiders with large leg spans. It's not so much that I fear stings or bites as that I experience a visceral response deep in my nervous system that compels me to put distance between myself and the small animal in question. The scientific notion of "here's a creature interesting to observe and learn about" comes to me eventually, but on a sort of cognitive delay: the shiver comes first. (I still manage to rescue even the most formidable spiders trapped in our house and deposit them outdoors, but it requires some deep breathing on my part.)

This response makes evolutionary sense—our ancestors who were cautious around stinging, biting creatures may have survived longer and (most importantly) enjoyed greater reproductive success, and today we are dealing with a carryover effect. In another way, though, it is very strange. Insects, mostly harmless to us, are everywhere, even in our modern sheltered-from-nature lives. When fifty homeowners in or near Raleigh, North Carolina, volunteered their houses for an entomology study in 2012, the results were striking: over ten thousand specimens were collected in total—some living, some deceased. More than a hundred species of insects, spiders, centipedes and millipedes, and crustaceans like pill bugs were often found in a single home. Flies and beetles, ants, book lice, moths, silverfish, stinkbugs, cockroaches, cobweb spiders, and of course dust mites were among the common inhabitants. Crickets were less common, and bedbugs were absent entirely. The researchers who carried out the work, led by Michelle Trautwein from the North Carolina Museum of Natural Sciences and Rob Dunn and Matthew Bertone from North Carolina State University, concluded that many of us live inside a veritable, insect-favoring natural history museum. Shouldn't we habituate after a while?

Millions of people around the world do seek out insects and regularly, intentionally consume them. They do not pluck bugs from under the bed or the dusty attic, of course, but forage for sources of fresh protein and other nutrients in the wild or purchase prepared insects or insect flour at traditional markets. With a little help from anthropology, we may identify a global panoply of flavors that insects can provide to our palates.

ENTOMOPHAGY AROUND THE WORLD

Humans eat over sixteen hundred species of insects. "The Western abhorrence of eating insects is unusual on a global scale," note naturalist David Raubenheimer and anthropologist Jessica M. Rothman. Westerners may clamor for honey without fully recognizing that when ingesting it they are consuming regurgitated bee products, but people in many countries consciously embrace a wide variety of bugs as food. Raubenheimer and Rothman's cross-cultural report on entomophagy is stuffed full of intriguing data and forms the basis for my discussion of insect-eating patterns in this section.

The percentage of dietary protein people acquire from insects varies widely from population to population: up to 26 percent seasonally in parts of the Amazon region and perhaps as high as 64 percent in parts of the Democratic Republic of Congo. Yet it would be a mistake to connect entomophagy only with people who live in so-called undeveloped societies. The traditional diet in Japan and Thailand, for example, still includes insects. Thailand is a fascinating place for entomophiles. Regional preferences exist for different insects, but the giant water bug is eaten across the nation. Crickets are popular too and may be offered for commercial sale in abundant numbers. "400 families in two villages," Raubenheimer and Rothman report, "produce 10 metric tons of crickets in the peak production period, both for the domestic market and export."

Crickets are one thing. The idea of eating a giant water bug seems far more formidable to me, though I recognize this judgment is again a culturally grounded one. The Entomophagy Wiki project offers a video of a person called Bug Nomster who consumes on-camera a "massive" water bug, boiled and dehydrated and sold commercially in a silver pouch. Bug Nomster first bites into the posterior end of the intact bug, then decides to remove the legs and wings in order to get at the interior meat. He tastes "a hint of apple" but decides overall that the bug, in this desiccated form, offers too little meat in too much shell, and concludes that fresh-fried water bugs would be preferable. Beyond the lukewarm review, the video prompted me to wonder if consuming a water bug at home differs so very much from cracking into a lobster at a fine restaurant? Many people might covet the lobster as a delicacy but reject the water bug as a disgusting snack. Yet both these animals (and crab and shrimp, and insects too) are arthropods—animals with a shell, a segmented body, and jointed limbs. (Full disclosure: I don't eat lobster, thus this bit of comparative reasoning implies no necessity of my consuming water bugs for consistency's sake!)

Bug Nomster's comment about the giant water bug's shell illustrates a key point. Amid a great deal of cross-cultural variability—including whether insects are eaten as staples, as fallback foods in hard times, or as delicacies—one general rule is that people prefer insects at the peak size of their life cycle and those with the lowest proportion of exoskeleton. (The water bug, in its prepackaged form, succeeds on the first point but loses points on the second.) These preferences make good sense, as larger-package protein makes the energy expended in acquiring and processing insects more worthwhile, and the exoskeleton or shell must be distressingly crunchy for some tastes—a factor I didn't have to contend with when eating cookies made with cricket flour. The exoskeletons were in the flour, to be sure, but so finely ground that the crunch factor was entirely absent.

When I lived in a national park in Kenya in order to carry out my research, I observed the behavior not only of baboons but of tourists, most of whom quested to see the "Big Five"—lion, leopard, elephant,

Cape buffalo, and rhinoceros. I was thus amused to learn that there is also a "Big Five" of the entomophagy world. Of all insects, species in five orders—Coleoptera (beetles), Hymenoptera (ants, wasps and bees), Isoptera (termites), Lepidoptera (butterflies and moths), and Orthoptera (grasshoppers, crickets, locusts, and katydids)—show up most regularly in human diets. These insects tend to occur in abundance, often (except for Coleoptera) in large clusters, and are rich sources of protein, fat, and micronutrients, although species variation in nutritional content is considerable.

Entomophagy, as it catches on outside traditional cultural practices, builds on some of these patterns, yet there's an edgy new element to some of the current fascination. After all, Bug Nomster isn't in Thailand partaking of the local cuisine: he's showcasing his experimental entomophagy for, presumably, a heavily Western viewing audience. His fans include serious food enthusiasts—chefs and their customers who crave new dining experiences and work hard to bring them about.

Dining on escamoles is a good example. Often referred to as giant ant eggs, they are more correctly understood as ant larvae (species *Liometopum apiculatum*). In Mexico, escamoles were popular in Aztec times and are still highly prized. Looking a bit like pine nuts, they are often described as slightly nutty in flavor. (Are most insects nut-flavored, like my cookie-embedded crickets?) These larvae can't be bought easily in the United States. When writer Dana Goodyear shadowed Laurent Quenioux, a French-born chef now cooking in California, the pair sought escamoles from Mexico. Quenioux "knew a guy," Goodyear writes, "who knew a guy who would bring them across the border from Tijuana; we simply had to drive down to a meeting place on the US side and escort them back." In other words, the delicacies were smuggled into the country. Once at the pickup site, Quenioux exchanged a $100 bill for a half kilo of frozen larvae. This shipment ended up as part of a tiny dish graced also by Japanese noodles; at other times, Quenioux may prepare a corn tortilla

Cricket-topped dessert at Montreal Insectarium. Photo courtesy of Norman Fashing, College of William and Mary.

with escamoles among the ingredients. Part of the zest with which Quenioux cooks these dishes stems, Goodyear makes clear, from the illicit nature of the goods—and a profile of Quenioux in *LA Weekly* (as well as Goodyear's book) makes it plain that his smuggling has been a fairly routine practice.

A major report on future prospects for entomophagy, released in 2013 by the Food and Agriculture Organization of the United Nations (FAO), notes that tamping down sensationalism when promoting insect-eating is a worthy goal. It's a fine line between sensationalism and pure excitement when it comes to any cuisine, I admit: does Bug Nomster cross the line into sensationalism by posting online a video of himself biting off the end of a massive water bug? Are the smuggled *escamoles* as much about the thrill of the illicit as they are about flavor? While it's hard to know, it *is* nice to visit restaurants that incorporate insects into their menus without hype and hoopla.

Oyamel Cocina Mexicana in the Penn Quarter neighborhood of Washington, DC, is just such a restaurant. Stepping inside on a cool June evening in 2014, my friend Stephen Wood and I were immersed in the colors and smells of Oaxaca, Mexico. *Oyamel* is the name of the fir tree native to central Mexico where monarch butterflies rest upon migrating from the United States and Canada, and the décor had a lepidopteran theme: the glass door at the entrance was studded with transparent red, yellow, and pink butterflies, and butterfly mobiles hung from the ceiling.

But it wasn't butterflies that Stephen and I had come to sample. Our quest focused on *chapulines*, soft tacos stuffed with grasshoppers. Taking our order, the waitress noted our luck: the grasshoppers sometimes get held up coming through customs from Mexico, but that night they were readily available. Stephen and I ordered a number of small, *tapas*-like dishes, and when the *chapulines* arrived, I saw insect body parts right away. A delicate grasshopper leg tumbled onto the table when I raised the taco to my mouth.

So long to the land of cricket cookies. Here was the crunch factor at last! To our mild frustration, neither Stephen nor I could summon the adequate vocabulary to convey the grasshoppers' taste. What stayed with me was the sound (the crunch), the texture (many insects to chew), a smoky taste, and a spicy heat, which stemmed not from the insects but from the guacamole. Hot foods don't agree well with me, so I contented myself with eating only part of the grasshopper taco, then moving on to entirely delicious Mexican potatoes.

As I dined at Oyamel, I pondered some questions not often addressed by fans of entomophagy, whether they write popular books or government reports, or make edible art in the kitchen. What happens when we view insects through the lens of "animals we eat," as we do for chickens or pigs? What do we know about insect intelligence, personality, and sentience?

The ants, grasshoppers, spiders, and crickets that appear in prepared edibles are not much like the other animals we will consider in this book. They don't utilize underwater tools like octopuses or exhibit easily recognizable (to us) emotions like joy or grief as do farm animals. To include insects in a book that also embraces our supersmart, emotional, highly individual closest living relatives the chimpanzees takes us from one end of the thinking-and-feeling animal continuum way over to the other.

And can we really imagine anyone mourning the crickets baked into the Little Herds cookies or the grasshoppers that grace Oyamel's tacos the way we grieve for our companion animals once they die? Or for individuals of charismatic species like pandas or gorillas, whose deaths may be met with an intensely compassionate response in the media? Very few of us go around naming insects we encounter—or considering them as distinct individuals. Can we imagine, for that matter, insects mourning each other in ways akin to those I documented in *How Animals Grieve*, which explored the emotions expressed by animals as diverse as dogs, ducks, and dolphins?

The first step in taking these questions seriously is *seeing* these tiny animals. Yasmin Cardozo, an entomologist at North Carolina State University, grew up in Honduras. As a child, insects were among her first toys; in imaginary play she went about "collecting June bugs to treat as seriously injured hospital patients." We can picture this little girl interacting with her many-legged or winged "patients," an image that underscores how wide may be the range of our interactions with insects. And it's not only in "other" cultures that children interact with—or at least observe—insects with enthusiasm. Growing up in the New Jersey suburbs, I loved whiling away an hour watching the scurrying yet remarkably well-organized activity visible within an Ant Farm, peering into anthills in the yard to trace the stream of red ants as they flowed in and out, and watching fireflies on a summer's night as they blinked messages in code through the humid air. What I *don't* remember is thinking of any of these small creatures as individuals; they existed for me in an abstracted sort of aggregate, in a way that my pet cat Queen and dog Shadow, or even the elephants and monkeys I met on family trips to the Bronx Zoo, never did.

Insects aren't primates like chimpanzees (or us), and they aren't, usually, our pets. What might happen, though, if we tap into our natural curiosity about insects and spiders and ask how they live on their own terms? We do these tiny animals a disservice if we fail to ask questions that only relatively recently in recorded history have humans begun to ask about chimpanzees (or cats and dogs). Do insects learn? How do they interact with their world in intelligent ways? Do they experience the world via distinct personalities?

INSECT INTELLIGENCE

Wasps may strike us as buzzing, sometimes stinging, annoyances when we spend time outdoors. But there's another way to look at them: as animal with busy brains. Paper wasps, with a brain less than 0.01 percent the size of our own, recognize individuals who are important to them. Neurobiologist Elizabeth Tibbetts discovered this fact when she altered wasps' facial features by applying modeling paint to them. Nestmates of these suddenly different-looking wasps responded in an atypically aggressive way, while their behavior toward control wasps, who were daubed with paint but whose facial features remained unaltered, didn't change at all. The specificity of the hostile response indicated that the wasps recognized faces, using that recognition to determine who belonged in their community. Nestmates with painted faces were suddenly seen as strangers, and the reactions were not friendly.

Queens of the species of wasp used by Tibbetts in this experiment (*Polistes fuscatus*) work together cooperatively within shared nests, but they also experience female-female competition. Facial recognition is adaptive in this context because queens need to distinguish potential rivals from potential allies. Tibbetts went on to train these wasps to distinguish pairs of images of various sorts. "Most strikingly," she and her coauthor Adrian Dryer write, "simply removing the antennae from a wasp face image or rearranging the face components dramatically reduced their impressive face-learning capacity." This fact suggests to Tibbetts and Dryer that the wasps process faces holistically in specialized parts of the brain, as we humans do.

Tibbetts then expanded her study to include a second species of wasp (*Polistes metricus*) in which solitary queens—instead of clusters—establish nests. In this case, paint-altered nestmates elicited no immediate facial-recognition response. But here's the fascinating part: in the training phase, these wasps did learn to discriminate faces. Presumably, this ability had not been directly selected for in this species over evolutionary time. The mental capacity is there but doesn't emerge under natural conditions. Reviewing studies of wasps and bees in general, Tibbetts and Dryer conclude that "there is ever so much more going on their teensy brains than we could have imagined possible."

Does that conclusion apply to other insects? Yes, if we're talking about learning. In entomology, learning is defined as the ability to acquire, and represent in one's brain, new information. Historically, the working assumptions in entomology were all about instinct. The reigning equation "simple nervous systems = behaviors driven by hard-wired instinct" was straightforward enough—and also spectacularly wrong.

One spring morning when I was writing this section, my Twitter stream lit up with the news that fruit flies make decisions, and what's more, they take longer to do so when the information presented is difficult to evaluate. In an ingenious experiment, fruit fly subjects were first trained to avoid a certain strong smell, then offered a choice between two samples of that smell whose intensities varied by degrees. The insects took longer to make their choice when the difference in smell was subtle (or minimal) than when it was pronounced (or maximal). Neuroscientist Shamik DasGupta and his team concluded that the experimental outcome "bears the behavioral signature of evidence accumulation." In other words, these insects wait until they have gathered enough information to make a reasonable choice when presented with options that complicate decision-making. This weighing of variables according to context is linked in the fruit flies to one specific gene (*FoxP*) and about 0.1 percent of the flies' total neuron count—right around two hundred neurons.

Far more famous an example of insect learning is the honeybees' waggle dance. In this case, the acquiring of new information happens socially. Performing in the dark hive, the dancers, experienced forager bees, clue in younger, naïve bees about how far to fly, and in what direction, to find suitable flowers. Thanks to scientific experiments, we know that the dances do not operate like the GPS devices that send us, via detailed driving instructions, to a pinpoint location. Instead, they convey information that directs the observer bees to the right general region. There, the flowers themselves provide sight and smell cues; the bees zero in on these beacons and begin to forage.

Decision-making fruit flies and information-sharing bees are joined by a host of other examples: learning, both individual and social, is a robust phenomenon in the insect world. At the end of a 2008 review paper, Reuven Dukas concludes, "Learning is probably a universal property of insects, which rely on learning for all major life functions." Don't be thrown by that qualifying word "probably"—we scientists are trained to assume that we can't know what *always* happens, even when we do know what *almost always* happens. Dukas is exhibiting appropriate caution. Even so, he expands his assertion soon enough, writing that the "widespread assertion" that insects' small brains and short lifetimes prevent them from learning "has been rejected" by new data.

No mindless drones, insects are intelligent in the sense that they evaluate information coming into their senses and their brains from their physical and social environment, and in some striking cases, they think about how to act on the information they have learned.

THE PERSONALITY OF BUGS

Given my culinary connection to crickets, it was startling to come upon this provocative sentence at the top of a science-news post on the BBC Nature website: *The experiences of youth can change the adult personalities of crickets, a new study has found.* The very fact that biologist Nicholas DiRienzo and his colleagues had hypothesized such a connection tells us something important—that established animal-behavior researchers by now *expect* indicators of personality to be found in some insect species.

DiRienzo explains in a technical article published in *Animal Behaviour* that degree of boldness—an organism's willingness to expose itself to risk—is a trait expressed consistently in individual crickets at different ages and in different situations. Boldness tends to co-occur with aggression. "We consider aggressiveness to be a personality trait in this species," the researchers note, "particularly since aggressiveness and boldness are correlated and thus form a behavioral syndrome."

The scientists experimentally manipulated the sounds experienced by young crickets (*Gryllus integer*, commonly found in the American West). They started with males too young to have yet developed an ear, called a tympanum and located in crickets on the front legs. As they were reared, the crickets were separated into two groups: those in one group had a chorus of male calls played to them, mimicking what they would have heard in the wild; those in the other group experienced only silence.

The males reared *without* hearing the cricket chorus, referred to as "acoustic sexual signals" because the calls are uttered during male-male competition for females, were more aggressive and more likely to become dominant. I enjoyed reading the details of this experiment, imagining the researchers at work avidly watching cricket male-male grappling matches, the events through which they assessed aggression levels. But I couldn't work out on my own *why* males reared in silence should be better and more dominant grapplers.

DiRienzio and his coauthors, it turns out, think that crickets use the sounds they hear—or don't hear—to figure out population density. The crickets who hear nothing assume that they will face little competition from other males in their forays to find females, and act accordingly—asserting greater dominance than they would if they had discerned evidence of greater competition around them. In other words, signals from the surrounding environment alter cricket personality.

Now, measuring levels of boldness and aggressiveness in crickets admittedly affords a limited perspective on animal personality. Hanging out with crickets, we would not likely feel that we were in the presence of highly distinct individuals the way we would with chickens or chimpanzees. Some animals vary one from the other along more complex dimensions, not just bold/less bold or aggressive/less aggressive, but gregarious/socially shy, emotionally volatile/phlegmatic, spiteful/easygoing, and so on.

Insects are not, though, cookie-cutter copies of each other when it comes to their ways of being in the world. The chorusing-cricket experiment shows that personality is not merely a matter of in-born genetics, because the rearing environment plays a role. (Recall from the preface that for some scientists, animal *personality* is affected in part by the environment, whereas animal *temperament* stems from genetics.) In short, when I ate those cricket cookies, I swallowed animals who had experienced the world in some individualistic ways. In this, crickets are not alone among insects and spiders.

"Tarantulas tend to taste somewhat like smoky lobster," reports Daniella Martin. Based on the involuntary shudder reaction I have mentioned—while I am fascinated by insects' and arachnids' biology and evolution, and try to minimize harming these animals (with some exceptions, including mosquitoes), I need to repress shivers when I get close to them—I'm not going to experiment any time soon in order to find out if I agree with her description.

My reaction is, once again, culture-bound. No documented death of a person has ever come about because of a tarantula bite. Yes, these are large animals for arachnids (the biggest known boasts a leg span of twelve inches and a weight of five ounces), and their hairy appearance can be startling. Negative reactions to tarantulas based on their size and physical traits may be exacerbated when there's no great fondness in the surrounding culture for these creatures. 'Thanks in part to Jiminy Cricket," Martin notes, "[crickets] have pretty good PR in Western society." Tarantulas have anything but.

Yet the tarantula's hairiness *should* lead to fascination rather than fear, because it's a lovely example of evolution at work: tarantulas don't build webs but like other spiders they do sense their world largely through vibrations; the hairs help detect those and thus help the animal capture prey. I learned these and other cool tarantula facts from an online interview with Nicole Atteberry, curator of ectotherms at Zoo Miami. Atteberry went on to distinguish between shy and aggressive tarantulas, evoking tarantula personality.

The key here is to find a reasonable balance in how we think about insects' individuality. Samuel Marshall, an arachnologist who has studied wild tarantulas in French Guinea (considered by some the tarantula capital of the world) and has clocked countless hours with tarantulas in the lab, cautions that because of their rudimentary nervous systems, we shouldn't go too far down the road of thinking in cognitive or emotional terms about tarantulas. He doesn't believe, for example, that tarantulas can become anxious or depressed in the way many vertebrate creatures may. Talking with *Discover Magazine* in 2004, however, he embraced the word "personality" as applying, for example, to how different tarantulas from a single population of the same species respond to handling. These variable tendencies form part of a suite of potentially fairly complex behaviors. Two of Marshall's students, Melissa Varrecchia and Barbara Vasquez, discovered that Indian ornamental tarantulas prefer to associate with their siblings over other possible companions. "Long-lived, giant spiders," Marshall said at the time, "have a lot more going on than we have any idea of."

In exploring the science of spider personality, I contacted Marshall, who, in the wonderful way of science networking, sent me on to Susan Riechert, a spider biologist at the University of Tennessee–Knoxville. "As spider behavior is highly repeatable," Riechert told me, "it has a very strong heritable component and thus I always refer to spider behavioral tendencies as temperament." The "always" in her statement startled me because, as I have understood it from other scientists, environment does sometimes influence spider behavior. The comment conveys, though, that variability within a species' repertoire doesn't invariably stem from *learned* complexity. One of the coolest bits of research I've read in a long time demonstrates this neatly: Riechert's and Thomas Jones's paper on variation in spider social organization shows (in this specific case) an imperviousness to environmental influence.

Riechert and Jones study *Anelosimus studiosus*, a social spider found in North and South American forests. In this species, there's maternal care, which is atypical for spiders: the mothers guard their young offspring and offer them food via regurgitation. When the mother dies, a dominant daughter often assumes control of the nest and forces out her siblings. Working in the United States, the scientists identified two *studiosus* sites (each with many spider nests), accessible by water, at 2-degree intervals in latitude, from south Florida's Everglades (26 degrees) to east Tennessee (36 degrees). Solitary nests were, they discovered, the most frequent type at all latitudes. The presence of multifemale nests and a cooperative-female social structure was first found at 30 degrees and increased in frequency as latitude increased.

With a laboratory phase added to the field research, the results get really interesting. Riechert and Jones collected nests from two cold-water and two warm-water sites, and raised the juveniles from those nests in the lab. Then they transplanted this second generation back into the wild at various latitudes. In this way, some of the juveniles from solitary nests were transplanted to latitudes where multifemale nests were common, and vice versa. All of these juveniles tended, in the scientists' words, "to express the social structure of the parental nest, regardless of the warm- or cold-water environment of the transplant site." When multifemale nests were transplanted, for instance, into the Tennessee habitat that favors single-female nests, new multifemale nests resulted. Even though social structure correlates with latitude, it's *not* the case that certain environments induce certain social structures. Social behavior in this spider species is resistant to environmental factors and doesn't demonstrate plasticity. Can there even be such a construct as personality under such conditions, given that personality is shaped in part by the environment? It would seem not, but there's definitely evidence for temperament in these spiders.

The ecologist Jonathan Pruitt found that *studiosis* individuals can be categorized as more aggressive or more docile. He became a sort of arachnid matchmaker, creating in the lab ninety spider couples; some paired an aggressive male and an aggressive female, some a docile male and a docile female, and others one of each. The next generation's temperaments were consistently (but not completely) predictable: an aggressive pair's offspring were nearly all aggressive, and so on. Pruitt then moved the ninety nests out into the wild, shielding half of them from other invading spiders and allowing the other half to exist amid the interspider competitions that naturally develop in the wild. All of the spider colonies in the predator-managed areas did equally well. Among the homogeneous colonies transferred to natural conditions, the docile colonies did better initially, but over the longer term the aggressive ones survived and reproduced more, apparently because they were less frequently consumed as prey. As a write-up in *Science Now* about Pruitt's research noted, "It turns out nice guys do finish last, at least among arachnids." Pruitt observes, however, that when mixed colonies were introduced to the wild and aggressive *studiosis* individuals lived side by side with mellow ones, all the spiders did well, perhaps because spiders of different temperaments excel at different survival tasks.

Future studies along the temperament-personality continuum in spiders and insects will be exciting to track. Focusing on the social insects, biologist Jennifer Jandt and her colleagues explain in a 2014 review paper that differences in individual behavior within social colonies of ants and bees are usually explained in terms of task specialization. Guards, for example, naturally behave differently from foragers. But the authors suggest that something beyond a division of labor may be involved. Individual ants may be bolder or shyer, more or less aggressive, more or less ready to explore the environment. As we have seen with temperament in the *studiosus* spider, this kind of variation (whether based in temperament or in personality) may be adaptive:

> Mixtures of behavioral types within a colony might affect the flexibility of the colony to react to changing environmental conditions. For example, colonies could become more active when environmental conditions are favorable. The more variation among workers, the more types of individuals are available for each ecological condition, and indeed, high variation among workers increases colony productivity.

Going back to tarantulas, I wonder whether shyness or aggressiveness, a tendency to hide or to strike, is more effective in evading hungry *human* predators. *Some* tarantulas (temperament or personality unknown) *are* successfully captured, prepared, and eaten, in certain regions of the world. When visiting Cambodia on her global food tour, Daniella Martin set out to find and consume fried tarantulas. Driving the roads outside Phnom Penh, she found a place called Sugar Palm World, its entrance flanked by two large cement tarantulas. And there she found her prey. In Cambodia, Martin reports, tarantulas are eaten whole. Apparently that's the practice Martin followed as well. She compares the variety she sampled, fried in soy oil and seasoned, not to smoky lobster but to "extra-chewy Korean barbecue crossed with a Dorito."

THINKING THE WAY FORWARD

Insects learn, and may make thoughtful decisions as they learn. Though we often think of them in the aggregate, they may be distinct in their personalities (or their temperaments). It's challenging to ascertain whether they feel pleasure and pain, and to the all-important question of sentience in insects and spiders I can find no ready answer. Given their sophisticated abilities for learning, though, it seems clear that the possibility of sentience should not be ruled out. As enthusiasm for entomophagy builds in the United States and Europe, hard questions like these should be kept front and center.

For some, no possible ethical justification exists for eating intentionally any living creature, even apart from the issue of whether those animals learn or think, express personalities, or feel pleasure and pain. After I ate the cricket cookies, I interviewed Robert Nathan Allen, the man who baked them and the founder of Little Herds, for a blog post. Allen told me that he "can't imagine a reason why" vegetarians wouldn't embrace entomophagy; as I have just indicated, I definitely *can* imagine a reason. For most vegetarians with whom I have talked (including my husband and my daughter), animal life is animal life, not to be consumed.

Yet people who consume insects still may operate within a thoughtful ethical framework. Abbey Alison McClain, an artist in Washington, DC, described for me the high and low points of her insect-eating experience so far. The best was "definitely the grasshopper doughnuts at Noma in Copenhagen," she said. "Not only were they delicious, but the idea of being served insects at what is ranked the best restaurant in the world is almost poetic." By contrast, she summed up an experiment with a grilled grub in Cuzco, Peru, in anything but poetic terms: "I was fairly grossed out."

What intrigued me most is that McClain identifies as a vegetarian. I asked her how she thinks about the costs and benefits of her entomophagy. "For me," she replied,

> vegetarianism has always been about sustainability and better solutions for a cruelty-free world hunger solution. While it is undeniable that insects are living beings, the ability to farm and raise insects can seemingly happen on a large scale and would greatly benefit most other living organisms.
>
> The toll that livestock farms take on the planet is intense. It may seem unfair or hypocritical to some to turn toward the bottom of the food chain for human nutrients, but when you consider that many humans eat animals that can live for decades on a daily basis, shortening the life of some of the quickest inhabitants of our ecosystems seems like a small price to pay for the benefits.

Of course, the small price McClain speaks of isn't so small for the insects. Yet the hungry world needs sources of protein, and we have to make choices about where that protein comes from—or more correctly, *some people in some populations* have to make those choices. Some of us in resource-rich countries may opt for largely or wholly vegetarian or vegan diets rather than deliberately taking in animal protein. Yet even when adopting those diets we contribute to insect deaths simply because industrialized food production kills insects, including through application of toxic chemicals to crops and use of heavy harvesting equipment. Organic farmers too must manage "pests," and ploughing at any scale sometimes kills insects. (I could find no reliable estimates as to the quantitative impact of farming practices on insect life.)

As I note throughout this book, not everyone has the luxury of choosing what foods to eat. It's precisely because of this global situation that Allen's goals for Little Herds merit hard consideration.

Allen reflects on the lives, and deaths, of the insects themselves. "Insects raised in farms," he told me, "live in teeming dark conditions (their preferable environment), with ample and abundant food supply, no natural predators, no risk of outside diseases or parasites, and when they're culled we lower the temperature so that there's no violent death or change in state (because insects are exothermic their metabolism slows until they go into a coma-like sleep without any pain). I can't think of a more humane way to raise our meat."

Skeptics may take issue with the notion that death-by-cold makes for a humane end for insects. It's a question that deserves further probing, along with others relating to insect sentience. Watching a scene in Andreas Johnsen's 2016 documentary film *BUGS*, about worldwide entomophagy, I felt slightly sick. Exploring edible insects out in the field in Kenya, a chef from Nordic Food Lab tosses a massive termite queen onto a skillet over the fire. As the queen writhes, the chef says, "She's in pain, she's being cooked alive." We don't need scholarship on termite sentience to recognize that that sort of practice amounts to blatant cruelty.

We also know that, compared to raising traditional livestock species for consumption, entomophagy is more environment-friendly, not least because insects don't require the huge stores of grain and soya that we feed to the mammals and birds we now slaughter for food. The 2013 FAO report includes the best summary I have read on this topic:

> The environmental benefits of rearing insects for food and feed are founded on the highfeed conversion efficiency of insects. Crickets, for example, require only 2 kilograms of feed for every 1 kilogram of bodyweight gain. In addition, insects can be reared on organic side-streams (including human and animal waste) and can help reduce environmental contamination. Insects are reported to emit fewer greenhouse gases and less ammonia than cattle or pigs, and they require significantly less land and water than cattle rearing.

Compared with mammals and birds, insects may also pose less risk of transmitting zoonotic infections to humans, livestock and wildlife, although this topic requires further research.

So in entomophagy do we find a one-stop solution to world hunger and environmental crises? No, of course not. Right now entomophagy is, at least in some circles, a cutting-edge thing to do (Jardin's "nerd cuisine"), either a playful adventure, a hopeful step forward in a world facing crises driven by climate change and expanding population, or both. Ophelia Deroy, a researcher at the University of London's Centre for the Study of the Senses at the School of Advanced Study, believes that insect-eating will catch on because it's fun, not because it makes environmental saviors of us. Writing in *Nature* in 2015, Deroy notes that presenting insects as "industrially farmed meat substitutes" is not an attractive basis on which to persuade skeptics. "We should think less about combating disgust and more about appealing to taste," she says, asserting that insects naturally lend themselves to desserts.

No one action, certainly no one diet, is a magic bullet for our environmental troubles. Writer and farm activist Wendell Berry, in his essay "In Distrust of Movements," expresses his dissatisfaction with movements that promote wilderness preservation, sustainable agriculture, or even the welfare of children. The notion, he writes, that "a thousand separate problems . . . can be fixed by a thousand task forces of academic and bureaucratic specialists" leads only to piecemeal solutions, neither comprehensive nor radical enough. By this standard, the entomophagy movement might seem to be just another misguided, overly specialized idea. Yet Berry doesn't merely throw up his hands, content to rail about the toxicity of environmental causes. He envisions ways we can do better in fashioning collective responses to pressing problems. A primary thing we can do better, he says, is to find and favor cheap solutions over those that require expensive administrators and bloated infrastructures. "Solutions within the reach of everybody," in Berry's words, are best. Entomophagy, its fans say, has a chance to make a difference for precisely this reason: it taps into resources that are globally available, and that could be made more available, more responsive to global need.

Entomophagy is poised on the verge of a major upswing, of spreading far beyond traditional contexts where it has always been popular. Meanwhile, scientists have begun in the last fifteen or twenty years to ask deeper questions about insect intelligence and personality than ever before. It will be a fascinating thing to watch as the two trajectories intersect, perhaps even collide: a growing interest in eating bugs and an equally growing interest in understanding the complexities of their behavior.

Generalizing about an enormous taxonomic group of animals, say, the "big five" orders of preferred edible insects, is risky. Nonetheless, writing in 2014, Oliver Sacks felt confident enough to offer a summary that resonates with the material reviewed in this chapter: "We often think of insects as tiny automata—robots with everything built-in and programmed. But it is increasingly evident that insects can remember, learn, think, and communicate in quite rich and unexpected ways. Much of this, doubtless, is built-in—but much, too, seems to depend on individual experience." It's precisely that *unexpected* angle that we need to keep our eye on. While it's far less easy to offer a definitive statement about sentience in insects than about intelligence or personality, insects are surprising us.

In Glen Stone and Jon Doyle's 2014 novel *The Awareness*, animals gradually emerge into a state of heightened consciousness about their treatment at the hands of humans. They begin to rebel. A war between humans and other animals breaks out, and the consequences are violent, even gruesome. But for the pig, elephant, dog, and bear who are the novel's central characters, revenge against humans becomes an empty act—it's not the right answer, they come to see, for smart, sentient creatures such as themselves. As this trajectory unfolds, animals—nonhuman and human together—fall into conversation about topics both monumental and mundane. Individuals of one species often explain to those of another their skills, strengths, and customs. At one point, a bear helps a human injured in battle. The man awakes from a sleep into which he had collapsed some hours earlier; the bear had been out foraging for insects in a log. The dialogue starts with the man:

"Where am I?"

"The place where I rest. Here. I brought you food." He extended his paws to the human.

The human, seeing the insects, shook his head. "Thank you. But we don't eat that."

Oh, but we do.

2. Octopus

Like 95 percent of the earth's animal species, including insects and spiders, octopuses are invertebrates. They are also, hands down, the most intelligent invertebrates on the planet. In 2009 marine biologists Julian K. Finn, Tom Tregenza, and Mark D. Norman announced a first-of-a-kind conclusion: veined octopuses off the coasts of Sulawesi and Bali carry around coconut shells in anticipation of needing them to construct a shelter. Four different times, octopuses were observed carrying halved and stacked octopus shells under their bodies as they traveled as much as twenty meters. I can't say that the animals *swam* those twenty meters, because the shells were so awkward and energetically costly to carry that the octopuses walked on the sea floor with an odd, stiff gait.

Finn and his coauthors coined the term "stilt walking" to describe this peculiar motion. I laughed aloud when I first saw stilt-walking on video. It reminded me of the gait of chimpanzees who load themselves down with fruit—not only filling their hands but stuffing the pockets between thigh and groin area—or of humans who rock from side to side as they trundle along carrying a heavy load. The payoff for the octopuses is apparently worth the hard labor: as is clear in the video, they may perch in one shell on the sandy ocean floor and then pull down a second shell to fashion a cozy clamlike shelter for themselves. Alternatively, they may partially bury the shells and inhabit an instant den.

These octopuses (*octopus* comes from the Greek, so "octopuses," not "octopi," is the preferred plural) project themselves a little bit into the future when they carry their coconut shells around, aiming toward a goal of greater safety and comfort. Certainly these coconut-carriers think about what they are doing and employ to a strategic end objects that exist in their habitat only because humans have altered the ocean (the coconuts are human refuse left in the sea). I love the way Finn and his colleagues conclude their *Current Biology* article on octopuses' tool use: "The discovery of this octopus tiptoeing across the sea floor with its prized coconut shells suggests that even marine invertebrates engage in behaviours that we once thought the preserve of humans."

Coconut-carrying is just one in a string of fascinating discoveries about octopuses that I discuss in this chapter. Whether in the wild or in captivity, octopuses solve problems strategically; in captivity, they pay keen attention to what humans do to or for them in their enclosures. As octopus researcher Jean Boal told me, they "certainly distinguish between kind experimenters that feed them (coming out of their dens and approaching them) and annoying experimenters that siphon-clean their tanks (squirting water, ink, and/or mucus at them). So they also communicate directly with us. And they certainly behave as if they have intentions and emotions."

Octopuses' well-being is threatened in far more serious ways than those deployed by annoying experimenters. In Korea, as a National Geographic video clip shows, the eating of live octopus is popular among some groups. Given the source, the video's narration is notably unscientific: first it incorrectly describes the octopus's "bulging head" (in fact that's the body), and then it highlights the animals' "beady eyes" and the fact that some people find them to be "ugly and disgusting". As the video proceeds, we see a young woman with a squirming octopus arm poking out of her mouth and, later, restaurant customers who are served octopuses, still in motion, on white dinner plates. The eating of living octopus is in Korea considered a means to ensure strength and stamina—if, that is, the diner doesn't choke as the octopus clamps its suckers onto his or her tongue. Indeed, some live-octopus eaters have choked and died, so that others who master the custom are lauded as courageous.

Blogger Michael Johnstone tells of his visit with friends to the Noryangjin fresh seafood market in Seoul. The goal was to experience *sannakji*, a dish for which an octopus is killed and the arm segments severed from the head. The disarticulated arms continue to move for up to half an hour, Johnstone says. Why would Johnstone want to consume live octopus? He explains it as a test—which he and his friends passed—"of our commitment to Korean culture and our willingness to choke back something that is instantaneously repulsive to the western palate."

A grasp of octopus biology makes clear why the arms' movement persists after the death of the animal. As Katherine Harmon Courage explains in her book *Octopus! The Most Mysterious Creature in the Sea*, the octopus brain is effectively distributed over multiple locations: "The central brain," she writes, "is wrapped around its esophagus, and to mire matters more, most of its 'brain' is in its arm." Observing an octopus's free-flowing, watery choreography, what we see is information-gathering in progress. A common octopus, Courage notes, has 240 suction cup–like suckers on each arm, and each one moves on a flexible stalk as it gathers data on matters of taste, pressure, and position: it really *is* a choreography, because the octopus integrates input from all eight tentacles.

Given an arm's skill at data-gathering, what might it experience in the process of being consumed? Might an arm try frantically to communicate to the now-distant (and deceased) central octopus brain that it's in harm's way? I don't know, of course. During the course of writing her book on octopus behavior and intelligence, Courage herself consumed *sannakji* at a restaurant called Sik Gaek in Flushing, New York. Perhaps her choice is not so different from my own experiments with entomophagy recounted in chapter 1. My bias reveals itself here, though; while I had little trouble consuming crickets and grasshoppers, I paled at the thought of Courage consuming the subject of her fascination. Arriving for the first time in Gabon, West Africa, to join a team studying the behavior and physiology of captive chimpanzees, I was offered monkey as a restaurant meal. Although I was mindful of the anthropological dictum to immerse oneself in the local culture, I couldn't bring myself to accept the dish. When my dinner arrived the French fries were studded with black hairs that the waiter agreed was from monkey, so I hadn't saved a primate's life by my refusal. Two years later I would sample exotic meats at Nairobi's Carnivore restaurant (as described in the preface), but not even during my meat-eating periods could I consume monkeys when I've devoted a big part of my professional life to observing and understanding our closest primate cousins.

By contrast, Courage embraces her *sannakji*-eating experiment: "On the plate," she writes, "the muscular arm segments look like little slugs, writhing about, gray and stubby, seething all over one another and the garnishes." Some cling stubbornly to the plate, and as Courage rips the last one up and toward her mouth, she hears "popping sounds all the way, like a tiny shower mat being ripped off the bottom of a tub." She loved the taste, but the glory of the experience for her went beyond the flavor: "It was the most intimate eating experience I've ever had. Although for the poor octopus it was not the best of times, to me, it felt almost as if we shared the dining experience."

From that last sentence, "poor octopus" resonated with me; the romantic notion that the animal somehow participated in his or her own consumption did not. Later on, during our correspondence about octopuses, Courage told me of more complicated feelings than she let on in the book:

I strategized my own research, so that I explored the world of octopus eating and culinary traditions before I dived too deep into the research on their biology and intelligence. The *sannakji* dish was, I will admit, truly delicious and an exquisite dining experience, although I am not sure I would order it again, knowing now all that I know about octopus intelligence and cognitive sophistication.

On the other hand, it is possible that these octopuses have been handled more humanely in their life and death than, say, most factory-farmed pigs, which are likely a good deal more intelligent. So, as octopus aquaculture is still in the research and development phase, most all octopus today that becomes food is wild-caught. I also think that for many of those in the United States, who have not grown up with octopus as a common food item (I count myself firmly among them), the animal takes precedence in our minds over the dish. To restaurant owners and chefs I spoke with in a small fishing village in Greece, the idea of an entire book about octopuses seemed curious, like writing a book about the chicken cutlet.

Octopus-eating is indeed a cultural matter, as is true with most foods, including the crickets, grasshoppers, and tarantulas considered in chapter 1. How we respond to one published suggestion for cooking octopus—"don't shy away from the eyes," since "many people believe fried octopus eyes to be the best part of the meat"—is influenced by whether we grew up with, or later came to experience, octopus primarily as a smart ocean- and aquarium-dweller or as a regular part of our cuisine (or, I suppose, both at once). Still, it's sometimes the newest cultural initiates among us who scrutinize traditions that otherwise are accepted as wholly natural. The dawning notion that an octopus has a head is what started three-year-old Luiz Antonio of Brazil thinking hard about eating one, a mental experiment that ended with his refusal to eat the octopus gnocchi his mother had offered him for lunch.

Recorded on video, the little boy in dialogue with his mother became famous around the world in 2013. Speaking in Portuguese,

Luiz starts by asking if the animal in pieces on his plate is real, and is assured by his mother that he is not. When Luiz asks more specifically, "He doesn't speak and he doesn't have a head, right?" the mom replies no, there's no head, only chopped-up legs; the head is back at the fish market. As the mom elaborates, explaining that we also chop up cows and chickens to eat, Luiz begins to protest, to ask why animals die in this way. "So we can eat, love," his mother replies. This doesn't satisfy Luiz, who states that he doesn't like that they die: "I like that they stay standing up." In the end, brushing a tear from her face, moved by her son's compassion, the mom urges him to eat only the potatoes and rice.

Around the world—even aside from traditions and rituals of consuming live ones—octopuses are prized more for their meat than for their moxie. Cuisines from Greece, Spain, Italy, and Japan favor the octopus, whether in salads or grilled, fried, or boiled as a main course. In some Greek fishing villages, a common sight is a string of octopuses hanging up to dry in the sun. For people who dwell outside the octopus-besotted zones, the quest for high-quality octopus meat involves extra effort. In Brooklyn, New York, the store called Octopus Garden is invariably crowded in the run-up to Christmas Eve, as customers, many of Italian ancestry, prepare for the Feast of Seven Fishes. This ritual meal originated in the days when Roman Catholics were forbidden by their church to eat meat on that night. Despite the fish-focused name, the feast often features the serving of octopuses, ranging in size from babies to eight-pounders.

Octopus Garden boasts state-of-the-art octopus-preparation equipment, including a huge walk-in freezer capable of preserving forty thousand pounds of frozen seafood and octopus-washing machines that tumble and spin the dead animals through salty water in a thirty-minute tenderizing process. Photographs in a *New York Times* profile show octopus after octopus lying on ice beds, ready for purchase, presumably having already gone through the freezing and tenderizing processes.

ALPHA INVERTEBRATE

Octopuses are invertebrates, as I have mentioned; more specifically, they are mollusks. Shells, hard ones made of carbonate material, come to mind when we think of mollusks like clams and snails, but the Latin root *mollis* means "soft," and the octopus exemplifies just that quality, existing with no shell and no bones. More specifically still, along with the other equally soft mollusks the squid and cuttlefish, octopuses are cephalopods (from the Greek "head feet"), sometimes called "inkfish" for their ability to squirt ink from their bodies. Unlike animals who are bipedal striders, sky flyers, or fishy swimmers, these cephalopods get around by contracting their bodies and shooting water out through their funnels. When on a dry surface, an octopus propels herself along using her tentacles and a sort of half-flowing, half-creeping motion.

Octopuses are my favorite invertebrates for fascinating fun facts. Like chickens, octopuses lay and guard eggs—but in a most unchickenlike quantity, as many as seventy thousand for a giant Pacific octopus. They pump blue blood, tinged by copper, through their three hearts. One heart ensures blood flow to the organs, while the other two dedicate themselves to shunting blood through the gills. The array of habitats occupied by octopuses is vast, ranging from the cold, dark ocean depths at three thousand feet to deeper but intensely hotter hydrothermal vents. An octopus may squeeze his boneless self through remarkably small openings, as one six-hundred-pounder did for National Geographic cameras when provided with a Plexiglas playland that featured narrow tubes. Even octopuses of this substantial bulk can fit themselves through openings the size of a quarter.

Most fascinating of all may be an octopus's ability to camouflage his body, both because it's visually stunning to witness and because it reveals more information about the octopus brain. Here again, it's best to see the evidence, and video by researcher Roger Hanlon captures the moment: as we gaze at the dull colors of an underwater plant, it flashes white, then white and brown, and suddenly the body of an octopus becomes plain to see. All along the octopus was there, attached to the plant but exquisitely camouflaged. Hanlon, who had been tracking the individual for some time, caught the moment of transition back to normal-octopus color.

And when I say "the moment," I'm exaggerating only a little: it takes the octopus just seven-tenths of a second to complete the transition. Hanlon explains that this isn't some reflex reaction but an act of neural processing and decision-making. The octopus changes shape, color, texture, and pattern only after evaluating the nature of the substrate against which his body is arrayed. Hanlon duplicated this observation in the lab using the octopus's cephalopod cousin, the cuttlefish. In the same documentary video, Hanlon places a cuttlefish in a pan of water resting on three different artificially pat-terned backgrounds; the first is solid white, the others black-and-white checkerboards, one with small and one with large squares relative to the size of the cuttlefish. The cuttlefish rapidly assesses the contrast of each background and mimics it with one of three pat-terns, which Hanlon terms uniform (against the solid background), mottled (with the small checks), and disruptive (matching the large checks). Hanlon calls this a cognitive act; the visible result of the cuttlefish's neural activity is represented on the animal's skin.

Marine biologists had long thought that almost all social be-havior among octopuses was related to reproductive activities like mating and egg-guarding. In *Octopus: The Ocean's Intelligent Inverte-brate,* Jennifer Mather, Roland Anderson, and James Wood describe the behavior of Olive, a giant Pacific octopus who laid her eggs just offshore from Seattle, in Puget Sound. Olive made a nest attached to wooden pilings in the sound and lined the deeper of two open-ings with rocks. This arrangement meant she was highly visible to local divers, a boon to those of us who crave an up-close, if vicarious, glimpse at octopus reproduction.

Divers first noticed Olive's eggs, deposited in a massive string on the underside of the pilings, on February 25, 2002. No egg census was conducted, but based on her size of about sixty pounds, it's thought that she exceeded the average of seventy thousand eggs for her species. In the next weeks, Mather and her coauthors report, Olive was seen "blowing water through the eggs and caressing them with her arm tips." Was Olive an attentive cephalopod mother, then? At this stage of affairs, yes. She guarded her eggs that summer, repelling predators and altering her own behavior markedly so that she did not leave the den to forage.

When on September 22 the eggs were first seen hatching—209 days after they were laid—Olive expelled many of the hatchlings from the den by forcible water-blowing. At that point, Olive was white in color (not a good sign for an octopus of her type), and clearly her health was deteriorating; she suffered from visible ulcers. Her eggs continued to hatch until Halloween. One week later, on November 7, Olive was dead.

By this point, at least in the Seattle area, Olive was one famous octopus, and her death was mourned; people responded to the life and death of a cephalopod individual, an octopus seen not as an exotic American meal but as a living creature with goals and motivations of her own. At the same time, octopus biology must be our frame of reference, and it's not as though Olive's hatchlings suffered deprivation due to the trauma of a mother's premature passing. The timing of Olive's death was perfectly natural, part of the octopus life cycle. Males die soon after mating, females not long after their eggs hatch.

I would argue that there *is* fierce, protective maternal care (and by contrast, no paternal care) in octopuses, but apparently only before birth, a state of affairs that evolved over eons in octopuses but may seem utterly strange to mammals like us. Once hatched, octopus babies survive initially on the nutrients contained in the yolk sac; quite soon, they must find their own food. From that point forward, they often live in solitude until it's time to mate.

Octopuses excel at surprising us, though. In 2016, the recorded behavior of gloomy octopuses, a small species (*Octopus tetricus*) studied in the shallow waters of Jervis Bay, Australia, rocked the world of cephalopod science. Here was evidence, published in *Current Biology* by David Scheel, Peter Godfrey-Smith, and Matthew Lawrence, of extensive social behavior outside reproduction: the octopuses used color changes not as solo camouflage or an antipredator tactic but as socially communicative cues. At times, the gloomy octopuses performed what the researchers called a "stand tall" move, in which they raise their head on extended arms, then spread their arms, raise their mantle, and turn dark. The move was observed as part of one-on-one encounters in aggressive-submissive displays. Here's the coolest part: "Interactions in which dark body color by an approaching octopus was matched by similar color in the reacting octopus were more likely to escalate to grappling. Darkness in an approaching octopus met by paler color in the reacting octopus accompanied retreat of the paler octopus." There's no reason, Scheel and his coauthors point out, for dark color to be physiologically linked to aggression *except* in a communicative context: there's highly social signaling going on.

Octopuses do live alone in their dens, which they may construct or modify in innovative ways, as we will see. Males approach females, who are sometimes tucked away in their dens, for the elegant choreography of mating. One of my favorite animal videos, filmed in Indonesian waters by Christine Huffard of California's Monterey Aquarium, reveals a different sort of octopus surprise. A male algae octopus extends an arm toward a den, only to discover that the octopus near it is not a female at all but a large male guarding the female who hides inside the structure. This guarding male looms up large and aggressive, and a tangle of sixteen arms is the result. The two males fight until the intruder fires his jets and departs, in a rush.

When I blogged about this startled male, I learned from Katherine Harmon Courage a good reason for the male's initial caution in approaching the den. In one notable case—albeit in a different species, the day octopus—the female, the larger octopus of the pair, strangled her partner at conclusion of the mating act. She then carried him off to her den, where, marine biologists think, she consumed him; octopuses are cannibals, and presumably the cache of protein gained explains their choice to sometimes eat their own.

No wonder octopuses are often solitary! Our most vivid accounts of octopus intelligence come from researchers who witness solo performances. In Bermuda waters back in the 1980s, Jennifer Mather was engaged in intensive observations, from 6 a.m. to 6 p.m., of two octopuses. One of her subjects was in his or her den, making arm motions that to Mather signaled he or she was cleaning the area; earlier, this octopus had hunted, then eaten a meal. Then, three times in quick succession, the octopus swam down to the sea floor, collected a small rock, and dropped it at the den entrance. Finished with housekeeping, the octopus repaired to the den and slept. That was Mather's "aha" moment. But why?

Mather already knew that octopuses tend to select dens with small entrances. This octopus, though, hadn't made that choice. Rather, he or she had envisioned a small den entrance and employed rocks as tools to reduce the existing entrance to the mentally imagined size. Mather later wrote that this "smart sucker" had "wanted, planned, evaluated, chose[n], and constructed" in his or her actions that day. At the time, her observation of this simple instance of octopus tool use was just as groundbreaking as the report of coconut-carrying octopuses would be in 2009.

Truman, an octopus at the New England Aquarium, demonstrates time travel in the other direction: just as the octopus observed by Mather planned for the future, Truman remembered the past. There was one aquarium volunteer this octopus just didn't like. Repeatedly, he soaked this person by jetting streams of salt water at her out through his funnel, the anatomical structure octopuses use to pulse their bodies through the water. No one else received Truman's obnoxious treatment. The volunteer left for college but on a visit back to the aquarium several months later found herself soaked once again. Truman hadn't forgotten her; in fact, he squirted her at first sight.

Can octopuses learn from each other socially, even if they mostly do not? In 1992 a paper appeared in *Science* declaring that they can, at least in a laboratory context. Graziano Fiorito and Pietro Scotto reported that in the common octopus, untrained observer octopuses learned to discriminate between red and white balls by watching same-species demonstrators who had undergone training on the task. The learning response occurred significantly more rapidly among observer octopuses in this situation than among octopuses trained by classical conditioning techniques to solve the same problem on their own.

Copying of a model was considered by Fiorito and Scotto a notable feat of cognition for an invertebrate. Reading their article, I am distressed at how the demonstrator octopuses were trained: if the red ball was deemed the correct choice in the testing trials, an octopus who selected that color was rewarded with a tasty piece of fish attached to the side of the ball he or she couldn't see. If instead the white ball was selected, the octopus received an electric shock. This experiment was conducted a quarter century ago, and I hope this method would not be used today.

Some cephalopod scientists have suggested that the observer octopuses may have been cued inadvertently by researchers to select the correctly colored balls. I wonder also if the fish treats (affixed to one ball and not the other) might have been sensed by the octopuses' information-seeking arms, even if they remained invisible to the eyes.

In any case, octopuses in their natural environments certainly do pay attention to what others are doing in the world around them, and some social learning may therefore occur. The consensus among marine biologists, as I interpret it, is that the octopus lifestyle is primarily but not exclusively conducive to a solo approach to learning; that is, octopuses' formidable intelligence is built primarily on individuals' perceptual engagement with the world and on their ability to learn from the information that constantly streams in to their eyes and arms.

THE SHY AND THE SENTIENT

Five years before Fiorito and Scotto's octopus social-learning study—keep in mind that 1987 was quite early in the scientific quest to understand octopus behavior—volunteers at the Seattle Aquarium bestowed names upon three octopuses in their care: Lucretia McEvil, Emily Dickinson, and Leisure Suit Larry. It was more than twenty years after Jane Goodall had won her battle to name individual wild chimpanzees (Flo, David Graybeard, and so on) rather than referring to them by numbers, but still, to name invertebrates wasn't exactly a routine thing. Lucretia, the volunteers had noticed, was a turbulent force of nature in her tank; shy Emily hid from prying eyes; and Larry acted in ways we might call "forward," to the extent that he would have been "ripe for citation of sexual harassment for excess touching if he'd been human." Through sharp-eyed observation of their charges, the volunteers stumbled upon an insight that marine biologists would later prove by way of controlled experiment: octopuses show differences along the personality spectrum, though I could find fewer detailed studies than those published on insects and spiders.

Marine biologists instead report different behavioral tendencies in whole *species*. Just as I know, having observed great apes, that on the whole orangutans are more phlegmatic and chimpanzees more excitable, with gorillas somewhere in the middle, these biologists observe that common octopuses are feistier than the giant Pacific octopus—on average at least, with exceptions always possible. Variation *within* a species is where things get more interesting, and in octopuses that seems to occur along a quartet of dimensions: active engagement, arousal-readiness, aggression, and avoidance-disinterest. Poke octopuses with a test-tube brush and what happens? Some rush away from the threat, squirting ink as they go; others face the challenge head on, grabbing and pulling the brush. When we describe octopuses' behavior, whether Olive's curating of her eggs or the large male guard's aggression in chasing away his rival at the underwater den, it's good to remember that the *quality* and *nature* of these individuals' responses don't generalize well, any more than your dog's, cat's, or rabbit's play behavior generalizes to how all other dogs, cats, or rabbits might chase, jump, or cavort.

Octopuses express themselves distinctly, and certainly may express themselves intelligently when engaged in foraging or constructing shelters for themselves. Still, these are invertebrates we're talking about. What hard evidence do we have that they are sentient?

"How to Anesthetize an Octopus" is a video available on the Internet that displays an esoteric skill, but an important one: how to render an octopus unconscious. Research illustrated in it shows that administering the anesthetic isoflurane to the common octopus puts the animal right out. How is it possible to tell when an octopus goes unconscious? Watch the minute-long clip: the octopus test subjects, bathed in seawater, first go pale, then cease responding to gentle poking when isoflurane is added to water in the appropriate concentrations. Within an hour of being placed back in fresh seawater, the animals regain their color and their sensation, and thus, their consciousness.

The timing of this work, in 2014, was no accident: the year prior, the European Union declared that cephalopods must be treated humanely when used in scientific research—the only invertebrates so protected (insects certainly aren't). To make sure that the animals don't feel pain when studied, trials on anesthetics were carried out. Perhaps it is no revolutionary conclusion to say that octopus feel pain, given their acute and well-distributed sensory systems. Note, though, that this humane declaration is European in origin; it is far from universal, although the international Cambridge Declaration of Consciousness in Animals does mention the octopus—again, the sole invertebrate chosen—which may signal that the notion is spreading. If so, perhaps we will see no more of the type of US-based research published in *Neuroscience Letters* in 2014. Biologists Jean S. Alupay, Stavros P. Hadjisolomou, and Robyn J. Crook subjected five algae octopuses in the laboratory to arm crush injuries, which sometimes resulted in what's called autotomy, self-removal of the arm by the animals. The octopuses were decerebrated under anesthesia (their cerebrums were removed) "to permit sequential harvest of each arm without distress," and the arms were later stimulated by electrodes. Although the steps taken in these experiments are not entirely clear to me from the published report, any way you cut it the results for octopuses both before and after arm "harvest" make for troubling reading:

> All animals inked and jetted at the onset of stimulation and showed immediate wound-grooming behavior, where the arm stump or crushed site was held in the beak . . . in two individuals for at least 20 min. By the 6 h behavior test no animals expressed ongoing grooming, and mechanical stimulation did not re-induce it. Instead the injured area was contracted and held close to the body, and some animals (n = 3) used adjacent arms to curl around the injured site. This guarding behavior was provoked further by stimulation of the wounded arm.

Stunningly, Alupay and her colleagues don't conclude from this work that octopuses feel pain, because the responses observed either are considered insufficient to indicate pain or aren't known to be pain responses in invertebrates. I'm all for scientific rigor, and it's true that invertebrates may not process pain in the same way vertebrates do, but is it so hard to read these acute signals as coming from animals who wish to experience no further pain at the hands of experimenters—even experimenters who write that they intend their results to inform regulations regarding use of octopuses in scientific research?

The psychological aspect of octopus suffering, as well as the physical, deserves notice, and speaks also to octopus sentience. Biologist Jean Boal and her student Marie Biegel tested octopuses' responses to an enriched environment as compared to an impoverished one. Using California mudflat octopuses as their test subjects, Boal and Biegel fashioned two distinct types of clear Plexiglas tanks, each placed in the lab such that their inhabitants could see other octopuses nearby. Into the impoverished tank went flowerpots, including one big enough to be a den, and other assorted objects like stones, beads, and shells. Into the enriched tank, twice as large, went the same objects plus more: a crushed-coral bottom, plants, and an adjacent mini-aquarium containing a wrasse (a type of fish that, as we discover in chapter 3, is a cognitive star of the fish world) for the octopuses' viewing pleasure.

Each of the six octopuses spent two weeks in the less-than-great habitat, then an equal time in the enhanced tank, and finally a week back in the impoverished habitat. The octopuses let the experimenters know what suited them and what didn't, including by the mechanism of color change. When in the low-stimulus, small tank, the octopuses more often paled to an unhappy white or flashed colors that the researchers knew correlated with anger: the animals threw themselves against the tank walls in apparent stress (three times more often than in the fancier cephalopod pad) and interacted less often with enrichment objects. Outside of the formal data-collection periods, observers noticed great stress in the impoverished tank: there, octopuses ate their own arms, a behavior called autophagy that thankfully was never seen in the better habitat. It's telling, I think, that the worst of the autophagy occurred the *second* time the octopuses encountered the sterile tank: after they had dwelled in a more stimulating home, adjusting to the small, boring one wasn't so easy.

I had just read about Boal and Biegel's experiment when, in March 2015, I visited the Virginia Aquarium and Marine Science

Center, located not far from Virginia Beach's famous oceanfront. It's evident even from a relaxed family-oriented visit such as mine that this aquarium, as its name indicates, orients itself toward science and conservation. A short distance from the large tank housing massive, gracefully swimming sea turtles (including loggerheads, greens, and Kemp's), as well as a variety of fish, was the glass-walled hatchling nursery, where aquarium visitors may watch the tiniest sea turtles, who are raised and cared for intensively. In a separate building, three male river otters tumbled through the water, climbing out to a concrete ledge to groom each other, then sliding back in to swim through and play with enrichment objects. By contrast, the single Atlantic (or common) octopus in the aquarium, housed in a small dark tank that featured what seemed to be a quite shallow recessed den, sat immobile, suckers attached to the glass window. No enrichment objects were visible.

This habitat for the octopus concerned me. Trained as I am to consider other individuals of the same species to be the most exciting and valuable "enrichment objects" for captive animals, I had to remind myself that a lone octopus makes sense given these cephalopods' solitary nature. Still, why such a small, sterile habitat? When I emailed that question to the aquarium's senior curator and dive operations supervisor, Beth Firchau, she explained that the aquarium team moves objects in and out of the habitat in order to offer the octopus variable stimulation, and sometimes that process means no enrichment in the tank at all—on purpose. Maybe, I thought, my visit had by chance fallen on one of those sterile days. It did seem a lost opportunity, doubly so in that the octopus was offered nothing as stimulation, and there was no signage to explain to aquarium-goers the enrichment process, which surely would grab the interest of animal lovers. Firchau wrote also that "daily and quite often, twice daily, the aquarists engage the octopus in creative enrichment activities that challenge its puzzle solving abilities, work its muscles, and encourage natural exploratory behaviors about the exhibit."

Two months later, thanks to Firchau, I was able to observe, together with my husband Charles Hogg, just such an enrichment session with the Atlantic octopus. We arrived in time for the aquarium's 10 a.m. opening and joined Firchau and aquarist Evan Culbertson behind the scenes. I learned that only a third of the exhibit that had concerned me is visible to the public; the 120-gallon enclosure had been designed after a team of aquarists visited wild-octopus dens right off the Virginia coast. Because there's not much natural rocky rubble—prime octopus habitat—in our area, octopuses here often build their dens near human-made features like riprap structures or light towers. The Atlantic octopus's tank features subdued lighting and recessed areas to which the octopus may retreat. Firchau emphasized that as important as it is that the octopus feel safe and not stressed, it must also be visible to the public: the balance between animal welfare and accessibility to aquarium visitors is all-important.

Although aquarium staff refer to the octopus as "it," she's almost certainly a she, given the evident lack of specialized arm features that a male uses to deposit sperm into a female. Wild-caught in North Carolina waters, she was about three years old, judging from the size of her mantle. That's an elderly octopus, one nearing the end of her life.

After this basic information was shared, Culbertson got to work. Earlier that morning he had cleaned the tank, a task that doubles as tactile enrichment for the octopus, who often touches him or his equipment. Consulting a randomized computer program, Culbertson determined the mechanical type of enrichment to be used that day: "hamster tube with pegged block," a colorful oval tube with small open holes into which were inserted rewards of food (peeled shrimp) and objects (small toys, essentially).

Immediately after Culbertson placed the ring in the tank, the octopus pulled it deeper into the water, "tented" over it with her body, and began to explore the holes with her tentacles. We were watching a choreography of information-gathering behavior, with the octopus's neuron-studded arms drawing in all kinds of data. For thirty straight minutes, the octopus was occupied with the ring and its enclosed food and object rewards. Later on, I learned that she hadn't been offered the hamster ring in about three months, so the comparative novelty of the object probably added to the intrigue. Soon, she broke the ring open and manipulated (or ate!) the rewards. Her motions appeared to me purposeful. Her chromatophores were active too, and the color shifts from red to dark red that we could see indicated that she was probably excited. Had my husband and I been able, we would have been color-changing too: watching this thinking creature in action was an elating experience.

Right around the half-hour mark, the octopus released the ring and drifted off. We debriefed with Culbertson, asking him how he thought the session had gone. Using a five-point scale, with precise behavioral criteria assigned to each number, Culbertson rated the session a 5 for the octopus's interest and a 5, as well, in terms of visibility to the public: the best outcome. Every three months, using this sort of data, the "octopus team" evaluates which enrichment objects work well and drops from the rotation those that don't.

I left the aquarium awash in mixed feelings: impressed by the octopus herself, full of admiration for the aquarist team's dedication to the octopus's welfare, and dismayed that the octopus had been plucked from natural waters to spend her short, and reproductively barren, life in a tank.

That very week, as I was mentally steeped in all things octopus, naturalist Sy Montgomery's book *The Soul of an Octopus* came out. At Boston's New England Aquarium, Montgomery joined the aquarist team to observe and interact with octopuses on a sustained basis. In this way, she comes to know octopuses with names like Athena, Octavia, Kali, and Karma. "They have changed my life forever," Montgomery writes. "I loved them, and will love them always, for they have given me a great gift: a deeper understanding of what it means to think, to feel, and to know." Here was a book with a different goal than the others I had read: to convey good science about octopus behavior, intelligence, and emotion, yes, but to do it with an unbridled sense of personal involvement and wonder. This volume I inhaled, reviewed for the *Times Literary Supplement*, and purchased for friends.

Montgomery dove off the French Polynesian island of Mo'orea in order to observe wild octopuses, but the bulk of her octopus-watching occurred in captivity. Wild-caught in British Columbia and transported to the Boston aquarium by Federal Express, giant Pacific octopus Octavia is the animal Montgomery came to know best. On one occasion, Octavia and Montgomery held on to each other for an hour and fifteen minutes, in an instance of apparently mutual tactile pleasure. "I stroked her head," Montgomery reports, "her arms, her webbing, absorbed in her presence. She seemed equally attentive to me." Montgomery excitedly describes Octavia as she lay eggs—thousands of them: "Mottled with dark patches, Octavia is radiantly beautiful, the very picture of a healthy octopus and a diligent mother. She fluffs the clusters of eggs nearest the window with one arm, like a mom sitting on a park bench might jiggle a baby buggy." How reminiscent this account is of Olive's behavior in the waters off Seattle. Octavia's eggs, though, unlike Olive's, would never hatch; they were inert, infertile, sending no signs of life back to their caretaker. Never having had the opportunity to mate with a male, Octavia would not experience the evanescence of octopus motherhood shortly before death in the way that wild female octopuses do.

Montgomery acknowledges the ethical issues inherent in seizing octopus from their natural ocean homes in order to confine and display them for our entertainment and education. She worries about factors that conspire to keep a new young octopus called Kali off-exhibit in a fifty-five-gallon pickle barrel inside a sump awaiting her turn—presumably upon Octavia's death—to inhabit the main tank. "Can this young, growing animal thrive in a space so small and barren?" The answer requires no soul-searching.

Octavia guarding her eggs. Photo courtesy of Tianne Strombeck.

About Octavia herself, Montgomery notes the trade-offs implicit in an unnatural longer life in the aquarium. "In the wild, virtually every hour of every day would have brought the risk that a predator would bite off part of her body, as had happened to Karma, or that she would be torn limb from limb and eaten alive." Confinement brings benefits as well as costs. The skill and compassion of the senior aquarists whom Montgomery comes to know are notable as well, reminiscent of my experience at the Virginia Aquarium.

Skeptics might worry that Montgomery's obvious adoration of her octopus companions colors her objectivity in describing the animals' profoundly intelligent nature. I'm not among them. What Montgomery writes, with a few exceptions (in musing about universal consciousness and a Creator's thinking, she departs the realm of science), is of a piece with marine biologists' reports. In Jean Boal's lab, octopuses preferred fresh frozen squid for a meal. Once, when

Boal distributed less-than-fresh squid instead, one of her charges took note. After dropping squid bits in each tank, Boal circled back to the first one, in which a large female octopus resided. No squid was visible. The octopus locked eyes with Boal, made her way to the back of her tank, and forcefully propelled what she had hidden under her body—the stale squid—straight into the tank's outtake drain. Recounting this story for me, Katherine Harmon Courage noted how "curious" this behavior is "in light of the octopus's largely antisocial nature. So the fact that octopuses engage with us at all—through eye contact, even—is fascinating and strange, and I think, hints at their neurological complexity and cognitive flexibility. Of course we need controlled experiments to start to suss all of this out. But these simple, daily interactions with octopuses can teach us a lot about where to look—and what to look for."

Earlier in this chapter, I quoted Boal's observation that octopuses distinguish between kind and annoying experimenters, but in fact, she told me, the same is true of all cephalopods: "I find no objective reason to distinguish between the cognitive abilities of octopuses, cuttlefishes, and squids, yet people have very different responses and expectations of them, apparently based on how they interact with us. Octopuses seem very human-like in their attention and manipulation of objects, but cuttlefish seem to be every bit as capable, and squid have all the neural machinery of cuttlefish and octopuses but jet around like fishes, which we routinely underestimate." Boal's point about fish aligns perfectly with material I present in chapter 3. I hope there to avoid underestimating fish, and here, to steer clear of the tendency to elevate octopuses above their closely related cousins without adequate reason. At present, though, evidence about cephalopods' smartness and sentience is far more readily available for octopuses than for cuttlefish and squid.

Here's what we know: the conscious, thinking, strategizing octopuses evaluate what's going on around them, and express their upbeat or not-so-upbeat moods accordingly, so visibly and strikingly that even we land vertebrates can understand them. Unfortunately, we too rarely make the effort to do that, instead seeing octopus only as a succulent meal to give our palate a half hour's worth of pleasure—or, bizarrely, as a tool with which to symbolize loyalty to a sports team.

HOCKEY PUCKS

Certainly it wasn't octopus intelligence, personality, or sentience that two Detroit Red Wings hockey fans had on their minds in 2010 when they drove from Michigan to Phoenix to watch their team play. Preparing for the game, they donned red shirts, made a fan sign, and planned their postgame "brewskis." They also enclosed dead octopuses in plastic wrap. On home video, one of the men describes them as "little baby ones" and exults about the plan to throw them out onto the ice during the game.

The octopus-tossing tradition at Detroit hockey games is over half a century old. It began on April 15, 1952, during the Stanley Cup playoffs, and represented no random choice of animal: at the time, eight wins were needed for a Stanley Cup victory, so the eight-armed creature was thought ideal. The Red Wings won the championship that year, sealing the octopus's fate as a sort of deceased team mascot. It's not only babies that are tossed: the National Hockey League reports that even fifty-pounders have landed on the ice.

As the two fans' home video shows, during the Detroit-Phoenix game's third period, the men did manage to lob the octopuses into the center of the action. Crowd reaction ranges from cheers and claps to high-fives, even as security is seen coming to lead the men away. A later scene shows them, high on victory, paying bail money for their freedom; the NHL prohibits throwing "objects" on the ice, out of concern for player safety, so there's a price to pay for this brand of sports tradition.

I can't help but think back to Olive, the octopus who guarded her eggs so fiercely in Puget Sound. The baby octopuses tossed onto the hockey-rink ice, or laying atop ice at Octopus Garden in New York awaiting Christmas Eve customers, had doubtlessly been nurtured too, before their birth. When, at a young age, they were left on their own, they managed to survive—for a time.

If some food entrepreneurs have their way, octopus will in the near future be bred and farmed in great numbers. Jake Conroy, CEO and president of Kanaloa Octopus Farms, told a Hawaiian newspaper in 2015, "Octopus are fascinating animals and almost all aquariums have them—and that's just the ornamentals." His goal is to "move up to a scale to provide octopus for eating." If his vision comes true—and I hope it does not—many thousands of the smartest invertebrates on earth could soon join the millions of fish confined in close quarters in aquaculture tanks.

3. Fish

Groupers, a warm-water type of coral reef fish in the sea bass family, may hunt their prey together with giant moray eels and Napoleon wrasses. This three-species cooperative system, which increases the chances of the groupers' hunting success, stunned me in its sophistication. As zoologists Alexander Vail, Andrea Manica, and Redouan Bshary explain, the groupers tear off after prey using their burst-speed swimming capabilities; the giant moray eels swim their slender selves into tight hiding places among the reefs; and the wrasses have "powerful protractile jaws that can suck out hidden prey or smash the reef matrix around it." What a formidable hunting team!

As someone who has studied gestural communication in African great apes, I frankly did not expect that when hunting, groupers may alert their eel and wrasse partners to the presence of hidden prey by using a referential gesture, a sophisticated type of communication long thought to be used only by the cerebral apes and ravens. To be counted as a referential gesture, five stringent criteria must be met; the action in question must be (1) made without mechanical force (unlike a push gesture on a partner's body, for instance), (2) performed with intention, (3) directed toward a communicational partner, (4) about some object or event in the world, and (5) followed by a voluntary response from the partner.

One of the grouper's signals is a full-body shimmer, made while positioned horizontally in front of an eel who is inside a shelter. The grouper will signal repeatedly to the moray, taking breaks to look at the moray, if the moray at first resists joining in a prey search. That amounts to thoughtful communication intended to motivate a hunting partner, but it doesn't amount to referential communication because the grouper isn't directing the eel's attention toward an object or event.

All five criteria for a referential signal are fulfilled, however, when the grouper signals to alert the hunting partners to a spot where potential prey is hiding. In this case, the grouper assumes a vertical position, head down, and shakes his or her head with pauses in between shakes, acting in this way—and here is the significant point—only in locations directly above prey that had already been chased but not caught. In fact, the grouper skids to a stop after high-speed swimming, then performs the gesture. As Vail, Manica, and Bshary emphasize, this deliberate head-stand and head-shake directs the partners' attention to a specific crevice adopted as a lair by the escapee animal. The zoologists' analysis of the communicational context around the head-shaking is impressive: their data show, for instance, that in all thirty-four observed cases of the head-stand and head-shaking, performed by nine different groupers, a potential recipient for the message was nearby; eels often responded actively to the signal and wrasses always did, exploring the crevice the grouper had pointed out immediately. In five instances, the prey was caught after the signal was made: twice by a grouper, twice by a moray, and once by a wrasse.

Like the groupers, certain sea trout also use a head-stand and head-shake referential signal, in this case directed toward octopus hunting partners. Octopuses, as we already know (chapter 2) are intelligent cephalopods who are well-prepared to respond to attention-directing signals of this sort.

These referential gestures don't sway me into thinking that groupers rival chimpanzees or other great apes in the intelligence department. But does that even matter? The fish are smartly solving the problems that need to be solved in their own environment. There is thinking going on in the groupers' minds, as is especially obvious in the groupers' sensitivity to their communicational audience and the specific context in which they gesture to bring about a particular result.

Groupers are not the only smart fish in the sea. Abundant in the tropical and subtropical waters of the Atlantic, Pacific, and Indian Oceans are fish—about six hundred species in a single taxonomic family, the Labridae—called wrasses. Mostly small to moderate in size and often brightly colored, these fishes have a thick-lipped appearance (*labrum* means "lip" in Latin), forage in reefs or among rocks for tiny invertebrates, and under the right conditions change sex, from female to male or vice versa. Small wrasses are popular choices for home aquariums, where they are often displayed with aquascapes that feature rock structures meant to mimic reefs.

Some wrasses are cleaner fish. If those of us who took college biology years ago dusted off our old class notes, odds are we would find cleaner fish represented as a classic example of mutualism, defined as an interaction between different species of animals that benefits each. When the cleaners remove and eat other fish's ectoparasites, both they and their clients benefit. Textbook examples of mutualism, wrasses are a vertebrate parallel to the insects of the invertebrate world (chapter 1): intriguing in their biology and behavior, yet rarely understood as individuals who go beyond genetically programmed actions to make choices in the world.

Fish biologist Culum Brown, reviewing the literature in a groundbreaking survey paper called "Fish Intelligence, Sentience and Ethics," makes wrasse behavior downright exciting precisely *because* of what individuals intelligently choose to do. First, the cleaner wrasses set up work stations among the coral, in order to pick off parasites and dead skin from their "regular customers" and also from transient fish who are just passing through. The wrasses seem to distinguish between residents and transients, choosing to serve transients first because residents will linger in the region whereas transients won't, and also between predator and nonpredator clients. They wisely choose to nip nonpredators at higher rates than predators when, even while working to provide the cleaning service, they cheat and try to thieve a bit of extra food in the form of their customers' body scales or mucus. The customers often have a choice of where to be serviced—there are rival cleaners nearby, after all, with their own cleaning stations at the ready.

Zoologists Redouan Bshary and Manuela Wurth, who scuba-dived in order to observe cleaner wrasses in a national park near Sinai, Egypt, observed that a client fish may visit the same cleaner fish again and again in the same day. Sometimes in the course of cleaning, the cleaner bites the client; the client (understandably) reacts with a jolt and may respond aggressively to the cleaner or depart the work station altogether. Adopting rather poignant language, the zoologists note, "The behavior of clients following jolts clearly indicates a momentary disturbance in their relationship with the cleaner." But here's the most fascinating part: when a client flees, the cleaner may pursue and coax the offended party back into a calm state. The cleaner hovers about the client and touches the client's dorsal fin area with his or her own pectoral and pelvic fins, but without carrying out any cleaning service, a behavior called "tactile stimulation." Through this practice—Brown dubs it giving the client a back rub—the cleaners sometimes calm their clients and halt their clients' departure. The wrasses offer tactile stimulation selectively: predators receive more than nonpredators, and as I have noted, the behavior occurs more often after cleaning sessions that end with jolts and aggression by the clients than after sessions without them.

At this Egyptian site, cleaner wrasses interacted with more than a hundred different clients of numerous species. In describing this system, Bshary and Wurth use language borrowed directly from studies of monkeys and apes who repeatedly encounter each other during complex cognitive interactions. The wrasses, they say, *manipulate* their clients and *reconcile* with them. These terms signal that, as with the groupers, we're dealing with intelligent animals who act with intention.

When headlines around the world reported the first videotaped proof that fish use tools, it was a wrasse species at the center of the media storm. Evolutionary biologist Giacomo Bernardi recorded an orange-dotted tuskfish who first digs a clam out of the sand, then transports the clam to a rocky area and hurls it at the rocks until it breaks open. "It requires a lot of forward thinking," Bernardi noted in an interview accompanying the video's release, "because there are a number of steps involved. For a fish, it's a pretty big deal." In a paper for the journal *Coral Reefs*, Bernadi explains that in July 2009, he was in Palau observing fish in four feet of water. After he saw the tuskfish crack a clam using anvils in two separate bouts, he turned on the camera and made fish-cognition history. Have a look at the video and you'll see what Bernardi means about forward thinking. For me, the clincher is that, between acquiring the clam and smashing it on the rocks, the fish travels a distance estimated to be about five meters (though on video it looks longer to me). A brainy search is under way here for a way to extract food from a stubborn mollusk.

Knowing that those three tool-using events together lasted about twenty minutes, I asked Bernardi about the wonder I imagined he felt as he watched the tuskfish. He told me:

> I spend a lot of time underwater and all fish fascinate me, so I tend to be excited very easily about the littlest things. When something major happens, I tend to go overboard. About twenty years ago, my wife and I spent ten days living in an underwater habitat in Florida. There, a colleague witnessed another wrasse, the yellow head wrasse, doing exactly what I [later] saw the tuskfish doing. I tend to

forget where my keys are, and pretty much everybody's name, but I
can remember every fish factoid I hear, so when I saw my tuskfish,
it was more of an aha moment, where it was more like something I
was expecting but had to wait twenty years to see and enjoy.

Though Bernardi's is the first video documentation of wrasse tool use,
it was the fourth instance described formally by zoologists. Notably,
three genera (*Choerodon*, *Halichoeres*, and *Thalassoma*) of wrasses are
represented; because these three are not closely related evolution-
arily, but their tool-using behaviors are nonetheless similar, Bernardi
predicts that tool use may be widespread among wrasses. If he's right,
then wrasses are extractive foragers, meaning that like a number of
birds and mammals they use external objects to break open a matrix
of some kind in order to liberate the food inside.

Why the wrasses, in particular? Are they smarter than the run-of-
the-mill fish? Do wrasses learn tool use socially from each other? In
conversation, Bernadi reveals how much we have left to learn:

> Wrasses are carnivores, with well-developed olfactory lobes that
> allow them to smell prey. Talking to a brain specialist, I understand
> that this region of the brain may be related to cognition, so it is
> tempting to associate the natural development of the wrasse brain
> and its potential ability to connect the dots and realize that tool
> use might work.
>
> In my experience, two tuskfish next to each other don't learn
> from each other, but I can't know for sure. Since my observation,
> I have looked at them more carefully and did not see the behavior
> again, but I did not go back to the same place to see if it was a trait
> that would be common in a specific population (something that
> has been seen in primates).

It's unlikely that wrasses match the complexity and sophistication
of tool use by chimpanzees, who place nuts on platforms and bring

down wooden or stone hammers to smash them open, and insert wands into termite mounds to extract the delicious protein morsels inside (chapter 8). Again, though, we need to keep in mind that what the wrasses do is smart and strategic behavior, *equally effective* at solving the problems in their habitat as the behavior of apes in theirs— and not what most people expect from the fish on their plate.

We do eat wrasses. The largest coral reef fish in the world, weighing as much as four hundred pounds, is the humphead wrasse, a fish considered a palate-pleasing delicacy in high-end restaurants, most famously in Hong Kong. A favorite of poachers and subject to a great deal of population pressure, the humphead, with its thick lips and bulging forehead, has been described by the World Wildlife Foundation as "one of the most spectacular sights in the ocean" (see the video clip from Australia's Great Barrier Reef, cited in the reference list). The humphead wrasse is even a WWF priority species, designated as one of the most ecologically, economically, or culturally important species on our planet and thus selected for a protection campaign. Naturally occurring in low numbers, and with a slow rate of breeding, this wrasse is an endangered fish; its popularity as a food fish has led to the humpheads' decline by 50 percent in the last few decades.

The smaller, more abundant Labridae escape the menu of fine-dining seafood restaurants, but this doesn't mean they aren't food fish for humans. When the question of their suitability for a meal was posed to a free-diving, scuba-diving, and spearfishing discussion group online, the forum mentor, located in the UK, replied with enthusiasm:

> Bigger wrasse have more solid flesh with nice big, firm flakes. Down in Cornwall, I was fortunate to get a couple well over 5 lb (maybe 6–7–8 lb)—wish I'd weighed them now as I found out later they were in record territory. We cut them into big, meaty steaks (salmon-style, cutting across the strong, thick, spine—these were

big, hefty fish) and BBQ'd them, wrapped in foil with butter. It surprises me that people have such low opinions of them—often having never eaten them—they seem as good any fish I have eaten and far better than anything you'd find in a supermarket.

It's precisely in the supermarket, and eventually on our dining tables, where human-fish encounters generally occur—although "encounter" may not be the most apt word when one of the pair has already become food. "Few of us ever see fish behaving naturally," Culum Brown notes, especially given that the actions of aquarium fish cannot be counted as natural. "The vast majority of people only ever see fish on their plate." In the food cultures of much of the world, fish dwell at the opposite end of the consumable spectrum from the insects of chapter 1: whereas entomophagy is either a traditional cultural practice or a relatively new fad, eating fish is a staple of nearly every culture.

The World Bank estimates that fish—defined as finfish, mollusks, and crustaceans together—account for 16.6 percent of the world's protein supply from animal sources and 6.5 percent of all protein consumed by humans. The impact of fish on global nutrition far exceeds these statistics, the World Bank notes, because fish as food contains, in addition to protein, key vitamins, minerals, and polyunsaturated omega-3 fatty acids that are crucial for health, nowhere more than for people in impoverished areas.

At the same time, owing to severe pollution of our oceans and waterways, we may also consume alarming levels of toxins when we eat fish. When in 2014 an article in *Nature* announced that "anthropogenic perturbations to the global mercury cycle" have tripled the mercury content at the ocean's surface, a new estimate of the problem's scope came to light. Mercury levels in fish range widely, so health concerns must be taken up on a species-by-species basis. Most adult humans, according to comparative-fish reports, can eat nearly a pound of salmon per day and be in the clear, at least if we accept governmental levels for safe intake. Eating a single forkful of swordfish catapults that same person into the danger zone, however, and routine consumption of tuna may be harmful as well.

When in 2015 I visited Florida Bay in Florida's Everglades National Park to observe marine life, I was startled at the severity and specificity of an online warning:

> High levels of mercury have been found in Everglades' bass and in some fish species in northern Florida Bay. Do not eat bass caught north of the Main Park Road. Do not eat bass caught south of the Main Park Road more than once a week. Children and pregnant women should not eat any bass. The following saltwater species caught in northern Florida Bay should not be consumed more than once per week by adults or once per month by women of child-bearing age and children: spotted sea trout, gaff-topsail, catfish, bluefish, jack crevalle, or ladyfish.

Statistics for safe ingestion by geographic region; fish species; and our own age, sex, and health indicators take work to ferret out and update over time, and the picture becomes only more complex when we take into account the skyrocketing importance of farmed fish. Salmon make an instructive example. Famous for their long-distance migrations, salmon nowadays are increasingly confined to tanks and tubes, and when we select (or are served) salmon for dinner, it's increasingly unlikely to be the wild-caught variety. Norway produces more than a million tons of farmed Atlantic salmon annually—four times the country's total production of meat and an amount equivalent to twelve million salmon meals a day. Thanks to its immense, steeply increasing investment in aquaculture, Norway is now the world's leading producer of farmed salmon, and it's far from an isolated industry. In California, according to a 2016 *New York Times* report, "virtually all salmon" are now raised in hatcheries.

Both Atlantic and Pacific salmon are born in fresh water, migrate to the salty ocean where they live as adults, then navigate back to their natal waters in order to breed. Environmental cues ranging from chemical signals to the position of the sun may act as guiding factors for the salmon on their watery treks home, which may be quite lengthy. A chinook salmon, the largest of the Pacific species, was first tagged in the Aleutian Islands and then found a year later in the Salmon River, Idaho, a swim of about thirty-five hundred miles, just about the distance between New York and London.

The salmon's migration is often depicted as a sort of hero's journey, undertaken by an individual aiming to return home despite formidable obstacles along the way—a challenging navigation problem, river rapids with turbulent water, hungry bears or bald eagles, people who fish along the route, and so on. In *Salmon*, the environmentalist Peter Coates gives salmon their cultural due: "Inspired by its remarkable life cycle, we have selected the salmon as a symbol of indomitable fortitude and endurance, self-sacrifice, loyalty to place, untamed wildness, irrevocable fulfillment of destiny and the powerful intimacy between life and death." Quite an honorable list, but note its absences: Coates offers no praise for the salmon's cleverness. The hero's journey, it seems, is firmly rooted in instinct rather than intelligence. Are salmon as smart as wrasses? Outside of fisheries-management questions, it seems that salmon smarts are rarely explored.

In any case, we eat salmon in numbers that far exceed those for wrasses or most other fish mentioned in this chapter. Since 1980, consumption of salmon has increased threefold, in large part owing to the salmon-farming I have mentioned. The World Wildlife Fund reports that salmon aquaculture is the fastest growing food production system, accounting for 70 percent, or 2.4 million metric tons, of the global salmon market.

When I typed into the Google search engine the words "why eating salmon is healthy," the first hit, ironically enough, was titled "Top 10 Reasons Not to Eat Salmon," a posting from the animal advocacy group People for the Ethical Treatment of Animals (PETA). "Salmon are smart" is PETA's alpha reason—a fascinating (and in my view, pretty nifty) decision, to list a feature inherent to the salmon, albeit one rooted (because we know so little about salmon cognition) in generic statements about fish intelligence. Concerns about salmon's relation to human health follow closely; reason number two refers to high levels of chemicals in the fish we eat, including salmon. Third on the list is "harm at the (fish) farm."

Two eye-opening reports taken together offer a grim picture of salmon lives on those farms. In *Farmageddon: The True Cost of Cheap Meat*, Philip Lymbery notes that up to fifty thousand salmon may be confined in a single sea cage:

> Often suffering from blinding cataracts, fin and tail injuries and body deformities, and infested with parasites, they are forced to compete for space and oxygen. Salmon are reared in stocking densities equivalent to a single bathtub of water per 75-centimetre fish. . . . Fins and tails are rubbed sore as the fish press against each other and the sides of the cage.

These numbers fit with the statistics offered by Marianne Elisabeth Lien in her brilliant ethnography of salmon production in Norway, *Becoming Salmon: Aquaculture and the Domestication of a Fish*. Using the participant-observer method, Lien herself engaged in caring for farmed salmon as she observed aquaculture practices and interviewed industry workers and managers. She emphasizes the mutuality of interaction between the salmon and the aquaculturalists—no passive beings, the fish make choices and demonstrate agency—but equally brings home the severe limits of that mutuality. Observing the process by which salmon are flushed through a pipe to be slaughtered—first stunned electrically and then bled out—Lien is shown how the stunning machine works. At this point, because the mechanical process has been interrupted, the system fails; the fish flop about in visible distress, anything but stunned. Yet distress is a product of planned aquaculture strategy as well as the occasional accident. In the final two weeks before being killed, the salmon "go on hunger," meaning that they are no longer fed, in order to ensure that their stomachs will be empty upon their slaughter.

If salmon aquaculture is the way of the future, unanswered questions abound. Here's just one: because salmon are carnivorous, their feed is made up largely of other fish, including anchovies. How sustainable is the harvest of these smaller fish taken from our oceans, to feed not only the millions of farmed salmon every year but also the farmed chickens and pigs we will meet in subsequent chapters?

THE SENSORY WORLDS OF FISH

We evolved from fish, and our bodies reflect that evolutionary history even today: if this piscine perspective sounds familiar to you, thank Neil Shubin. Shubin's wildly popular book *Your Inner Fish* invited us to travel in our imaginations back to a time well beyond famous human ancestors like the three-million-year old Lucy from Ethiopia, to the 375-million-year-old fish named Tiktaalik from the Canadian Arctic (the name means "large freshwater fish" in Inuit). Tiktaalik represents, Shubin writes, a "beautiful intermediate between fish and land-living animals," a mash-up of fins and scales with a flat head and body that presages what's to come. "Bend your wrist back and forth," Shubin instructs his readers. "Open and close your hand. When you do this, you are using joints that first appeared in the fins of fish like Tiktaalik."

Shubin's connecting of the evolutionary dots between fish and people brings fish to our notice in new ways: after all, we seem prone to attending most seriously to other animals when their lives are explicitly related to our own. Read Shubin's book and "you'll never again be able to look a fish in the eye (or eat seafood) without thinking about shared evolution," as I put it in my review for the *Washington Post*. If we see our present bodies reflected in our fish ancestors, what can we find in fish of our minds, our individuality, and our emotions? We may start with looking a fish in the eye.

If we glimpse an underwater world, our vision may fill with the brilliant colors that dress these animals' weird and wonderful bodies, shaped in all ways from the impossibly slender to the rotund. That's the thrill I experienced from my perch in a glass-bottomed boat miles out from Florida's Key Largo, hovering over an Atlantic coral reef: I saw wrasses, tangs, barracuda, and other fish going about their daily lives in a way that could never be replicated in an aquarium. Yet the water-air barrier was still firmly in place, and I felt walled off from the fish's world. Divers, by contrast, may directly experience something of a fish's seascape.

If a diver tries to catch a fish's eye, chances are the animal will look back using the eye preferred for viewing unfamiliar, potentially threatening objects or creatures—not the eye most often chosen for looking at familiar fish of the same species. For primates like us, with our forward-facing eyes, overlapping fields of vision and depth perception, it's challenging to grasp what it would be like to experience distinct streams of information entering the brain visually, as fish do because of this division of labor between their two eyes. It would be as if our right eye trains itself on whoever approaches us as we traverse crowded city streets, while the left eye devotes itself to viewing our partner who walks alongside us.

Imagine now that our diving person begins to take in underwater sounds as well as sights. Fish vocalize to each other, as when minnow males growl in wooing a female or utter a knocking noise in fighting rivals. Haddock and cod make percussive noises when certain muscles drum against their swim bladders. Culum Brown estimates that as many as 50 percent of fish species "make some kind of meaningful noise for communication." Those growling and knocking minnows even resort to yelling if they encounter noise in their environment. When fishery biologists piped white noise into blacktail shiners' tanks through underwater speakers, the minnows vocalized more loudly than they did during normal, quieter periods. If this finding holds true for fish in oceans, rivers, and lakes, it may allow a valuable behavioral adaptation to emerge: when boat and car motors rumble and groan near fish habitats, not to mention when our own loud words and cries carry through the air into the water, fish may increasingly need to shout to be heard by each other.

By highlighting fish vocalizations, I don't mean to paint fish communication systems as just watery versions of our own. In the same way that the workings of fish vision depart from ours, so too are other fish sensory systems fine-tuned by millions of years of evolution to specific environments, some of them unimaginably alien to terrestrial mammals such as ourselves. In 2015, when researchers sent a small robot down through a hole drilled in Antarctica's 740-meter-thick Ross Ice Shelf, they were thrilled—and shocked—to discover that fish live in cold, dark waters where common sense insists little life should thrive. This isn't just an unfamiliar ocean ecosystem, it's a location that Douglas Fox, writing in *Scientific American*, describes as "so remote and hostile" that Antarctic glacial geologists expected to find only "scant microbial life."

The robot's descent to the rocky, black depths below the ice mass made for tense moments for the scientific team watching on the video monitors showing transmissions from the robot's camera. Bits of debris knocked loose as the robot disturbed a landscape no eyes (artificial or human) had ever before seen. A meter above the sea floor, the robot was brought to a stop. As Fox reports:

> Then someone started to yell and point. All eyes swung to the screen with the down-looking camera. A graceful, undulating shadow glided across its view, tapered front to back like an exclamation point—the shadow cast by a bulb-eyed fish. Then people saw the creature casting that shadow: bluish-brownish-pinkish, as long as a butter knife, its internal organs showing through its translucent body. The room erupted into cheering, clapping and gasps.

Somewhere between twenty and thirty fish, of three types, were counted that day: the large translucent fish and two smaller types, one orange and one black. Sources of food for the fish and of energy for the ecosystem as a whole are not yet clear, and it's even harder to guess what the sensory perception systems of these fish may be like. Some fish sense the world in part through production or reception of electricity, and many fish sense vibrations (motions of the water, changing pressure, and so on) through the sensitive cells that make up their lateral lines. But the Antarctica fish? We just don't know.

Fish, then, live in habitats ranging from the colorfully vibrant to the inky black, and in each landscape their sensory systems act as the gateway to fish learning and intelligence. As we have seen, some fish use tools in thoughtful ways. While we don't know much about whether knowledge of technology is passed along social lines in fishes, we do know that some fishes closely attend to and learn from others around them.

FISH LEARNING

Evidence that I have already described, on referential signaling (groupers), selective coaxing of clients (wrasses), and tool use (also wrasses, specifically tuskfish), helps us identify behaviors that we tend to rate as among the most advanced *using a human scale of measurement*. An anthropocentric frame of reference, however, is very limited precisely because it notices and preferentially rewards what we humans consider smart.

Looking more broadly, we see that fish readily share information with and learn from each other socially. In their watery worlds, fish aren't only predators, of course; they are also prey. Strategic avoidance of hungry hunters who may wish to consume them is an excellent skill for fish to possess, and thus natural selection is likely to reward sharing of social information about predators. "Many fish," concludes biologist Jean-Guy J. Godin, learn how to recognize and respond to predators they've never before directly encountered. They do this, Godin explains, by "associating visual or odor cues emitted by a predator with chemical alarm cues released from the skin of other fishes when they are frightened, injured, or captured by a predator." *Frightened fish*—I like Godin's statement because it bundles together fish emotion with fish social learning. When we watch scenes (in real life or filmed) of fish being hunted for food, it's all too easy to focus on the powerful animals who gulp down smaller, less savvy ones. How about when those smaller animals—like fish— deploy all their sensory and learning capacities to avoid such a fate? Do they become scared when those tactics don't work?

Touring Florida Bay in the Everglades National Park by boat, I was lucky enough to see a dolphin net-hunting some fish, though I couldn't discern what type of fish. Stirring up sand and silt with rapid movements of his or her tail, the dolphin made a visible ring in the water around the fish. Often Florida Bay dolphin work cooperatively to do this, with the ring-maker driving the fish into the path of wait- ing companions—but on the day I watched, a single hunter created the net. Marine biologists describe the technique as cultural because it's learned and characteristic of *these* dolphins. In Florida Bay they learn how to do it from each other, just as dolphins in Shark Bay, Australia, learn socially how to forage using sponge tools. Even as I felt excited to witness Everglades dolphin culture in action, I realized that the prey as well as the predator might have thoughts or feelings about what was unfolding.

Or consider the orcas who, in the waters off northern Norway, work together to hunt herring, as we see in a video excerpt from an *Animal Planet* documentary. Dolphins also (though nicknamed "killer whales"), the orcas cooperate as families to first encircle, then close in on, large schools of herring. Physically, the fish are, in the words of *Animal Planet*'s video narrator, "stunned and disoriented" by the orcas' tail slaps; as the orcas communicate with each other and cut off the fishes' escapes routes, the herrings are propelled or leap into the air. Soon, the orcas are feasting.

I have for years marveled at the orcas' dynamic dance in coordi- nating movements to bring about a robust and delicious meal of this type. We tend to think of schooling fish like the orcas' prey only in the aggregate: to our eyes, they make up a herd of identical animals, while the orcas are, to our eyes, individuals. Each orca may consume four hundred herring a day, and we may slip into thinking of those four hundred as an undifferentiated cluster of orca-resources. What might be the experiences of the individual herrings, though, as they become entrapped by these huge relentless hunters? What do the herring who manage to escape learn from their close call, and what information might they pass on to other herrings? Rarely are these questions asked. I don't have answers to them, but given Godin's conclusion about fear and social learning in *many* species of fish, I believe they deserve study. It will be impossible to discern precisely what fish feel, or don't feel, during predator encounters—including encounters with humans who fish—but the social behavior of fish survivors in the wake of predator attacks should be amenable to research.

Predation is not the only context in which fish social learning unfolds. Blue-head wrasses—we return once more to the multi-talented wrasses!—migrate to specific places on coral reefs where they spawn. Over time and across generations, they return to those same locations. In an experimental intervention in Panama, fish ecologists removed all the wrasses residing in one particular location and brought in a new group naïve to the area. The newcomers established their own spawning sites different from those that had been used by the original inhabitants. Nothing in the genes or in the environment compelled the wrasses to choose one spawning site over another; information is acquired by new generations from the older ones. Similar instances of social learning were found in an experiment with another species of coral-reef fish, French grunts in the Virgin Islands. It's worth underscoring that both experiments were carried out in habitats natural for the fish, indicating that natural selection has acted strongly on these fish to learn from each other.

ONE AMONG THOUSANDS

On a visit to California's Monterey Aquarium years ago, I stood in front of a blue column of ceaselessly circling anchovies, marveling at the anonymity implicit in that herd. (These anchovies or their descendants are observable on video.) Not one of the thousands of silvery bodies, or the behaviors they exhibited, differed from the others. A quarter century later, I still vividly recall my wonder at the vast gap between the aggregated fish in that tank and the individually distinct monkeys and apes in the wild and captivity I had observed.

Many fish school, and for good reason. A study of juvenile golden gray mullet captured in the Mediterranean Sea off France and tested in captivity shows that individuals expend less energy when aggregated, no matter their position in the geometry of the school. Even the mullets who glided along at the front of the pack did better energetically than when they swam alone, although as expected, fish who swam in their neighbors' slipstream enjoyed the greatest energy savings. Schooling probably evolved because of energy boosts like these, plus the fact that individuals in groups do better than singletons in avoiding predators and finding food. (If group foraging incurs some costs—many mouths feeding in a limited area at once may be risky—those costs must be offset by the advantages.)

Are fish who school really as interchangeable as my memory of the Monterey anchovies might suggest? In fish like guppies and sticklebacks, social networks are expressed within schools: certain individuals associate with each other repeatedly and preferentially; it's not as if all fish just hang out with others at random. Nor are all fish of a given species alike behaviorally. Some are bold.

About twenty years ago, ecologist Sergey Budaev showed in experimental work that guppies differ in what he called personality dimensions. Some guppies tended toward exploration and sociability, others toward behavioral inhibition and escape. Budaev interpreted these as alternative styles of coping with stress. In black-lined rainbow fish, as studied by Culum Brown and Anne-Laurence Bibost, wild individuals were bolder—more apt to take risks—than their captive counterparts, probably because of the higher threat of predation in the wild. Males were not bolder than females, but in a fascinating twist, boldness did vary according to whether individuals did or did not have lateralized brains. A question immediately springs to mind: How do we even *know* when one hemisphere dominates in a fish? To answer this question, Brown and Bibost set up underwater mirrors and observed how the rainbow fish gazed at themselves: fish introduced to a flume with mounted mirrors who spent over 80 percent of their time viewing their image with the right eye were scored as having a right preference; fish who spent less than 20 percent of their time viewing their mirror image were considered left preference. All others were decreed to be nonlateralized.

To test for boldness, the fish were let out of a holding tank into a novel environment, which they could explore once they crossed a high-contrast shape of white plastic. Speed of emergence was used as the measure of boldness: the faster the fish, the more of a risk-taker she or he was judged to be. The nonlateralized fish win the boldness prize in this experiment. Next boldest were the left-eye-preferring fish. Brown and Bibost review a number of possible technical explanations for why boldness varies in these ways, based on where fear is processed in the fish brain (which hemisphere, or perhaps both hemispheres).

The key point is that fish vary in their personalities. What's true in my houseful of rescued cats—small Marie bounds from coffee table to chair back to even higher mantel in a whirl of fearless jumping, watched by larger and heavier Diana, who runs nervously into a cabinet to hide when startled—holds true for many other animals, and fish are no exception, though we hardly know the dimensions of this phenomenon yet. More information will emerge not only from formal experiments but also as people share their experiences with their companion fish.

One of my favorite tales in Jonathan Balcombe's *What a Fish Knows: The Inner Lives of Our Underwater Cousins* was recounted by a woman who kept a fantail named Seabiscuit and a black moor named Blackie. One day, she told Balcombe, she returned home to discover that Blackie had somehow become lodged inside a decorative pagoda in the fish tank. Struggling and scraping his body against the tight walls, Blackie didn't look good at all. Meanwhile, Seabiscuit charged at Blackie over and over again, which the woman saw as an attempt to free his tankmate. This generous interpretation might well meet with skepticism, especially once we learn that the pair's history had featured Seabiscuit's not infrequent aggressive chasing of Blackie. Couldn't Seabiscuit again be acting aggressively toward the trapped Blackie, perhaps in part out of fear at this unusual disturbance in his habitat?

That conclusion might have carried the day with me, except for what happened next: the woman freed Blackie, who had suffered rubbed-off scales and a swollen, raw eye because of his ordeal, and for the next few days Seabiscuit stayed by Blackie's side as he began to recover. Seabiscuit's aggressive chasing did not recur. What exactly these two fish thought and felt as a result of Blackie's unsettling experience, I cannot say, but the distinct change in their relationship—coupled with what we know of fish generally—indicates that they thought and felt something. I would predict that not all fantails would act as Seabiscuit did, any more than all our companion dogs act the same when another dog is in distress; to the extent that I'm right, this story shows off fish personalities too.

In a fun video clip available on the Internet, a small orange-hued fish housed in a large tank, possibly a red devil cichlid, repeatedly circles back to a man who leans in to interact with him or her. First the man gently bats the fish with his hands, then he picks up and tosses the fish—again, gently—in an arc through the air and into the water. Instead of swimming away from the man, a response I would find understandable—being launched through the air by a large biped might not be every fish's idea of a good time—the fish asks for more. Some fish are bold and others aren't, and surely some fish are playful are and others aren't, with their own kind as well as with us.

Needlefish leaping over floating sticks, fish like mormyrids and stingrays batting around balls, cichlids striking a thermometer that snaps back into position: animal behaviorist Gordon Burghardt considers all of these behaviors to be playful. When such behavior occurs in captivity, where fish have extra time, resources, and freedom from fear of predation, we shouldn't dismiss it as irrelevant on the grounds that captivity is unnatural. Before field primatologists discovered that wild great apes like orangutans and gorillas sometimes make tools, along with their chimpanzee cousins, they saw the apes making and using tools in zoos (sometimes to escape their enclosures). Some behaviors seen in in captivity have no equivalent in the wild, of course, but many times what animals do under confined conditions clues us in to their behavioral capacities, and what to look for in the field.

WHAT ABOUT SENTIENCE?

Fish may feel fear; that much is established. Do they experience pain? The default assumption for years has been that if fish suffer at all, it's in a comparatively weak and unimportant way. "There is a sense," Philip Lymbery writes in *Farmageddon*, "that because they're not mammals or birds, it doesn't matter as much if they suffer." Lymbery recounts a day in France, at a Council of Europe conference focused on fish-farming standards, when he set out with EU officials, advisors, and veterinarians on a field trip to explore inland fish farms. At the third such place they visited, a factory farm with high densities of fish, conditions were poor compared to the other two. The fish were in appalling shape. Some had eyes popping out, either from impact damage or infection; others had raw flesh around the tails. The water was far from clear, and the fish crowded around the oxygen-injection systems. "I stood incredulous," Lymbery writes, "as government people, vets and other experts watched fish in obvious distress without a word of criticism or alarm."

Fish lack a neocortex, the central seat of intelligence in some other vertebrates, and in large part because of this, doubts have been raised about the degree to which fish may feel pain. Writing in 2016 in the open-access journal *Animal Sentience*, biomedical scientist Brian Key flatly concludes, "Fish lack the necessary neurocytoarchitecture, microcircuitry, and structural connectivity for the neural processing required for feeling pain. . . . What then do noxious stimuli feel like to a fish? The evidence best supports the idea that they don't feel like anything to a fish." Peer commentary published alongside Key's article was swift and lacerating in rejecting his conclusion. People whom I have cited in this book—Culum Brown, Gordon Burghardt, and Jonathan Balcombe in this chapter, octopus expert Jennifer Mather in chapter 2—explain that a neocortex is not required to feel pain, identify specific brain areas (primarily the telencelphalon) that almost certainly function to process pain in fish, and point to the sophisticated, flexible behavior of fish to support the growing certainty that fish do feel pain.

To be preyed upon by humans isn't easy on fish; if as most experts assert, fish do feel pain, they are feeling a lot of it. A *New York Times* report from 2015 on the three-thousand-year-old Spanish tuna-fishing method known as the *almadraba* pulls no punches: "Dozens of bluefin tuna rose to the choppy surface, thrashing wildly until, exhausted and asphyxiated, the fish gave up the fight, and the fisherman hoisted them onboard by the tail." In this region, a shift is under way to ranch fishing. But more to the point, it's not traditional practices but large-scale *commercial* fishing that is responsible for the lion's share of suffering and environmental damage. Particularly deadly and damaging is trawling, in which huge nets may be used to sweep up marine life as far down as the ocean floor.

In considering fish as seafood, we are catapulted back to challenges similar to those that surround insect-eating. The world's human population is skyrocketing; people need to eat, and fish provide desperately needed nutrition. If, as Brown recommends, we expand our moral circle to include fish, what would that look like?

Tool use and complex communicational signaling by fish have emerged from scientific study only very recently. It's problematic to designate only certain fish as *not to be eaten* based on assessments of fish intelligence, because we have next to no information yet on this subject. Besides, a focus on smartness may turn us away from thinking about sentience. Fish do feel pain, and because of this fact the vegetarian/vegan option will be the most attractive for some people. I struggle with this issue on a weekly basis. My admiration for vegetarians and vegans, coupled with the knowledge that their plant-based diets leave the ones whom I know robustly healthy, sits uneasily alongside a profound sense that I myself (owing to some long-term health challenges) feel healthiest when I supplement my almost-vegetarian diet with an occasional fish.

For those of us who eat some fish, how may we make good choices? Paul Greenberg wanted to devise a three-phrase mantra as powerful as Michael Pollan's famous "Eat food. Not too much. Mostly plants." What he came up with ("clunky," he admits) is this: "Eat American seafood. A much greater variety than we currently do. Mostly farmed filter feeders." About 90 percent of the seafood Americans eat is imported, Greenberg notes, including most of our "big three" favorites: shrimp, tuna, and salmon. If seafood eaters instead embraced farmed oysters and mussels, overfished species would get some relief. The trick, of course, is to avoid duplicating the same mistake that pushes us toward these species in the first place: overharvesting the oysters and mussels would cause harm to their populations. Moreover, oysters and mussels clean our waters as they filter them; when feeding on phytoplankton, a single oyster may filter thirty to fifty gallons of water a day. We don't want to disrupt that process to a destructive degree.

Ideal goals for environmentally minded fish-eaters could be to refuse endangered wild fish, fish taken by particularly cruel and unsustainable harvesting practices, and fish from high-yield industrial farms where close confinement at high density arguably leads to the most prolonged and intense suffering of all. The Safina Center, founded at Stony Brook University by ecologist and conservationist Carl Safina, who has long been invested in issues of overfishing and ocean conservation, offers a guide to eating "ocean friendly" seafood. On the center's website, chef and sustainable food advocate Barton Seaver recommends specific "swaps" to move us away from the more damaging choices. Instead of bluefin tuna, for example, we might select pole- or troll-caught yellowfin or albacore tuna, or wahoo. (*Trolling* is the drawing of baited lines through the water, a method of fishing wholly distinct from *trawling*.) Wild Alaska salmon makes a good substitute for Atlantic farmed salmon; striped bass is a better choice than grouper, and so on.

As the world of fish as individual, thinking, and feeling creatures opens up to us, we may begin to really *see* fish, and hear ourselves talk about fish. In the movie *The Trip*, British comedians Steve Coogan and Rob Brydon drive across the UK, sampling fine restaurant meals. In one dining room, the waiter announces their meal with a flourish: Manx queen scallops resting on baby gem, with parsnip. (Gem are fish; scallops are mollusks.) Brydon dryly observes to Coogan: "Rather optimistic to say 'resting.' Their days of resting have been and gone." True for the gem as much as for the scallops. Even though Brydon and Coogan were about to tuck into their meal, I still loved that moment for its quiet recognition of life and death in mollusks and fish. It's a start.

4. Chickens

At first appearance he was a small and unassuming bird. But when Mr. Henry Joy rode the halls of the Golden Living Center nursing home in Charlotte, North Carolina, carried along in his basket, the residents and staff came to know they were in the presence of an unusual personality. Mr. Joy evidently relished his up-close interactions with the elderly and seemed to tailor his actions to his audience. Center resident Kathryn Black wasn't much for socializing with people, but she warmed to Mr. Joy. "She would hold on tight to Mr. Joy like a teddy bear," remembered Alisha Tomlinson, Mr. Joy's caretaker and primary basket-bearer. "He never once squirmed or flapped his wings in protest. He just seemed to know that she was frail and meant him no harm."

Mr. Joy was a therapy chicken and, by breed, an Old English Game Bantam, a variety of rooster that tends toward small sizes. (Male chickens over a year old are called roosters.) White except for his bright red comb and wattles, Mr. Joy had been raised from an egg by an elderly man named Mr. Wallace. This man had earned a certain reputation for crankiness—at least around his own species. With Mr. Joy, it was different. Mr. Joy perched on Mr. Wallace's shoulder during the man's daily chores, and the pair sat close together when

Mr. Wallace watched television: they were inseparable, a fact that was a source of great pleasure to Mr. Wallace.

I can only speculate whether the later blossoming of Mr. Joy's skill with the elderly stemmed from these experiences with his aged friend, but it's pretty clear that his comfort with people generally originated in these early interactions. When humans raise animals from babyhood, the effects on the animals' subsequent behavior may be profound, as we have known since ethologist Konrad Lorenz's famous imprinting experiments with graylag geese starting in the 1930s. In the delightful 2011 PBS Nature film *My Life as a Turkey*, Joe Hutto raises wild turkeys from eggs he receives in a basket at his cabin in Florida. As the sixteen young turkeys hatch from an incubator and imprint on Hutto, and as man and birds explore together the land around the cabin, Hutto glimpses how turkeys come to sense their world. He even helps to guide that process by acting as the youngsters' substitute mother. "Imprinting gives the observer an opportunity to see into the lives of creatures that you would never have an opportunity to see otherwise," Hutto (speaking through an actor) says in the film.

Perhaps Mr. Joy didn't imprint specifically onto Mr. Wallace but instead on the experience of relating closely with another species, in a way that then generalized to all people. When Mr. Wallace had to go into a nursing home, Mr. Joy had the good luck to be adopted by Tomlinson. A number of contingent events then unfolded that in combination reinforced Mr. Joy's people-oriented tendencies. First, Mr. Joy fell ill with a foot condition that required the amputation of many of his toes, a state of affairs that ensured he was fussed over by Tomlinson. During his recovery, he began to ride around in a basket, a method of transport he found entirely satisfactory. Around this time, Tomlinson brought Mr. Joy along with her to visit a bedridden woman. The effect on the woman of Mr. Joy's calm and agreeable presence was so great that Tomlinson launched his career as a therapy chicken almost immediately: "It was then I knew I couldn't keep his charms to myself. Mr. Joy had to spread the message: chickens are sentient, loving creatures."

Tomlinson described for me how "present and alert" Mr. Joy was to events going on around him. He had his preferences, like all sentient creatures do, and vocalized in ways that conveyed his moods of surprise, fear, and joy. For some reason, Mr. Joy despised anything on wheels, to the extent that he rushed after and pecked at any cart or stroller that came near him. Happily, his congenial experiences extended to other chickens, not just to humans; Mr. Joy had, as Tomlinson calls them, "two wives," the hens Henrietta and BeBe. Speaking generally of roosters' relationship with hens, Tomlinson noted that while roosters can be rough on hens during mating, they also show a nurturing streak and "are always picking up morsels and offering them up to the ladies. No matter how many treats I gave them, roosters almost always call the ladies over and give them [away], taking none for themselves." Mr. Joy was "gentlemanly," she reports, toward Henrietta and BeBe.

Chickens are, of course, domesticated animals. They descended from the red jungle fowl in an evolutionary trajectory that has been shaped and guided by humans for at least seven thousand years. Unlike cats and dogs, the domesticated animals we are most likely to welcome into our homes, individual chickens rarely have their stories told the way Alisha Tomlinson enjoys telling Mr. Joy's. In North America and Europe, chickens are more often imagined as they are made to live now, in industrial farms, densely crowded together and seemingly indistinguishable. But chickens may be resplendently different one from the other, as was immediately apparent when I made six hen acquaintances at Wilder Ranch State Park near Santa Cruz, California, in the summer of 2015. These beautiful birds, with names like Goosey and Bella, ranging in color from white to gold and yellow, sometimes with patches of a soft iridescent blue, live in an outdoor coop outfitted with a chicken swing for exercise. During my visit they were turned out into a vegetable garden; there among the planted rows, one sunbathed and several foraged. Some invited human interaction, and others did not. I gently picked up Bella—so white, so soft—and held her against my chest in a serene encounter that I enjoyed greatly and that Bella seemed to soak up pleasurably as well. Nearby, Burt the rooster looked on.

That I held, stroked, and talked to a chicken for the first time in my fifties is very much a product of my time and place. In her book *Chicken*, Annie Potts notes that before World War I, many families raised chickens on small farms or in their backyards, where the birds moved around freely and soaked up the sunshine. Confined to barns or cages, the birds fared poorly; the lack of sun, and thus vitamin D, caused leg weakness. Research in the 1920s led to commercial chicken feed fortified with vitamin D additives, a critical change that paved the way to where we are now, a time when ten million birds may be confined on a single egg farm. It is all too easy to become desensitized to these staggering numbers and what they mean for the lives of animals.

As I write this chapter, the H5 virus, popularly known as the avian flu, is slowly advancing across a large swath of the United States. One morning, I find an update on the situation in the business section of the *New York Times*. A new case of H5 in Dixon County, Nebraska, "brings the number of states affected by the outbreak to 16, and the tally of birds that have died or will be killed to 32 million." Imagine the outcry, even the panic, if thirty-two million cats or dogs were dying from an advancing viral outbreak. Unless we raise chickens, these birds are probably more familiar to us as ten-piece nuggets selling for $4.29 at the local McDonald's than as animals with thoughts, feelings, and personalities. Recent exploration of chicken behavior and cognition, though, is gradually bringing back a more nuanced awareness of chicken lives.

CHICKEN WISDOM

If chickens are "birdbrains," that derisive term deserves a shiny new connotation. In impressive feats of memory, chickens keep straight over one hundred chicken faces and recognize familiar individuals after months of separation. They reason out the best outcome when given two choices: hens trained to peck colored buttons choose nine out of ten times to forgo an immediate (lesser) food reward for a slightly later (greater) one. Potts notes that this feat involves some consideration of the present moment versus the future.

When they guide their chicks in how to behave, hens modify their own routine behaviors, showing sensitivity to their chicks' skill levels. Veterinary scientists Christine J. Nicol and Stuart J. Pope demonstrated this in an ingenious way with experiments using palatable and unpalatable foods. Nicol and Pope already knew some key things about the foraging of hens and chicks from prior research: New hatchlings can't distinguish between food and nonfood items, and so they peck at both. Hens attract the chicks to food items by their food calls and pecking motions, and give longer, more intense calls for food that they perceive to be of higher quality. Nicol and Pope wanted to know how twelve hens would respond if they observed their chicks making errors in choosing what to eat.

The hens were offered two types of food, each having a distinct color and presented in a bowl of matching color: chicken feed (palatable food) and chicken feed sprayed with quinine hydrochloride (unpalatable food). The chicks, fed separately from the hens, received only palatable food, with some color-coded to match the hens' palatable food, some to match their unpalatable food. When the hens observed chicks eating what they had been trained to perceive as unpalatable food, they responded with more ground pecking and scratching than when observing chicks who appeared to be eating palatable food. These behaviors, Nicol and Pope concluded, were designed to reorient their chicks' choices, an action that may relate to teaching behavior.

In collaboration with veterinary scientists J. L. Edgar and E. S. Paul, Nicol showed in a later study just how exquisitely attuned to their chicks hens can be. The trio had previously demonstrated that hens who witness their chicks experiencing air puffs every thirty seconds show increased alertness, vocalizations, and heart rate. The conclusion from that work was plain: the hens were aroused when observing their chicks undergo mild stress. In a parallel to the Nicol and Pope study, which separated hens' responses to chick cues from hens' state of knowledge, this study asked: did the hens feel distressed themselves because the chicks acted distressed, or did they acquire knowledge about the situation that affected their own cues?

By now, you will probably have guessed the answer: when hens perceived their chicks to be threatened, no matter what the chicks were doing or the signals the chicks were sending, they increased their vocalizations and their walking, and decreased their preening. The experimenters discovered this by conditioning a dozen hens to associate a particular location with danger, specifically with administration of an air puff. Even though the chicks experienced no danger (they were never air-puffed, just as in the earlier experiment no chicks were given unpalatable foods), the mothers' behavior changed in the ways described when they observed chicks put into the "dangerous" area. This isn't to imply that chick cues don't matter at all: the hens showed signs of stress-induced hyperthermia, measured by temperatures in the head and eye, when their *own* expectations caused the chicks themselves to exhibit distress. The chicks "spent more time producing distress vocalizations and less time preening when they were in the coloured box that the hen had been conditioned to associate with danger," the experimenters report.

From an ethical standpoint, it's important to know that the chicks in the two experiments were not actually exposed to major stressors. It's unfortunate that the hens went into a state resembling hyperthermia at times, but that stressful state seems relatively mild and short-lived, and perhaps should be weighed against what we learn regarding chicken cognition, and chicken empathy, as a result.

Sensitivity to the state of others isn't confined to mother-chick relationships. The bond between a hen called Mary and a rooster called Notorious Boy amounted to a monogamous coupling; the pair spent all their time together at Animal Place, a farm sanctuary in California. In an echo of Mr. Joy's actions with his two hen "wives," Notorious Boy summoned Mary to eat food treats first, before indulging himself. While they perched together one stormy night, Notorious Boy sheltered Mary from the rain by completely covering her with his wing. Two chicks called Violet and Chickweed, a brother and sister rescued by the Eastern Shore Sanctuary in Maryland, were similarly inseparable. When Violet died suddenly of an infection, Chickweed veered from sadness to anger. Having watched the sanctuary caretakers bury his sister, over the next several weeks he returned to the location of the grave and stood silently there.

A New Hampshire women named Ellen Chase recounts what happened when one of her dozen mixed-breed hens went blind. A second hen took on the role of companion to the first. This helper hen followed the blind one around, roosted next to her even though the blind hen bedded down for the night at an unusually early hour, and once dropped a worm in front of the blind one and left it there for her. According to Annie Potts, the zoologist Maurice Burton reports a similar relationship between two hens, one old and nearly blind, the other younger and sighted. In this case, the young hen was an outright guide for her friend, collecting and offering food items to her and leading her around the garden during the day and toward a roosting spot at night. When the older hen died, the younger one could no longer bring herself to eat. She died within a week.

Grief so profound that the survivor cannot recover is not uncommon when two animals form deep friendships, as I found out when writing *How Animals Grieve*. While I had little to say about chickens in that book, I did share a story recounted by my friend Jeane Kraines about chicken empathy that remains one of my favorites to this day. Kraines, who raises hens in suburban New Jersey, told me this:

> One day I was in my kitchen when I heard a tremendous hullabuloo amongst my feathered friends. They were screaming and crying so

loudly that the birds in the trees started chiming in. The chickens rushed onto the deck, knocking furiously on the sliding door with their beaks. I ran outside immediately and they rushed off with me behind, trying to keep up. Straight to the pool we dashed. There I saw Cloudy, everyone's favorite hen, flailing her wings in the swimming pool. I reached in and lifted her out. She was only very wet: saved by the fast thinking of her loving flock.

Chase's chicken tale from New Hampshire isn't all happy endings in the way that Kraine's is. The least dominant hen in Chase's group, whom Chase describes as "fearful and isolated from her short lifetime of harassment," assumed a new boldness once she realized that her now-blind group-mate was in a weakened position. "All her pent-up anger," Chase writes, "came out in merciless attacks, random and unprovoked." Sometimes others in the flock defended the blind one from the assaults, but mostly they did not. Chase's flock seemed to include both an empathetic altruist and a smart, formerly oppressed hen who wished to join the ranks of the oppressors, plus other birds who remained relatively indifferent to a blind companion in their midst (but who no doubt expressed their distinct personalities in other ways).

Both experimental and anecdotal evidence, then, tell us about chickens' ability to take in and act upon another's perspective of the world. Yet anyone acquainted with the story of Mike the Headless Chicken might be forgiven for wondering what really goes on in bird brains. A Wyandotte rooster, Mike would have become dinner for the Olsen family of Fruita, Colorado, on September 10, 1945, if things had gone normally. They did not. When Lloyd Olsen endeavored to decapitate Mike, the chop of his ax must have gone in at a peculiar angle. Although Mike's head came off, Mike continued to walk about and peck for food—and not just for a few moments as commonly happens when fatal blows are administered to chickens. Mike had survived his own slaughter.

At this point, as Elwynjohn Johnston notes in a film clip about Mike, "any normal man would have reached down, picked him up and cut his damn head off, again." Instead, Olsen made a decision to care for Mike. Feeding Mike with an eyedropper that funneled food right into his esophagus worked well. After driving to a consultation with experts 250 miles away at the University of Utah in Salt Lake City, Olsen learned that Mike's jugular had escaped the ax blade; blood had then clotted at the site of the blow. Mike's brain stem was left mostly intact (as well as one ear). In this healthy, if headless, state, fueled by hand feedings of cracked corn and eyedroppers of water, Mike was able to live for another eighteen months.

During this period, Mike became a celebrity. Featured in *Life* and *Time* magazines, he toured nationally from Los Angeles to Atlantic City, Salt Lake City to Chicago. Money earned from these sideshow performances became a driving force for the Olsens, as they dreamed of a debt-free life and improvements to their farm. Public reaction was mixed. The family received hate mail from people who believed it had been an act of cruelty rather than kindness to keep the beheaded animal alive. At times, Mike began to choke on mucus that had built up and that he couldn't expel on his own. When this happened, the Olsens quickly had to deploy an eyedropper to clear his airway. For many months, the system seemed to work just fine. When at home in Fruita, Mike still mixed with the other chickens and led something akin to a rooster's normal life. Then, one night at an Arizona desert motel, on the way home from a public appearance, Mike again began to choke. This time the Olsens could not locate the eyedropper in time. Mike died. Now, seventy years later, Mike has a Facebook page and a fan club. Since 1998, the town of Fruita has hosted a festival every spring meant to honor Mike's will to live. Musical entertainment, 5K runs, rooster-calling, and, ironically, wing-eating contests ensure that the event is a lively celebration.

What then, *does* go on in the chicken brain, given that Mike survived and functioned with only his brain stem? Quite a lot. The research of neuroscientist Lesley Rogers shows that avian brains, including those of chickens, are as lateralized as our own, meaning that the right and left hemispheres divide up some tasks rather than duplicating the work necessary to accomplish them. Rogers was the first to discover lateralization in the chick forebrain, and she did so at a time when cerebral division of labor was assumed to be uniquely human (it is, we know now, common in vertebrates). By comparing chicks who were lateralized with chicks made visually nonlateralized through experimental intervention, Rogers showed that lateralization allows chicks to simultaneously find food (a left-hemisphere task) *and* attend to predators (a right-hemisphere task), a benefit of the hemispheric specialization. The right avian hemisphere controls fear and escape responses, while the left takes charge of details.

An international group of scientists going by the fabulous name the Avian Brain Nomenclature Consortium announced in 2005 that it was time to update the century-old terms used for the avian cerebrum, to reflect new understandings of the neocortex-like functions of one particular part of the bird brain. That area, called the *pallium*, the consortium members wrote, "supports cognitive abilities similar to, and for some species more advanced than, those of many mammals." The tired old dichotomy that mammals think with their neocortex and birds act on instincts rooted in their basal ganglia is inaccurate. The specific renaming accomplished by the group is challenging to track ("We renamed the avian palaeostriatum augmentatum and LPO as the lateral and medial parts of the avian dorsal striatum," and so on), but the two central take-home points are crystal clear: birds express behavioral complexity that is made possible by their brains, and the supposed gap in reasoning ability between mammals and birds is illusory. Examples of avian cognition offered by the authors range from feats of memory by scrub jays to tool use by crows. The question of whether these stars of the ornithology world out-think chickens has not yet been properly studied. I suspect that biased assumptions are made about domestic chickens *within* the bird group as much as the consortium members say are made *between* birds and mammals.

Americans now eat sixty pounds of chicken each year on average, a figure that has soared from sixteen pounds during the 1950s. When enjoying dishes made from chicken, people are unlikely to think much about the architecture of bird brains or the outcomes of behavioral experiments focused on hen-chick interactions. For many people, "chicken" translates simply to "delicious."

CHICKENS ON THE TABLE

Walking through the kitchen of Julia Child's Massachusetts home, which she donated to the Smithsonian's American Museum of Natural History in 2001, I hear all around me that unmistakable voice. Her "almost operatic vocal tonalities, the here floating, there plunging falsetto" as *Vanity Fair* put it in a 2009 article, originate from a monitor inside the exhibit that loops old clips of Child. Still, it's easy to picture Child, television personality and author of *Mastering the Art of French Cooking* (now in its forty-seventh printing), here in the flesh; when I do, she's surrounded by chickens, plucked and ready for cooking. This image I take from her program *The French Chef*, which aired on Boston's WBGH television station from 1963 to 1973. The second year's second episode plunges right in with startling visuals and narrative.

Wielding a large knife, an apron-clad Child energetically proclaims, "Julia Child presents . . . the chicken sisters!" One by one she taps six chickens, working right to left as if knighting them, each headless and propped up in a peculiarly humanlike posture: "Miss Broiler!" Child cries. "Miss Fryer! Miss Roaster! Miss Caponette! Miss Stewer! And Old Madame Hen!" This day's spotlight, Child explains, will be on the roaster. Chicken cackling noises and jaunty music takes over as the words "To Roast a Chicken" blaze across the screen and the camera zooms in on the six "sisters." As Child details differences among the various types of birds in front of her, with special care she hoists and pats her "beautiful birdie" roaster and offers vital statistics: weight six and a half pounds, age between five and a half and nine months. Child proclaims this bird to be "in the full glory of its chickendom."

Although that distancing pronoun "its" creeps into Child's narrative, I am struck by how personalized, even intimate, the presentation is otherwise. Child refers to the chickens as "who," not "that," even as she tacks between her affectionate term "the sisters" and the pronoun "he" to refer to individual birds. Child knows her chickens, explaining fine points of chicken anatomy to her viewers, yet of course her discourse is entirely in the service of constructing a flavorful meal. At times she veritably wrestles with Miss Roaster, first plunging the knife in between the vertebrae to tear out the neck. (Child's knife-wielding led to a now-famous *Saturday Night Live* parody in which Child, played by Dan Ackroyd, suffers an extraordinarily bloody accident while deboning a chicken to roast and tries to adapt a chicken bone and cheesecloth into a functional tourniquet.)

Next, Child uses shears to extract the wishbone, and pierces the flesh and muscle as she passes an iron trussing needle under the bird's knee joint. It's almost as if there's some animating spirit remaining in Miss Roaster as she rallies for a final fight, but naturally that's just my flight of fancy, and once she is trussed and herbs are being applied to her skin, no anthropomorphic allusions can possibly work any longer. Even when Child recommends giving the chicken "a butter massage," there's no trace of animality left: the chicken is now merely an object. It's as if Miss Roaster briefly enjoyed, at the show's start, what the anthropologist Arnold van Gennep would call a liminal status, no longer a living animal and not yet someone's meal, instead a chicken poised on the threshold of becoming consumable. All that is over now, and we don't see "Miss Roaster" any longer: we see meat.

As this episode of *The French Chef* comes to a close, the images on the screen are worlds apart from the sitting-high chicken sisters depicted at the start of the show. Child jiggles the legs in testing whether the browned bird is truly well roasted, but otherwise the ready-to-carve animal sits tamely on the cutting board. Indeed, Child begins to carve it ("it" now seems the only plausible choice of pronoun), and we soon view a disarticulated carcass. The jaunty music returns and Child's cheery "Bon appétit!" closes the program.

The transformation represented by what happens to Miss Roaster is both commonplace—it happens every day in millions of households—and, seen with fresh eyes, astounding. We start out in that liminal state—*close* to living creatures (the seven sisters) yet *far* from them (they are naked and headless)—and end up with a meal wholly unrecognizable as ever having been a breathing creature. Taste and flavor become paramount as the animal transforms into an object. My taste buds awakened as I watched and pondered how delicious that juices-running-clear chicken from Julia's kitchen would taste. I do not eat chickens, though. I didn't rush into my own kitchen and try to duplicate Child's patting, trussing, and roasting, or head out to a restaurant where a chef would do it for me. Instead my senses filled with the memory of a splendid meal years ago in a Parisian restaurant: an unadorned, unfussy roast chicken with salad, potatoes, and baguette. (We had chosen the restaurant at random while on vacation, so this was no Michelin-starred establishment, just a very good local place. I dream of that meal still.)

The romance of cooking chicken has not diminished since Child's day. A steady stream of chicken cookbooks is published each year, each one muscling out room on bookstore shelves next to the trendier paleo-diet or gluten-free or let's-eat-insects-for-our-environment volumes. The emphasis, both in print cookbooks and in online recipes, is often on novelty, as home cooks crave fresh ways to update the tried-and-true chicken dinner. Internationalizing the flavor fits the bill: Diana Henry's *A Bird in the Hand: Chicken Recipes for Every Day and Every Mood* from 2015 travels from Portugal to Thailand, gathering round-the-world recipes in a single volume. Quick-and-simple is also a major draw. Who has the time with our hectic twenty-first-century lives to truss and spit a chicken, then let it roast for hours, as Julia Child used to do? The word "easy" seems to move online chicken recipes higher in search-engine results. Some Google results marry these two factors of novelty and ease: a men's fitness website trumpets "an easy chicken recipe that won't bore you to death." It features onion, green pepper, frozen peas, cilantro, and dry white wine, and a preparation time clocked at under thirty minutes.

Chicken finger food, quick and convenient to purchase and serve, wouldn't thrill the French Chef but has become wildly popular. The National Chicken Council reported ahead of the 2015 Superbowl matchup between the Seattle Seahawks and New England Patriots that, on game day, Americans would consume 1.25 billion chicken wings. Taking us far from the individuality of Mr. Henry Joy or even the anthropomorphic labeling of Miss Roaster into the realm of mass-produced commodities, these statistics are cited with a tone as jaunty as Child's televised music: "If 1.25 billion wing segments were laid end to end, they would stretch back and forth from CenturyLink Field in Seattle to Gillette Stadium in Foxborough, Massachusetts . . . almost twenty-eight times. With the Super Bowl being played in Arizona, 1.25 billion wings would circle the Grand Canyon 120 times."

This playful language is mirrored in a whimsical desire to invent new chicken novelty dishes. Comfort food with a sweet twist was served at Chocochicken restaurant in downtown Los Angeles, where chicken was coated with bittersweet chocolate from locally based Coco Suisse. Chocochicken's "high-quality, free-range, locally-sourced" chicken debuted to media buzz in spring 2014 in the *Los Angeles Times*, but the restaurant closed in December of that year. In terms of unusual chicken-eating experiences, there seems to be nothing akin to eating giant water bugs or live octopus (aside from the occasional sensational, tabloidesque live-consumption event). A sixteenth-century Italian cookbook translated into English as *Epulario, or the Italian Banquet*, includes a recipe for how to make a pie with live birds baked into it. The idea in that case was for birds to fly out of the pie, stunning and amusing the assembled diners, and thus *not* be consumed; in any case it's unlikely that chickens were involved. Closer to the "octopus challenge," though, again, not involving chickens, is a recently revived French tradition that involves eating whole (but not living) small songbirds called ortolans. Britain's *Independent*, in 2014, described the dining experience:

> The birds are cooked for eight minutes and served with their heads still attached. After [a] shame-hiding napkin is placed over the diner's head (helping, too, to trap the aroma of the dish), the ortolan is popped in its entirety into the diner's mouth, who then proceeds to eat everything including the head and bones. Those who have tasted ortolan rave about the hazelnut and gamey flavours.

Balut is a dish that involves eating an unhatched duckling in its shell, its eyes, beak, feathers, and bones swallowed along with the rest. Chef Chris Cosentino tried *balut* and pronounced it "pretty gnarly" but believes that eating *should* be a challenging act: crunching on eyes and bones may wake us up, he says, to the food choices we make every day. Based on this philosophy, Cosentino serves meals that features pig's brain prosciutto, lamb heart, braised pig's head with grilled liver and large intestine, and chocolate blood pudding, or more simply, raw pork, including slices of ear.

When it comes to chicken though, it's the wings and McNuggets that drive the market. We like our poultry best when it's very dead and very processed. As Michael Pollan has written, at this point the chicken nugget is its own genre of food for American children. Some kids eat nuggets every single day; I knew one child (not my own) who for many years refused to eat anything else for dinner.

COSTS OF CHICKEN CONSUMPTION

The one-time reputation of chicken as the healthy meat has been in tatters for some time now. Akin to the creeping spread of a lethal virus like avian flu, revelations about costs of eating chickens—for the birds and for human consumers—are becoming only more dire.

Poultry is a megasource of germs, the leading source of death attributed to campylobacter, E. coli, salmonella, and associated diseases, according to the Centers for Disease Control and Prevention. A 2014 study by the Food Standards Agency showed that 73 percent of fresh chickens sold in supermarkets in the UK were contaminated with campylobacter, a bug that causes food poisoning. Around the same time, *Consumer Reports* tested more than three hundred raw chicken breasts at stores in the United States and discovered potentially harmful bacteria in 97 percent of them—including brands labeled as "organic."

I vividly recall finishing my reading of Potts's *Chicken* early on New Year's Eve 2011. This passage in her chapter "Meat Chicks and Egg Machines" made an especially deep (and by now I can add "lasting") impression:

> Male chicks, extraneous to the egg industry (except as breeders), are destroyed within twenty-four hours of hatching. Each year in the US alone more than 272 million male chicks are disposed of by gassing, microwaving, smothering or maceration (also termed "instantaneous fragmentation"), their collective remains used as pet food. Industry experts claim that fragmentation by fast rotating knives is the most humane method of extermination because it is the quickest, yet the process is seldom highlighted by egg producers since it seems unlikely to win favour with a public for whom baby chicks are synonymous with cuteness, Easter, springtime and new life.

I had not known about maceration. I knew that fifty billion chickens are killed globally for meat each year, and that about eight billion of these deaths occur in the United States. I knew Potts had abundant reason to conclude that in a century's time, chickens had been transformed from animals beloved by family members for their personalities to the "least respected and most manipulated beings" on earth. I knew, living as I do on the East Coast not far from the Delmarva (Delaware-Maryland-Virginia) Peninsula with its abundance of broiler-chicken farms, that chicks raised for meat live for all of six weeks before slaughter in conditions of stress, filth, and pain. It was the lives of battery hens—the egg-layers who are industrially reared—and the whirling-knives death of their male chicks that I hadn't fully grasped.

Right from that moment of closing the cover of Potts's book, I ate no more chickens. The absence of hamburgers, bacon, and lobster salad from my diet for years by this point had caused no regrets or mad cravings, but giving up chicken was another story. I missed my favorite chicken dishes, and I still do: made-from-scratch chicken pot pie, chicken korma, and of course roast chicken. Leaving behind a half century of chicken consumption meant also leaving behind food choices intertwined with memories of family rituals, starting as a child when I sampled different preparations of fried chicken state by state as my dad, mom, aunt and I drove from New Jersey to the Midwest to visit our extended family.

In the years since Potts's book, reports from the field—that is, from the slaughterhouse—have reinforced her message about the devastating suffering of chickens. In 2015 *New York Times* columnist Nicholas Kristof reported on Mercy for Animals' undercover investigation at a North Carolina chicken slaughterhouse. The chickens are meant to be knocked unconscious by an electrified bath before the ride forward on a conveyor belt toward a saw that slices open their necks. The goal is for the birds to bleed out and die before they reach the next step, a bath in scalding water that serves to prepare their carcasses. (Here is the "Miss Roaster" transformation to an object made horrifyingly vivid.) Even with that lethal combination of electric bath and saw, however, some chickens survive to the end of the conveyor belt and are scalded alive. The US Department of Agriculture cites seven hundred thousand as the number of chickens "not slaughtered correctly" each year, a phrase that Kristof says is "often a euphemism for being scalded to death."

Kristof's plain language is as necessary as it is disturbing. The discourse around the deaths of food animals is sometimes opaque and even romanticized. No one joyfully embraces scalding deaths for chickens, although obviously such practices are tolerated. There is, though, a way of talking that claims "sweet" deaths for animals killed for our food, as I discovered in reading chef Dan Barber's *Third Plate: Field Notes on the Future of Food*. Eduardo Sousa raises geese in large fenced-in enclosures in Spain, allowing them to forage freely in his project to provide what he calls "natural foie gras." The typical approach to producing foie gras, or goose liver, involves aggressive and artificial force-feeding of grain down a goose's esophagus before slaughter. Sousa, by contrast, aims for a free-ranging period followed by painless slaughter, which he says is important for the liver's flavor as well as for the birds' welfare. The geese are killed, he told Barber, "in a state completely absent of stress, like when a person slits their wrists in a bathtub—the sweetest form of death." (Barber reports also on another person's description of the "cold and sweet" death of fish who are plunged into ice before their throats are cut.)

Like Sousa's free-range geese, free-range chickens (if they truly are allowed to range over a considerable area) lead far more comfortable lives than do their industrially farmed counterparts. An argument I hear regularly from meat-eating friends goes something like this: "I can in good conscience eat farm animals like chickens, pigs, and cows as long as I know the animals had a good life and a compassionate death." No reasonable person would contest the fact that free-range farmed chickens live a comparatively better life and experience a more compassionate death; whether they have it better *enough* is the meaningful question. Writing in the *Atlantic*, James McWilliams cites what he calls the free-range "albatross" factor: the fact that "better" is not acceptable when it comes to animal slaughter.

"Farm animals have a sense of individual identity within time and space," he writes. "They are beings with potential. To kill them is to erase that potential."

As with fish, then, a broad range of options is available to the person thinking about whether or not to eat chickens. In 2015 when I interviewed three prominent vegan animal activists, PETA's Alka Chandna noted that her food choices give her the comfort of knowing that she doesn't contribute to the factory-farming system, and that includes egg production. Occasionally when eating out she is mistakenly served a nonvegan dish. "If I'm given something that contains an egg," Chandna told me, "I think that my miscommunication resulted in a hen suffering in a battery cage for 34 hours (and all of the ancillary suffering inherent in the discarding of the male chicks, the eventual slaughter, and so on)." Chandna and other vegans go further than vegetarians who do eat eggs, who in turn go further than chicken consumers who seek free-range birds, who make choices quite different from people who eat factory-farm-raised birds.

Animal activists don't, of course, care only about chickens. But I've found that for many, chickens hold a special place in the heart. In his book *Eating Animals*, Jonathan Safran Foer writes that KFC (formerly Kentucky Fried Chicken) is "arguably the company that has increased the sum total of suffering in the world more than any other in history" because it buys nearly a billion chickens each year, including chickens that have been treated horrifically at slaughterhouses. Paul Shapiro, the Humane Society of the United States' vice president for farm animal protection, hesitated not a second when I asked him what animal-welfare issue he believes is the most urgent: the life of chickens, he responded, because they suffer intensely and in enormous numbers. More than nine out of ten land animals we kill for food are chickens, he noted. When I asked what difference activists, vegetarians, and vegans are making in their quest to reduce the birds' suffering, Shapiro told me

The biggest advancements for chickens so far have come not for broiler chickens, but for egg-laying hens, of whom there are far fewer. California's Proposition 2 [a statute that prohibits the confinement of farm animals in cages too small for them freely to turn around, lie down, stand up, and extend their limbs] and the slew of corporate policies requiring cage-free conversions (from Burger King to Starbucks to Aramark, and more) are among the biggest animal welfare advancements for chickens in the US so far. But in terms of broiler chickens, the biggest advancement is just that fewer of them are being raised/killed since American are eating less meat.

Any drop in meat eating, though, must be considered in light of the overall increase in rates of chicken consumption in recent decades that I mentioned earlier. Like the Humane Society, United Poultry Concerns, an activist organization founded by Karen Davis and based in Virginia, fights for better conditions for chickens. UPC has established May 4 as International Respect for Chickens Day and suggests that the entire month of May be devoted to chicken welfare. The idea is for supporters to take specific actions on behalf of chickens and chicken-related causes on May 4, then continue to agitate for chickens throughout the month, and indeed the year. Symbolic days like this matter because they heighten our attention; this one invites us to stop and think about chickens as brain-lateralized problem-solvers, smart mother hens, and friends or rivals who interact as big personalities.

A second chicken-themed holiday might be equally useful: International Respect for Small-Chicken-Farmers Day. Around the world live millions of small (nonindustrial) farmers whose very lives depend on chickens. Raising a chick to become an outgoing, thoughtful therapy bird like Mr. Henry Joy or celebrating the variable personalities of hens isn't an option for most of these millions, who need the food and the income that chickens may provide. When I lived in Gabon in West Africa and Kenya in East Africa in the 1980s, the local tradition of small chicken farms was evident all around me. Now on a large scale, African NGOs work to involve people, especially women, in chicken farming because it is profitable without being overly labor-intensive.

American and European tourists flock to the town of Buhoma, Uganda, a gateway to the famous "impenetrable forest" within Bwindi National Park. Preparing to trek into Bwindi to see the magnificent and rare mountain gorillas, some of the tourists stay at luxury lodges. When they select an egg-based meal from their hotel's menu, they support local small farmer Chance Christine's efforts to carve out a more comfortable life for herself and her children than they had in the days when she sold porridge on the roadside. As journalist Deepa Krishnan reports in her article "Chicken Farming as the Next Revolution," it's money garnered from selling eggs laid by her seventy hens that allowed Christine to afford a nice house for herself and her three sons, complete with a backyard suitable for planting banana trees. Krishnan notes that chickens are an excellent choice for small women farmers not only because of the relative ease of their care, but also because in many male-dominated cultures, it's cattle that matter to men.

When a batch of eggs is ready for sale, Christine boards a boda-boda, or motorbike taxi, a form of transportation that requires precise balance skills so that she may arrive at the lodges in Buhoma and Bwindi with an intact product and not crushed eggshells. She is successful enough to make about ninety dollars a month per client. Christine's sons will proceed in school further than the seventh grade, the point at which her own education ceased so that she could begin to earn money.

Given that Christine's business focuses on eggs, it isn't clear how often her hens are slaughtered and sold for meat. But of course that practice is routine for many small chicken farmers around the world. To tuck such practices under the umbrella of McWilliams's "albatross factor" and stop there is shortsighted, because it ignores what we might call an intersectional approach, one that acknowledges the constraining effects of poverty on people's dietary choices. Meatless diets based in plant and insect proteins may, as I wrote in chapter 1, gradually move us away from global dependence on meat. There's new excitement in Kenya, for instance, about "indigenous vegetables" such as nightshade, cowpeas, and amaranth, excellent sources of protein, vitamins, and minerals that are also well-suited to local farming conditions.

Chickens experience their world with heightened intelligence, sensitivity, and awareness compared to plants and insects. The trick is to honor that fact in our food system as best we can in the present even as we work to move away from factory farms in the future. If only there could be a team of Mr. Henry Joys who fan out to industrial farms and bring comfort to all the chickens who live and die there now, anonymously, by the billions.

5. Goats

Collective fervor for acquiring the current "fad" pet tends to cycle quickly in the United States, flaring up then burning out. When the recent potbellied-pig fad faded, pygmy, dairy, and Nigerian dwarf goats next claimed central stage. According to the *Los Angeles Times*, the number of urbanites who sought goat companions spiked in 2015. As the writer-director Ben Callner told the *Wall Street Journal*, goats are right now "a thing."

Given our consumer culture, Callner means primarily that goats are a marketing thing. Callner's ad for Doritos snack chips, starring an irascible goat, aired on television during the 2013 Superbowl football game and then went viral. Greedy and ill-intentioned, the snack-craving goat in this commercial chomps relentlessly through his owner's stash of Doritos ("42 bags later . . . 156 bags later . . ."). When the supply dries up, the goat rampages through the house only to discover the owner cowering in a room with a hidden cache of the chips. The goat's enraged demeanor together with the ominous nature of the background sounds we hear signal that things aren't going to go well for the man from this point forward.

During this filmed sequence, the goat screams. Loud humanlike shrieks from goats are central to the current goat meme (don't miss the startling two-minute "goats yelling like humans" video) and can be heard in music videos by pop stars like Katy Perry and Taylor Swift as well as in the popular Goat Simulator video game ("you no longer have to fantasize about being a goat"). To borrow an explanation of Goat Simulator from Wikipedia: "the player controls a goat aimed at doing as much damage as possible around an open-world map, without any other larger goals." That's a perfect summation of how goats are often portrayed in pop culture—destructive and aimless, all at once.

Historically, goats tend to be represented as sexually profligate, out-of-control, and a little (or a lot) on the devilish side. In Pliny's *Natural History*, we learn that goats are "more ardent" than sheep and "never entirely free from fever." Jesus, an exemplar of kind action toward all living creatures, said that sheep, sitting at his right hand, would inherit the earth, but he consigned goats to the left hand—and hell. And think of the Greek god Pan, that boozy, sexually insatiable, widely feared half-man, half-goat. (It's thanks to Pan that we say we "panic" in moments of sheer fright.)

In medieval times, the Knights Templar were accused of worshipping an enigmatic goatlike god with the name Baphomet. This deity, best known to us now from a nineteenth-century drawing, features a horned, unmistakably caprine head atop a person's body that also bears mixed masculine and feminine features and great sweeping wings. Over the centuries, Baphomet became heavily associated with the occult. In July 2015, hundreds of followers of Satanism, together with curious onlookers, gathered in Detroit for the dedication of a one-ton bronze Baphomet statue.

The satanic resonance of the goat has carried through the centuries. Even today, writes Henry Alford, goats are widely seen as "simultaneously dopey and satanic, like a Disney character with a terrible secret." Devilish goats are embraced by some heavy-metal musicians, a genre that doesn't shy away from invoking Satan, if only as provocation. As one heavy-metal website puts it, the goat is "a tough, ballsy creature with an incredibly hard head that it uses to bludgeon its brethren. Its eyes, with their horizontal pupils, are utterly grotesque and deeply unnerving. . . . Truly, these beasts represent humanity at his most basic. . . . Metalheads grasp this link immediately."

More prosaic symbolism is found at the United States Military Academy in West Point, where the cadet ranked last in any graduating class is anointed as "the goat." Along with this undistinguished nickname comes instant notoriety and a gift of one dollar contributed by each classmate—a cool grand for comparatively low achievement. Among the more famous West Point goats is George Armstrong Custer, who went on to become a Union general and hero of the Civil War.

If birds are saddled with the "birdbrain" label, it's not much better for goats. Their sexed-up, not-so-smart, paired-with-evil reputation doesn't, however, affect our palates: goat meat is second only to pig meat in terms of global consumption. When a Masai friend stopped by the baboon-research house where I was living in Kenya's Amboseli National Park years ago, it was a goat leg wrapped in brown paper that he proudly presented as a gift from his family. Cuisines in places ranging from India and Italy to Mexico and the Caribbean, as well as Africa, embrace not only goat's milk and cheese but also goat stew, sausage, and chili.

In an odd pairing with the soaring goat-as-pet phenomenon, goat consumption is catching on in the States, where the number of goats slaughtered has doubled every ten years for the past three decades. Goat-meat fans wax ecstatic about their meals. In Los Angeles, writer Nathaniel Rich set out to sample birria, a type of goat stew popular in Mexico. His description of the first birria he tasted is graphic enough: "tangy, red and full of bones in unusual shapes" with "bone flakes, sides of fat and gristle, thick black veins and stringy meat." At another restaurant, Rich discovered the menu came with a warning: Birria meat may contain bone fragments that may lodge in your throat and cause choking. Perhaps it's not as harrowing as stuffing a

live octopus, its tentacles still gripping, down your throat, or crunch
ing into a large grasshopper, but given the bony, stringy nature of
goat meat, it might reasonably be asked, what's to like? The flavor,
apparently, and too, a chunk of goat meat contains a quarter fewer
calories than chicken, and less than half the fat.

Milk and cheese play a role as well. Gandhi ate no meat and refused to drink cow's milk, but he adored goat's milk so much that he
traveled with a doe, even on a state visit from India to London. Caprine cheeses are among the most flavorful; brie, cheddar, and gouda
may be made from goat's milk. Historically associated mostly closely
with France, goat cheese began to catch on in the United States when
in 1981 Alice Waters served a goat-cheese salad at Chez Panisse
restaurant in Berkeley, California. The salad was graced with bits of
soft, creamy chevre coated in bread crumbs and toasted; the cheese
came from goats locally raised by a woman called Laura Chenel.
(Chenel's history is itself fascinating: feeling a close connection to
goats, she began to fashion chevre at her farm after a cheese-making
apprenticeship in France, and in 2006 sold that farm for millions to
a French corporation.)

If seen as the source for a delicious stew and exquisite cheeses,
goats may also be objects of curiosity. Goats in Morocco climb trees
in order to find food. Or rather, they *walk up* trees, then eat while
standing on horizontal branches. It's a startling image: arboreal ru-
minants are not what one expects to see. The traction afforded by
these goats' hooves makes for an efficient adaptation, though, one
that allows the animals to seek out the leaves and small fruits of the
argan (ironwood) tree, key sources of nutrition in less-than-lush regions.

The International Fainting Goat Association works to conserve
another curious sort of goat, a rare breed in which individuals inherit a muscular condition called congenital myotonia. These goats
experience muscle stiffness or "freezing" at certain moments, such
as when they are startled, and fall abruptly to the ground. (A short

video from National Geographic shows myotonic goats in action, as does the trailer—don't blink or you will miss it—for the 2009 film *The Men Who Stare at Goats* starring George Clooney.) The goats aren't truly fainting at all, but rather collapsing for a brief period before bounding up again. As they age, at least some of the goats seem to learn from experience how to stabilize the stiffness in their muscles and not tumble to the ground. The association describes the goats as "alert, good-natured animals" and warns sternly, "The IFGA requires a photo of your fainting goat in the down position in order to register your goat with our organization." IFGA members aren't alone in their fainting-goat fandom: the annual "Goats, Music and More" festival in Tennessee honors these animals.

In a utilitarian, even macabre, sense, goats figure in some sports, in ways not so different from the Detroit Red Wings' fans' persistent throwing of octopuses onto the ice during hockey games. In 2013 a severed goat's head was dropped off at Chicago's Wrigley Field in a package addressed to the owner of the Chicago Cubs baseball team. This ghoulish act is no doubt related to the "curse" placed on the team in 1945 by the owner of the Billy Goat tavern, who had been escorted out of the park during a World Series game because of the unpleasant odor said to emanate from his baseball-viewing companion, a goat. At that point, the Cubs had been leading the series, but they went on to lose. In subsequent decades, goats were on several occasions brought to Wrigley Field in an attempt to break the curse. The curse held fast until 2016, when it was broken in spectacular fashion: the Cubs won the World Series.

In buzkashi, the national sport in Afghanistan, the ball is a goat, headless and disemboweled. Ancient in origin, this game is part of the fabric of Afghan life, as NPR put it. NPR also makes plain how brutal it is for the goats: "The morning of the match, the goat is chosen and slaughtered in halal fashion. The throat is slit and bleeds out. The animal is then decapitated and gutted. The hooves are cut off. The skin is stitched back together. Game time." If this practice strikes you as repugnant, keep in mind what footballs and baseballs are made of in the United States. That we don't slaughter the cows who contribute their hide to our sports equipment right at the stadium before Sunday afternoon or Monday night football games doesn't mean the cow is spared.

Goats are everywhere in popular practice and discourse. Rarely, though, do goat themes and memes embrace what goats know and feel as they go about their everyday lives. For that, we need to meet individual goats every bit as personable as Mr. Henry Joy the therapy chicken.

REAL GOATS

Mr. G, a white goat, lays inert in his enclosure. Rescuers from Animal Place in Grass Valley, California, had saved Mr. G from an untenable living situation: a woman who couldn't care for animals properly had kept him, a burro named Jellybean, and other animals on her small property for ten years. Although surrounded by kindness in his new home, Mr. G won't eat; not even molasses or apples tempt him. He doesn't move either. Staff members work to propel him around, so that his muscles get some exercise.

A health checkup confirms that Mr. G is fine physically, and soon his caretakers begin to suspect it's his heart that's at risk—and not in a medical sense. Jellybean the burro had been taken to another sanctuary. Could it be that the friendship between the goat and the burro went deeper than anyone thought? On day six after Mr. G's arrival, Animal Place transports Jellybean to his friend, and Mr. G greets him with exuberant body language and bright eyes. The two animals touch muzzles. Within twenty minutes, Mr. G begins to eat, standing right next to Jellybean. (Don't miss Animal Place's video of Mr. G's transformation.) Goat and burro now live together at Animal Place's six-hundred-acre sanctuary.

About two hundred miles southwest of Grass Valley, in the town of Pescadero just off coastal Route 1 with its gorgeous blue views of the Pacific, lives a herd of two hundred Alpine goats at Harley Farms Goat Dairy. For over a quarter century, Harley Farms has been a farmstead dairy. The goats raised in this small operation are milked twice daily, and each goat's daily gallon of milk produces a pound of cheese. When, together with my husband and friends, I visited the farm in 2015, we admired not only a cluster of goats resting in a shady enclosure but also the regal-looking brown llama who strode calmly among them. The two species paid no attention to each other. This apparent mutual indifference changes markedly at moments of danger. Pescadero lies in the midst of mountain lion and coyote country, and the llamas are meant to act decisively, with these predators or with dogs, as the goats' first line of defense.

Bart, a llama of "extraordinary presence," was, during his life, effective in this guardian role. (Bart died some years ago at about age twenty-eight.) One night Dee Harley, the farm's founder, was roused from sleep by Bart's warning call. Katie Cox of Harley Farms recounted the story to me:

> Bart was in front of the goats, who were in a tight herd out in the field, with a staff member's Alsatian dog in between Bart and the loafing barn where the goats would have spent the night. The Alsatian had killed a sheep—we had two sheep in with the goats at the time. Thus Bart had maneuvered the goats out from the shelter to the field, remaining in between them and the predator. The sheep had not responded to the herding.

Another day, a visitor's dog darted into the pasture with the goats. Bart spat at the dog, quickly maneuvering himself between that animal and the goats. No llama, not even Bart, could successfully take on a mountain lion, but Cox does think the llama trio, along with the farm's electric fence, provide night security against more than dogs. "The llamas have certainly seen off many more night predators," she noted. "Coyotes are common here. Dee has seen the llamas sit by holes in or under the fence, made during the night, for days." Llamas' perceptual acuities are as notable as their patience; at Harley Farms, judging from their visual attentiveness to the road, llamas anticipate neighbors' walking their dogs past the farm up to ten minutes before the dog comes into view.

If the llamas seem to be the clever heroes here, the system highlights also the goats' ability to pick up on communicational cues across species lines (unlike the sheep), a skill no doubt rooted in their keen attunement to each other. After leaving Pescadero that June afternoon and traveling on to Wilder Ranch State Park near Santa Cruz (the place where I held chicken Bella), I was invited to walk right in among the goats. Primed by the morning's earlier caprine experience, I saw immediately how attentive the goats were to each other, especially to Peanut, the group's alpha female. Herding goats is very much *not* like herding cats: when Wilder Ranch's animal program coordinator Sunny Schacher wants to coax the goats from one location to another, she motivates Peanut, who is the key to motivating the rest. Not that Emma, Daisy, Violet, and the other goats in the group follow mindlessly behind; as they go, they attend to their own squabbles and concerns.

It's this social attunement that led Farm Sanctuary to choose the white Saanen goat Prince as a face of its "Someone Not Something Project," which highlights farmed animals' interior lives. Prince was one of the 2,621,514 goats who lived in the United States as of 2012. Each goat's location was plotted by the US Department of Agriculture; for cartography (or goat) lovers, it's a fascinating map to pore over. Prince made his small contribution to California's cluster of dots, each representing five hundred goats. The dots look even denser in central Texas where, in Edwards County, goats outnumber people 22 to 1. Nationally, over three-quarters of these goats are raised for meat. Like Mr. G and the goats at Harley Farms and Wilder Ranch, Prince gives us a glimpse into what life is like for the goats who aren't—even if, as in Prince's case, they had originally been intended for the pot.

As a tiny kid two weeks old, Prince had been discovered by police officers in the back seat of a vehicle when the driver was stopped for speeding. Prince was stuffed in a bag, almost certainly meant to become someone's dinner. Through animal-rescue channels he landed instead at Farm Sanctuary, where Susie Coston met up with him. At this point Prince was emaciated, covered with lice, pneumonia-riddled, and suffering from a pox virus called orf that causes mouth sores and, in turn, pain upon eating. With proper care, he began to heal and bonded with an old ailing goat called Molly. Perhaps Molly's slow pace made a good match originally with an ailing youngster's diminished energy—and then the friendship stuck, even past the point when both goats' health improved.

Prince's primary love, though, ranked right up there with treats of strawberries, bananas, and molasses: hanging out with *Homo sapiens*. On tour days at the sanctuary, he stood at the gate awaiting the first visitors. Hours later, he closed down the tour at its end. "Prince chose to really go out of his way to be close to the people in his world," Coston told me, "but also with new people who came to the farm. He was a very gentle goat with people."

Two years after his arrival at the sanctuary, Prince was diagnosed with CAE, or caprine arthritic encephalitis, an incurable virus that is transmitted to kids through their mothers' milk. To combat the arthritic pain that this illness caused him, Prince received medication; lapping up his beloved molasses, he also took in strengthening supplements. For about two more years, Prince lived well despite the disease. Then the inevitable decline began, and eventually his left leg stopped working altogether. One night, clearly in some pain, Prince rose from his spot in the barn and went one by one to each goat in the herd and touched him or her on the head. Why did he do this? Was Prince aware on some level that his remaining time was short? Was he saying goodbye? It's a romantic notion, but one I want to resist: not because it's out of the question that certain animals anticipate their own deaths but because there's no way for us to know. I think it's enough to say, judging from the physical toll they took, that Prince's actions were fully purposeful and carried meaning for him.

An experiment-driven look into goat thinking and feeling complements what we learn from Prince and the other California goats I've profiled here. It turns out, when tested scientifically, that goats don't rely on each other to learn—they acquire information individually rather than socially—but they do excel at tasks that require advanced thinking and long-term memory, and they show pronounced emotional responses to how they are treated.

FRUIT BOXES AND OTHER PROBLEMS

Compared to their wild counterparts, domestic goats have bigger bodies and smaller brains. This reduction in brain size is almost certainly explained by the nature of the goats' interactions with humans, during our mutual evolution over the last ten thousand years.

Wild goats live in societies in which small parties of males, females, and kids constantly form, then break up and re-form with different members, a mode of group living called fission-fusion that also characterizes chimpanzee societies. With this in-flux arrangement, social skills that allow the goats to be attuned to who's coming and going, and who's doing what with whom, are at a premium. Further, wild goats may live in hardscrabble regions where, as is the case with the argan-tree goats in Morocco, finding food is a considerable challenge. Yet they flourish. From this, we see that wild goats evolved to be clever at both food-finding and mastering rapid social change.

Over the millennia, as they increasingly associated with us, goats faced fewer of these challenges. The shrinking of their brains is one result, and it makes the conclusions reached by biologist Elodie Briefer about goat learning and memory all the more fascinating. She and her colleagues trained twelve goats at Buttercups Sanctuary in Kent, England, to solve what's called a fruit-box task. The goats were presented with a box and had to pull, using their lips or teeth, a lever with a rope, then lift the lever up with their mouth or muzzle. When this two-step sequence was carried out correctly, a food reward emerged from the box. Nine of the dozen goats successfully learned the task, requiring between eight and twenty-two trials to do so.

Here's the best part: the nine goats remembered how to solve the puzzle even over the long term. Presented with the task at various intervals ranging from 26 to 311 days after the initial problem-solving, the goats got it right in one try. Though constrained by the formal tone of a scientific journal where they published these results, Briefer and her team exult just a bit, noting the goats' "remarkable long-term memory." And it *is* pretty remarkable, given widespread assumptions (myths) about dull-minded farmed animals.

Some of the goats in this experiment were shown the task by another "demonstrator" goat, and others were not. In light of their social nature, I expected that goats would learn the fruit-box task more rapidly if another goat showed the technique to them first. This wasn't the case, however. The goats showed no tendency toward social learning. Citing other research, Briefer reports that domesticated dogs, compared to wolves, may learn more readily from humans than from other dogs. Maybe a pattern exists: Domesticated animals pick up on cues from each other less readily when solving problems that aren't social in nature.

Goats also demonstrate advanced thinking skills like object permanence and categorization learning. Christian Nawroth and colleagues found that Nigerian dwarf goats tested at Germany's Leibniz Institute of Farm Animal Biology rarely committed what's called the A-not-B error. Goats first watched as one of three cups was baited with a reward. Then, the bait was uncovered and the reward moved, as the goat watched, to a second location. The goats were mostly able to find the reward in the correct location, without "perseverating" on the first (but now incorrect) location. Follow-up experiments were of the "crossed transposition" type, where a reward is placed under one cup and another cup left empty; the two cups' positions are then swapped. The goats had trouble finding the reward when identical cups were used, but their success rate shot up when the cups varied in color and size. Based on the animals' significant object-tracking skills, the authors conclude that the goats have a "quite sophisticated perception" of their physical environment. (And who among us doesn't empathize with the goat who caused the authors, in offering results for one experiment, to report, "One subject had to be excluded due to a lack of motivation.")

At the same German research facility, Susann Meyer and her colleagues asked Nigerian dwarf goats to categorize artificial two-dimensional symbols. The symbols were shaped identically, with either an open or a filled-in black center. In each trial, four symbols were presented on an automated LCD screen; four was chosen as the number rather than only two, in order to present the goats with a greater challenge. Often in this type of research, animals are led into special locations for testing; this site, though, doubled as a sort of environmental enrichment for the goats because the screen was placed right inside their home pen.

The idea was for the goats to ignore the overall symbol shape and zero in on the center. Open-center symbols were rewarded, filled-center symbols were not, and within any set of four, only one symbol had an open center. The goats had trouble telling apart certain symbols, possibly because the jagged margins of those particular shapes caused some sort of perceptual dysfunction. Overall, however, their ability to categorize symbols was impressive: the goats established categories and then placed novel symbols into them.

As we have seen, goats tend not to learn from each other, and experiments tend to favor individual performance on object and symbol tests. Goats do, however, use their brains in their social lives. Briefer and her colleagues sought to discover whether female goats remember the vocal calls of their youngsters, even beyond the time of weaning, when the kids are about six months of age. Mothers are the sole caretakers; fathers do not participate, nor is there communal rearing by females. Right after birth, mom and baby recognize each other through smell. Gradually they begin to separate from each other, and visual and vocal cues for mutual recognition kick in. At a farm in the UK, Briefer's team recorded pygmy goat kids' contact calls at five weeks of age, then played the calls back to the moms at two different time periods: right away, and then after eleven to seventeen months had elapsed. At the time of this second playback experiment, the kids had been weaned for at least seven months; it was now their younger siblings who actively nursed from the moms. Mothers at this juncture were also made to hear calls of other kids familiar to them (but not their own). The calls of the mother's *first* kid were found to be more similar to those of her *current* kid than of the familiar but nonrelated kid.

Responses of the listening mothers was measured by how often and how long they looked at the loudspeaker, how often they vocalized, and the timing of these behaviors (latency times after the call was played back). Maternal memory for their kids' contact calls was strong even a year later (that is, at the time of the second playback). Although they responded more strongly to their kids' calls at five weeks, they also responded more strongly at a year to their now-weaned kids' calls than to those of the nonrelated kids. Could the moms have simply misunderstood, and thought they were hearing their *current* instead of their *previous* kid's calls? Briefer and her colleagues conclude that this is highly unlikely because, although the calls of the siblings were similar, perhaps due to genetics, they were definitely distinguishable. These findings, they say, "reveal surprising long-term memory for vocalizations in mammals"—and I would add, not in big-brained elephants or chimpanzees but in oft-underestimated *goats*! This prodigious vocal memory may help the females keep up close kin ties in the short run, especially in their fission-fusion societies; at an evolutionary time scale, it may be selected for because it helps related goats, like mothers and sons, to avoid the genetic risks of mating with each other.

GOAT MOODS

Unlike chickens, cows, and pigs, goats aren't regularly kept at factory farms. Even so, they don't always escape abuse and neglect. Buttercups Sanctuary, one of the locations Briefer has used to conduct her behavior experiments, teems with goats, about 135 of them. It's the sole registered sanctuary in the UK given over wholly to care of goats. On tours days, brown, black, white, and multicolored faces peer out as some goats boldly greet and seek contact with guests—like Prince did at Farm Sanctuary in California—while others hang back. This variation is familiar to goat-raisers. When the novelist Brad Kessler left New York City for the farming life in Vermont, he began goat dairying and soon spent his days surrounded by does Hannah and Lizzie, kids Pie, Nisa, Penny, and Eustace Tilley, and more. In some ways, the goats seemed to him of one mind: they liked routine, not novelty; during milking, they visibly responded to calmness on Kessler's part with calmness of their own. Lizzie, though, stood out. She was "the perfect milker and mother and protector of the herd who policed the barnyard at night and took up the rear when grazing."

When visitors came to the farm to purchase two kids—Lizzie's two young daughters—the herd crowded around. Lizzie, who had been ill, didn't join in, staying on a hill apart from the others. Then one of the kids called up the hill to her mother. When Lizzie called back, the kid went up and pressed her face against her mother. Soon the twins were placed in their new owners' truck. At this point, Lizzie did descend the hill and called to her daughters. The truck pulled away. Of all the goats, Lizzie alone remained standing there for a full hour. She stared down the driveway, Kessler writes, "high wind in her hair, looking at the place where her daughters last had been."

The more time Kessler spent with goats, he says, the more "complex and wondrous" seemed their emotional lives. Yet he also knows that bucklings—the boy goats—are destined to become food, more often than are the doelings. "Young, milk-fed *capretto* is meltingly tender," he writes. "Older kids are barbecued or spitted and roasted whole, and still older ones braised, stewed, jerked, or curried." Those goat stews so savored in Los Angeles and across the world come from somewhere, after all. At Harley Farms in California, where I watched the protector llama stride among the goats, and saw the good life the milked females have, no males are present. The reason for their absence is clear.

My struggle to fathom how these dual commentaries of Kessler's can coexist—his recognition of wondrous goat emotions alongside his savoring of roasted kids—no doubt seems hopelessly sentimental to farmers. Just as with chickens, goats are routinely kept around the world on small farms, where they are known as individuals *and* may be slaughtered for the family table. Vegetarians and vegans wouldn't eat Kessler's goats no matter how humanely they had been raised. As I noted in chapter 4, this essential difference in outlook turns on (among other issues) whether the concept "humanely raised and slaughtered" makes any sense. It's too easy, and wrong, to assert that the world divides cleanly into people who love and refuse to eat animals, and others who eat animals and are indifferent or neglectful of them.

In the midst of these moral discussions, goats are rescued from bad conditions, and the sanctuaries where they go may become venues for research into goat personality and emotion as well as goat cognition. Together with Alan McElligott, Briefer tested two different sets of goats at Buttercups Sanctuary to see whether goats' past histories may affect how optimistic they are in the present.

Nine of the goats tested had lived through awful conditions before coming to Buttercups. Lumped together in the "poor welfare" group, these goats had truly suffered: one had been housed in a pen so small that no turning around was possible; another had been confined on bare concrete without any shelter, even in winter. Others were fed so poorly they became obese, sustained injuries that were never treated, or were tethered to fences without any proper care whatsoever. Compared to these goats, the second group of nine, the control group, had enjoyed adequate diet and shelter, medical care, and social companionship, but could no longer be kept by their owners and so ended up at the sanctuary. All eighteen of the goats had lived at the sanctuary in excellent conditions for at least two years.

Briefer's experimental apparatus was stationed in a field familiar to the goats. Five corridors radiated out in a semicircle from a central arena. Directly opposite each other, at the two extremes, were a so-called positive corridor, baited with apples and carrots in a blue bucket covered with a lid, and a negative corridor that contained no food rewards, only an empty blue bucket. In between, at 45-degree intervals, were three "ambiguous" corridors, which also contained only empty buckets. Starting with the ambiguous corridors closed off, half the goats were trained to expect food on the right, the other half on the left. Once the goats could discriminate between the positive and negative corridors, the ambiguous corridors were opened as well. The measurement of the goats' behavior was quite precise. As the researchers explain, they recorded "the latency of the goats to reach the end of each corridor as the time from when one of their front legs passed the gate, until one of their front legs passed the line delineating the end arena." In this way, speed was used as a proxy for positive anticipation of what would be found in each corridor.

Surprisingly, females from the poor welfare group were more optimistic than those from the control group, as indicated by their moving faster in the corridors. This finding was the opposite of what Briefer and McElligott had predicted going into the experiment, but they emphasize that the difference didn't reach statistical significance. For males, the control group goats were faster than the others, but again, not to significance. In short, even though one group of goats had been abused, their expectations were not pessimistic compared to those of the others.

Why should males and females react differently? The male goats had experienced worse treatment in almost all cases than had the female goats, that much we know. Perhaps that factor is enough to explain the sex difference. Alternatively, females may generally be less susceptible to stress than males in this species, or individual variation in temperament might be the key, two hypotheses which could be tested in a larger sample of goats.

Is this research even really about personality, you might wonder? Yes, but in a specific way. Certainly a goat's response to living conditions—including kindness or abuse shown to him or her by humans—must be shaped by both inborn tendencies and specific life experiences. Briefer and McElligott focus, though, on goat mood, which they define as long-term diffuse emotional states that arise from an accumulation of shorter-term emotional states rather than from a specific event. Moods, they explain, are known to guide animals' (including humans') expectations, so that good moods lead to an optimistic bias and bad moods to a pessimistic one.

Might the goats who showed an optimistic bias in the experimental apparatus also be said to display distinct personalities in their interactions with other goats at the sanctuary? Are they more upbeat, outgoing, or playful? For now, we don't know. But the goat-mood study puts *me* in a good and hopeful mood: goats may recover emotionally even after they have endured abuse or neglect. This is precisely what animal rescuers hope might be the case.

Along with that welcome news comes a message: animals who are capable of anticipation and optimism are able to embrace the joys of life. Mr. G shows us that with his response to reuniting with his longtime friend, Jellybean the burro. When images of a cavorting, horny, and quite dumb goat are used to stereotype goats in our culture, an accurate reply emerges from both controlled scientific experiment and close observation of goats going freely about their daily habits: goats are clever, and they express their feelings about what happens to them.

Plainly, goats as "a thing," as shrieking, product-selling cultural memes, are not the goats known to small-scale famers, sanctuary workers, animal-behavior scientists, and other fans of real-life goats. I'm one of 192,000 fans of @EverythingGoats on Twitter, where gentle goats are featured over goats as malevolent agents of chaos. In keeping with this theme, perhaps I'll patent a new game called Gentle Goat Simulator that depicts goats who make friends with humans, show off by categorizing symbols, and bring joy and solace in the herd to their goat friends. Would it sell? Stranger goatly things have happened.

6. Cows

The beef rib is an instant conversation stopper, a long block of
impressively tender meat clinging to a Jurassic curve of bone. It surely
upstages the brisket in theatricality, and possibly in flavor as well,
though it's a close call.

New York Times review of Mighty Quinn's Barbecue in the East Village

The poetry of beef rib—the "Jurassic curve of bone"—in the epigraph may cause carnivores' mouths to water. The very next article I
consulted after the New York Times restaurant review, a piece called
"The Zen of Beef Ribs," also remarked upon the ribs' "Jurassic size."
It's enough to lead an anthropologist to wonder: what is it about cow
meat that evokes our prehistoric past? Early humans gathered plants
as much as (and in some places more than) we hunted animals, yet
when is the last time you heard a big delicious salad described as
being of Jurassic proportions?

Of course, we Homo sapiens or our immediate ancestors weren't
around in the Jurassic period, which started around two hundred
million years ago during the Mesozoic era. Our lineage only broke
off from that of the other apes at around six million years ago. Still,
it's clear that eating meat acquired by hunting, and by scavenging
from carcasses brought down by other carnivores, boosted the de-

velopment of our outsized brains. At least by 2.5 million years ago, our ancestors in East Africa were fashioning tools suitable for processing of meat from animal bodies.

Meat-eating was key to the human evolutionary trajectory. Does that mean a salivary response to the poetry of beef rib and brisket is somehow ingrained in our species? Is there an evolutionary imperative for us to consume meat now and into the future? No animal is more central to these questions than the cow. ("Cow" is used here as an umbrella term that includes the steer, a bull who has been castrated for beef production; I will use specific terms when necessary.)

COW OBSESSIONS

Demand for the foods the cow gives us—and it's not only meat—is astonishing. In the United States alone, we consume about sixteen billion burgers a year. Our cheese consumption has just about tripled in the last forty years. We drink less milk than we used to, owing in part to the continuing crazes for bottled water and large sugary drinks, yet six billion gallons of the stuff is sold still every year.

Each one of us spoons up forty-eight pints of ice cream on average every year, more than the residents of any other nation. Ice cream holds a special pull on our imaginations, tied often to childhood memories. A trip to a Howard Johnson's restaurant when I was growing up in New Jersey in the 1960s was a major thrill. There behind the counter, where my cousins and I perched on stools, sat a huge selection of ice cream, well beyond the familiar chocolate, vanilla, and strawberry ("huge" at that time meant a boast of twenty-eight flavors). Butter pecan and peppermint stick flavors felt to us downright '60s radical! When I recently started a conversation among friends about childhood memories of ice cream, my forty-, fifty-, and sixty-something friends suddenly reverted to their younger selves: a five-year-old boy in Indiana who drove with his parents to enjoy lemon ice cream in a nearby town; another young boy, this time in Ohio, who visited a dairy on a Sunday drive with his grandparents, where he fell hard for the fancy-sounding French vanilla. There was also a small girl in Massachusetts who rode in a red Mustang convertible with her friends' parents to buy a fresh black raspberry cone, and kids pretty much everywhere who raced outdoors on summer nights chasing a Good Humor truck, offering up dimes and nickels in exchange for Creamsicles. We ice-cream fans nowadays face resplendent options. My own current favorites, Graham Central Station and Chocolate Raspberry Truffle, are no match in the exotic category for selections like Avocado, Beet Goat Cheese and Candied Pistachio, or Szechuan Peppercorn Chocolate.

Ice-cream love is a formidable force, but it's perhaps back in the world of beef where the strongest cow obsessions emerge. Beef-eating challenges, culinary versions of Outward Bound expeditions, probe an eater's endurance and limits. At Kelsey's two steak houses in Indiana, diners may tackle the Six Pound Challenge: consume a 96-ounce sirloin, baked potato, salad or soup, and piece of bread within one hour, and your meal is free. In a twenty-year period, fewer than ten people succeeded in doing so. The low success rate is no wonder: that's meat enough for two dozen quarter-pound burgers. At Brand Steakhouse inside Las Vegas's Monte Carlo casino, it's even worse: the beef brought to the table runs to 120 ounces. It's a size meant for sharing; swallow it all yourself, and it's free. (I couldn't find success statistics for this one). Diners at Gus' Steakhouse in Norwich, New York, must force down a mere 80 ounces of steak and a single side dish for a free meal.

We might be forgiven for assuming that the carnivores who meet these formidable challenges are robustly sized, not to say beefy, males. Yet in 2014, at Sayler's Old Country Kitchen in Portland, Oregon, a woman named Molly Schuyler consumed a 72-ounce steak, plus sides and a salad, in under three minutes. An hour later, she ate a hamburger too. (She weighs 120 pounds.)

Seen in this light, the steak house takes on aspects of a ritual space. Food writer Josh Ozersky plays with this idea of ritual dining, applying it not only to extreme-eating contestants but also to regular customers: "Steakhouses are not really restaurants in the strictest sense: they are closer in spirit to strip clubs or spas, places to which people repair for rites of costly self-indulgence, Dionysian revels in which stressed businessmen or harried wives vent their hypertension." Swallowing six pounds of meat in three minutes can't be about the taste; at that punishing pace, there's no time to savor what Ozersky refers to as "the enormous slabs of blackened prime beef" on offer. Yet for most beef lovers, taste *does* matter, of course, as the ecstatic restaurant review quoted above attests.

Milk, though less poetic, perhaps, than curves of beef, is a staple food. Cows grace us with milk because, in the first place, they are mammalian mothers who nurse their babies. Knowledge of this basic fact of biology is eroding as more and more of us become disconnected from farming—and from the sources of our food. Four in ten British people aged sixteen to twenty-three who responded to a 2012 survey did not realize that milk comes from cows; 7 percent somehow concluded that it comes from wheat. (The problem goes far beyond cows, as 20 percent said that jam is derived from cereals.)

If beef-eating is celebrated by millions and our major source of milks fades from collective understanding, cows as animals with their own lives to lead are often invisible altogether. We may enjoy a glimpse of bovine grazers as we pass open pastures in a car or on foot, or gaze at sanguine cow faces on milk cartons and billboards. But how many of us who don't farm have spent time up close and personal with cows?

CONNECTING WITH COWS

If I could choose cow companions, high on my list would be Tricia and Sweety, who live at the Farm Sanctuary property in Watkins Glen, New York. Both are blind. Sweety was born on a Canadian dairy farm that featured concrete floors and no access to the sunshine. According to Farm Sanctuary, she "endured an unrelenting cycle of insemination, pregnancy and birth." Each time she gave birth, including when she produced two sets of twins, her babies were taken away from her immediately, the males because they give no milk, the girls because that is just the policy. No babies stay with their moms. After eight years as part of the herd, Sweety was marked for slaughter. By this time, she wasn't well. Thin and tired, she suffered from an infected foot.

Despite these hardships, luck was on Sweety's side when it counted the most. She was taken in by a horse rescuer who couldn't keep her but refused to see her killed. Farm Sanctuary stepped in, in part out of compassion for Sweety and in part hoping to brighten the days of Tricia, a blind cow already living at the Watkins Glen property who also had narrowly escaped slaughter. Earlier on, Tricia had bonded with a cow at the sanctuary who had been disabled by a hip injury. When this friend died of cancer, Tricia showed signs of grief, like hanging her head in a posture of sadness.

Bringing Sweety and Tricia together took time. Health checks were required for both animals, and all sorts of paperwork too given that Sweety was coming over the Canadian border into the United States. Susie Coston, Farm Sanctuary's national shelter director, described what happened when Sweety arrived at the Watkins Glen property in 2014:

> It was amazing watching them meet, really just bringing Sweety into the barn and Tricia smelling the air, realizing there was a cow next to her. Sweety had the same reaction. They talked a great deal back and forth—they could not touch for the first few days, but then they could touch noses. When they finally were put in together they quickly started eating from the same hay rack and checking each other out—awkwardly at first but by the end of the night they were licking each other.

They became inseparable, although, Coston adds, "Tricia is far more comfortable in her pasture, which has been her home for so many years. She sometimes gets too far away from Sweety, and you can hear her mooing attempting to find Tricia out in the pasture."

That mooing is a sound we'll encounter again, because it's the same vocalization mother cows and their babies make for each other when forcibly separated. In this case, the mooing allows two blind cows to find their way back to each other. Tricia's grief behaviors have disappeared; despite her long years of rough treatment, Sweety is relaxed when near her friend. Cows aren't just herd animals, each standing dumbly near the next, without notice or care. Cows care very much who is around them, and they feel the absence of their close companions.

I feel some envy for those who get to know cows on a more sustained basis than I ever will (though this yearning is coupled with knowledge that such an opportunity at sanctuaries or on small farms comes with fiercely hard work). Few of us today know cows the way writer Judy Van der Veer conveys in her wonderful books from the 1940s, including the novel *November Grass* and the memoir *A Few Happy Ones*. Growing up in ranch country near San Diego, California, Van der Veer saw cows as individuals who, like all of us, feel joy and sorrow at different times in their lives.

Van der Veer made sure (in real life, not fiction) that the cow Sally Anne, after losing her first two bull calves, who were sold away, kept the third. Finally a mother, Sally Anne cherished the role. "Long after he was old enough to be weaned," Van der Veer writes in *A Few Happy Ones*, "she treated [her calf] as if he were a helpless infant depending on her care needing her to groom him carefully every day and supply him with plenty of milk." At one point, Sally Anne disappeared and could not be located despite a search. On the third day, she reappeared with bruises and broken ribs, apparently having experienced a bad fall. The first thing she did was to feed her calf— and only then did she collapse. With veterinary help, Sally Anne recovered, and Van der Veer attributes the cow's strength of will to her fierce bond with her calf: "After her fall, she had lain day and night, until she was able to get up and make her way home to him."

Modern-day family farmers echo Van der Veer's connection with their cows. Lorraine Lewandrowski is a lawyer and fourth-generation dairy farmer in Herkimer County in New York State. At the turn of the twentieth century, her grandparents emigrated from Poland to the United States, then brought their own parents over as well; with about sixty cows in her care, Lewandrowski continues the family legacy.

I asked Lewandrowski to tell me about her cows as individuals. "Of course cows exhibit different 'styles' of doing things," she told me:

> Perhaps you have heard about alpha cows? Alpha cows seem to be rather brave in terms of leading the herd to new pastures, signaling when it is time to flee, keeping other cows in line. So, over the years, we have had many alpha cows who will be the first down the lane to go graze, who will determine that the herd should leave the pastures and head home if a storm is coming. This is in contrast to cows who are afraid of new things, refuse to leave the barn even when green pastures beckon.
>
> We have had some cows who, though hand raised like the others, were downright miserable. They would kick the milking machine off, kick people, buck other cows around. I hate to name names! I will name names of some pretty sweet little cows. We were recently gifted by a farming friend with a little half-Jersey, half-Holstein heifer. She is the sweetest little heifer, even though she was not raised with a lot of human attention. Her name is Silkie. Silkie will come right up to us humans, rub her head on us, say hello when the others are more intent on getting to their food.

In *The Moo Man*, we gain a glimpse of dairy-farm life. This film (available online) showcases the labor required in caring for cows while striving to know them as individuals. Its focus is the 180-acre Longleys Farm in Hailsham, East Sussex, England, run by Steve Hook and his dad Phil. The farm's Friesian Holstein herd contains, at the time of filming, seventy-two cows, each identifiable by distinct black-and-white markings. The cows, together with the Hooks, produce organic, raw, unpasteurized milk and milk products.

At Longleys, the heifers eat well. "We consider the cows' welfare and health are paramount," the Hooks write on the farm's website. "Cows in a conventional herd produce nearly 50% more milk than our cows. This means our Kates, Idas, Biddys and Rowenas and Rubys are not under so much pressure and stress." Grass and clover make up the cows' diet at Longleys; animals eat outdoors in spring and summer, and indoors during the colder months, when sunflower, lucerne, and sugar beet are added to the mix. Dairy cows in England typically live about six years, but at Longleys it's eight or nine. Ida, one of the cows featured in the film, lives considerably longer than that.

Watching *The Moo Man*, my husband Charlie comments that Steve Hook is "a patient fellow." We watch as individual cows run away from the herd, or cease moving altogether, in no mood to comply with what's asked of them. Steve Hook calmly approaches the stubborn ones. Sometimes he gently pulls or pushes an animal; more often he gentles the cow with his voice and contained coaxing movements.

When the Longleys cows are first turned out into the field after the winter, their exuberance is profound and wonderful to witness. A parade of loose-limbed, jumping, and kicking cows makes its way to fresh grass. On screen, the closed-caption phrase that accompanies this scene is "excited moo-ing," an apt if understated note: this is pure cow joy.

Of the cows, Ida is a clear favorite. Steve Hook distinguishes between having "a great relationship" with all the cows on his farm and the special closeness that develops with certain individuals. Hook's affection for Ida is visible and must be palpable to Ida herself when he speaks lovingly to her and pats or caresses her. She's the cow chosen one day to ride in a trailer from the farm to coastal Eastbourne for a promotional photo-op. Her body language telegraphs how much Ida enjoys the outing and her time with Hook away from the other heifers; more than a few nudges are required before she agrees to reenter the trailer for the trip home. A moving scene between Ida and Hook transpires near the film's end, at which point anyone who has ever shared years with an aged dog or cat will empathize with Hook's emotional state.

The Moo Man isn't a sentimental film, though. The realities of farm life are ever-present. In one scene, large chunks of beef grace Hook's kitchen, cut up into plastic bags; Hook works with the meat as he reminisces about the personality of the male calf the meat used to be. When males are born, a clock begins and inexorably continues to tick: at around two and a half years, they are slaughtered for beef. Bull calves cannot produce milk and, like the male goats in chapter 5, have no place on the farm. A "boy or girl" check is Hook's first act when a calf drops from a laboring cow to the ground. "Very disappointing," he says quietly, when Ida births a male.

When it's deemed time for the young ones to access their mother's milk from a pail instead of the teat, the moms become agitated. "It's the toughest day in the year" for the mum, Hook says. The mother's "upset" is visible in her body posture and audible in her bellows: a prolonged mother-calf duet is captured on film, as the new pail-feeding routine is instituted and the calf is held in a separate stall. Hook comments simply that this has to be done.

Family farms in England, Hooks says, are "dying very quickly." It costs the Hooks thirty-four pence to produce a liter of fresh organic milk that sells for twenty-seven pence. The farm is only sustainable, Hook explains, because of the extra money coming in from working family tax credits and the direct retailing schemes with which the Hooks have had some success. It's a precarious way of life.

Economic factors explain why the focus in industrial-scale farming—whether for dairy or for beef—doesn't resemble Hook's or Lewandrowski's. At that enormous scale, production concerns override matters related to cows' individuality or their thinking and feeling. The dairy farms of California's Central Valley make for an instructive and alarming case study. The term "dairy farm" may suggest that these megafacilities share features in common with the family farms we have been discussing: they don't (except of course for the killing, different in quantity and quality in the two locations, to be sure, but with the same result for the cows in question). In his book *Farmageddon: The True Cost of Cheap Meat*, Philip Lymbery refers to the industrial dairy farms as "milk factories where animals are just machines that rapidly break down and are replaced."

Here's the scene at one such place Lymbery visited: cows standing around outdoors, some in shade and some in the sun. Idle except for the moments in which they are fed or milked, the cows have nothing to do and no grass to cushion their feet. They stand on a mix of earth and manure (Lymbery describes the stench in the air as "a nauseous reek"). Swollen with milk, the animals move barely at all. They can't even look forward to a natural meal, since cows in megadairies are fed unnatural foods such as corn. "We saw these farms every couple of kilometres," Lymbery writes, "all with several thousand cows surrounded by mud, corrugated iron and concrete."

The misery in the Central Valley cuts across species lines; humans suffer health problems almost as dire as do the cows. The 1.75 million cows in California generate more fecal waste than the human population of the UK, and that waste matter has to go somewhere. Most of it flows to lagoons near the farms, but inevitably some escapes into the air as gas and into the ground and water supply through seepage. Water and air pollution, linked in part to the megadairies, is an immense worry for residents of Central Valley, where, Lymbery says, children have a rate of asthma nearly three times the national average and adult life expectancies are lower by up to a decade than the national average.

Cows consigned to short lives in megadairies go unrecognized as individuals with thoughts and feelings. Similarly, the intelligence, personality, and sentience of cows goes missing in factory farms and concentrated animal feeding operations (CAFOs) where the animals are slaughtered for beef. These cows do not eat their natural diet either. Michael Pollan, in *The Omnivore's Dilemma*, laid the situation out a decade ago: in CAFOs, cows "exquisitely adapted by natural selection to live on grass must be adapted by us—at considerable cost to their health, to the health of the land, and ultimately to the health of their eaters—to live on corn."

In the CAFO context, corn provides cheap calories for cows, fueling faster weight growth before slaughter, even as the cows' consumption solves the problem of surplus corn. While feeding cows in this way is meant to be an economic boon, it creates a cascade of human health problems. In the decade since Pollan's beautifully written, hard-hitting book came out, the lesson has been knocked into our heads over and over again: our diets are drenched in high-fructose corn syrup: if we are what we eat, we are nothing so much as corn. The same can be said about cows raised for beef slaughter. Of course, it's not only corn forced into these cows. "What gets a steer from 80 to 1,100 pounds in fourteen months," Pollan reports, "is tremendous quantities of corn, protein and fat supplements, and an arsenal of new drugs."

In our food system, with exceptions on family farms that dwindle in number by the year, our knowledge of cows' lives is severed from our action toward cows. This situation is all the more striking given the close association between our species and cows since prehistory—and I don't mean only through the hunting and scavenging that I wrote of earlier. It's not, after all, the Hall of Goats or the Hall of Pigs that graces Lascaux Caves in France, that most famous showcase for the art of our early *Homo sapiens* ancestors—it's the Hall of Bulls. A more accurate name would be the Hall of Aurochs, referring to the huge wild ox that is the ancestor of all domestic cattle and that the Lascaux people painted so frequently around fifteen thousand years ago. On the Internet you can find a short video clip that features gorgeously rendered bulls and horses from Lascaux: it conveys how closely our forebears observed these animals and perhaps admired them.

Evolving around two million years ago, the aurochs was known to Egyptian pharaohs, Julius Caesar, and European kings. After a long period in which they thrived, aurochs slowly fell victim to the combined forces of hunting, habitat loss, disease, and competition with their own descendants. By the 1400s they were found only in a single preserve in central Poland, and when the last individual died there in 1627, they became the first animal recorded to go extinct. (The second was the dodo.) By that time, of course, humans had long been surrounded by, and were living and working alongside, domesticated cattle. The "taming" process began perhaps eight thousand years ago as wild aurochs in Asia and Africa gradually integrated into human settlements. As with all animal domestication, this process relied in its initial stages on a sort of mutual contract between species. Hannah Velten writes in *Cow* that "it is no exaggeration" to note that domestic cattle "played an enormous role in shaping civilization," primarily through "the innovation of milking and the cultivation of land using the plough."

Were cows recognized as clever beings with personalities in prehistory and during earlier eras, and subject to mistreatment only in modern times? No, far from it. Hard labor was often required of them as the cows' price for domestication, and sometimes their sacrifice went beyond long hours of toil. Velten traces numerous cross-cultural instances of cow and especially bull slaughter over time, often connected with religious ritual. At the very least, though, these earlier cows were part of human lives, *visible* to all, instead of being shoved together by the thousands in factory settings to endure long days standing in muck and consuming corn.

COW MINDS AND HEARTS

A look at the intelligence, emotion, and personality of cows restores these animals to our visibility. This exploration embraces observational and experimental science along with the insights of those whose livelihoods bring them together with cows. When I write about animal intelligence and emotion—when I assert in a book or a blog post that crows solve a particularly difficult puzzle, elephants may suffer emotionally when they witness trauma to their loved ones from poaching, or monkeys in the wild grieve for their dying or dead partners—a response often comes in along these lines: "Huh! No one would be surprised by *that* except scientists; we all know that animals think and feel." But this isn't true of cows, much in the same way it isn't true of fish or goats or chickens, yet the evidence is compelling.

Cows recognize us as individuals. When we think of the many centuries' experience they have had with *us* just as we have had with *them*, this finding makes sense. Experimental trials by dairy researcher Pierre Rybarczyk and his team found that Holstein cows discriminated one person from another even when the humans were wearing the same color clothes. The cows used cues dependent on the situation. If they were presented with two people of different height who had their heads fully covered by masks, the cows had no trouble telling them apart. Peoples' faces may be used as a cue also. Encountering two humans of the same height, the cows succeeded in the discrimination task if the faces were visible. If *only* the faces were visible, though—if the experiment called for a person's face to be seen by the cows but the body blocked by a curtain—the cows were less often successful. Rybarczyk and his cowriters conclude, "Cows can therefore use either the face or the height to tell the persons apart but they do not need both cues. Thus, they seem able to store information about several cues that identify the person and to switch from one to another one depending on which is available to them." This degree of cue-based flexibility can be taken as a marker of mental acuity.

Dairy cows thrive when *we* recognize *them* as individuals too. Referring to cows as Bossie or Daisy may be a gentle form of humor for most of us, but farmers who name their cows, according to a 2009 study in the UK by Catherine Douglas and Peter Rowlinson, are rewarded with more milk: 454 pints more, on average. Now, a result quantified in pints produced sounds as if this research is all about *us*—about how farmers can increase production yields. But Douglas brings it back around to welfare of the cows themselves, noting in an interview, "Just as people respond better to the personal touch, cows also feel happier and more relaxed if they are given a bit more one-to-one attention." What seems to come naturally to cow caretakers on small farms—relating one-to-one with cows, as Steve Hook did with his favorite Ida and others in *The Moo Man*—yields benefits for all parties involved.

It's not only companionship with humans that cows crave, of course. For the first time in 2014, scientists showed that housing dairy calves singly impairs their cognitive performance: when paired with a peer, calves were better at solving problems. Charlotte Gaillard and her team worked with eighteen Holstein calves who had been separated from their mothers within six hours of birth, then housed alone for a period of four days, and thereafter kept either alone or with a peer. The calves in the social condition ("social calves") were quicker to solve what's called a reversal task. During choice trials in a Y maze, the young animals were first trained to associate the color white with milk, but not black: when calves chose the white branch of the maze they received a milk reward, but they received nothing—except a time delay before the next trial—when they selected the black one.

In this initial phase, and with the milk hidden from their view, calves in both groups did equally well. When, however, the calves suddenly underwent a "reversal," in which the hidden milk was now paired with a black stimulus, results for the two groups diverged. Social calves began sooner than isolated calves to recognize the switch and to select black in order to obtain the milk reward. In separate trials the social calves also habituated more quickly to a novel object, a plastic red bin, indicating that they learned to recognize it more readily. It's notable that the social calves were separated from their partners when they were made to encounter the red bin (just as they were in the color discrimination test), and yet if they felt any stress because of that separation from another calf they may have bonded with, no impaired performance resulted.

Why the social calves show increased cognitive performance—or to put it another way, why the isolated calves showed cognitive impairment—isn't strictly clear. One possibility, the authors say, is that the isolated calves experience anxiety being housed alone (for a much longer period than the social calves' brief interval of solo testing). We know in a general sense from the field of animal learning that anxiety interferes with learning; the experimental situation provides no confirmation of this factor as an explanation for the isolated calves' poorer performance, but it's clear that isolation had some negative impact on the baby cows. In fact I found the experimental setup—removal of the calves from their mothers, and the physical isolation of some of them, so soon after birth—to be an ethical concern.

When dairy calves are first separated from their mothers, emotions run high on both sides. This fact is abundantly clear from observation on farms, including small family farms (as in *The Moo Man*). Canadian animal welfare researcher Rolnei Daros and his colleagues wrote in 2014 about the "acute emotional response" of calves separated from their mothers at the time of early weaning in a farm context. Daros and his team set up a project aimed to measure effects on cognition of this separation process. Central to their experiment is the concept of judgment bias, already reported for a variety of animals (including humans) in the literature: when presented with ambiguous stimuli, individuals who experience low mood or who feel depressed tend more readily toward a negative interpretation than do others.

Thirteen Holstein calves were tested in this study. Twenty-four hours after birth, the calves and their mothers were put into a group setting. The mothers were fitted with udder nets so their calves could not suckle; the calves drank milk from a bottle and were given supplemental food. In a process similar to what happened in the white versus black color-discrimination experiment, these calves were trained to discriminate between white and red signals displayed on a computer monitor, then rewarded with milk if they approached the white signal and punished with a timeout delay of one minute before the next trial if they approached the red signal.

Next came the testing phase, when computer screens were presented in one of *three* conditions: positive (white), negative (red), or ambiguous (red and white blended to various degrees). In this research scheme, approach to an ambiguous screen was scored as a positive judgment bias. The big question was, would separation from the mother affect the calves' responses? The calves were tested when they had access to their mothers and again after forty-two days of age when they no longer did. The answer is yes, separation does have an effect, although the difference is not pronounced: calves approached 72 percent of ambiguous screens before separation from their mothers but only 62 percent after separation. In the language of animal research, this behavior after separation is interpreted as "a pessimistic response bias [that] is consistent with a negative emotional state" or "low mood."

It's fascinating and a bit upsetting to learn that the calves' emotions in the separation context mirrored another negative condition they experienced: dehorning. Calves were dehorned at thirty-six days of age. After a local anesthetic was applied, a hot electric iron was applied to each horn bud for thirty seconds. It is made clear by Daros and his coauthors that postoperative pain is considered normal in this situation. The negative judgment bias occurred in just about the same degree after dehorning as after maternal separation: calves approached 73 percent of ambiguous screens before and 66 percent after dehorning. Emotional upset affects the calves in much the same way that physical pain does.

These studies and others like them will, I hope, be used to better the welfare of calves. The presence of matter-of-fact statements in the scientific literature about compromised learning on the part of isolated calves or agitation on the part of calves and mothers held apart from either other, not to mention those about the dehorning pain the calves were made to feel, shouldn't be taken to mean that the research scientists are indifferent to the animals. The scientists' motivation indeed may be to make a difference in calves' lives within the food system these animals find themselves to occupy. When we are given a glimpse of how cows' lives are affected negatively by our actions, even outside a factory-farm situation—in both sets of experiments I have just described, the calves were housed at the University of British Columbia Dairy Education and Research Center in Canada—the science of cow feeling and thinking may be used to improve the animals' lives as well as to improve management of the animals.

I can't help but wonder though, do these calves really need to be prevented from suckling and subjected to dehorning pain, at least so early in life? I also wonder if rigorous animal-behavior testing truly is required to "prove" that cows need companionship and may suffer negative consequences when separated from their mothers or peers. That calves feel more pessimistic when apart from their moms, for instance, is entirely predictable given that these are mammalian babies, whose mothers are to them the most important beings in the universe. Now I sound like the people I describe earlier, who always want to tell me that we know enough about animals' thoughts and feelings without science! There *is* value in collecting and publishing the aggregate numbers, the statistics about performance in controlled trials: these data become a powerful complement to the practice of describing animals' behaviors as they go about their daily lives. The experimental work acts as a check against claims of anthropomorphism lobbed at reports of animal lovers, while the anecdotal information brings home the point that smart, sweet living individuals exist behind the aggregated numbers. It's just that some research studies that have passed ethical-review-board screening for animal welfare still include practices that strike me as not really so ethical.

Ethologist Helen Proctor's research shows that noninvasive behavioral experiments on cows may quite *directly* improve cows' lives. With her colleague Gemma Carter, building on previous work that suggested the amount of eye whites visible indicates cows' arousal and emotional states, Proctor designed trials to see if positive emotional states could be assessed by looking at easily visible changes in the cows' eyes. They compared the responses of thirteen dairy cows in the UK before, during, and after periods of stroking by humans. All kinds of precise requirements were put into place for the stroking: a rate of forty to sixty strokes per minute (the speed at which cows groom each other) by hands encased in canvas gloves; equal action on the left and right sides of the body; focus on the cows' preferred grooming areas of withers, neck, forehead, and cheeks; and most important of all, cessation of the stroking if the cows moved away, to ensure that the experience was voluntary. Results showed that the cows' eye whites were significantly decreased during the stroking as contrasted with the before and after periods. Close observation indicated that the cows enjoyed the soothing action offered by the humans: they stretched their necks, a behavior known to be a pleasure response, almost exclusively during the stroking rather than before or after; sometimes the cows leaned right into the person who was stroking, as if to underscore their delight.

In other studies, Proctor's team found that cows' ear postures and nasal temperatures are measurably affected by positive emotional experiences too. Surely this work reveals ways to effectively assess when cows are relaxed and remedy the situation when they are not. Proctor and Carter make an excellent suggestion along these lines: "If visible eye whites are found to be a useful measure of emotional state in a number of species, then it would be worth designing a hand-held instrument which can measure the percentage of visible eye white non-invasively and spontaneously." Individual differences across cows, or other animals within a species, they note, make it imperative to measure *changes* in eye whites across different contexts: aiming for a one-size-fits-all mean percentage number just wouldn't work well. I really like that nod to personality variation across different animals.

There's a third source of information, in addition to formal scientific reports and informal observations, that I find valuable and fun when exploring the lives of farmed animals: video clips. Admittedly, the full context or even much description may be missing from videos posted online (as opposed to full-length films like *The Moo Man*), and I take care to work only with clips that are, to the best of my knowledge, legitimate. In one of my favorites, a jazz band from the United States, visiting France, stops at a roadside pasture and begins to serenade some cows. At the start, the cows are scattered, some idly watching, others grazing and paying no attention. After the first few notes drift across the field, though, all the cows become intensely alert, and the grazers move up closer; the cows as a group face the musicians and listen. To skeptics who insist the cows are only moving forward in the hope that the humans will offer food, I say watch again: it's the shift by the cows precisely when the music begins to play (as opposed to when the people stand at the roadside with silent instruments) that tells us how curious and thoughtful these animals are.

A second favorite clip shows a boxer puppy about six months old in an English field occupied by a group of cows. As the puppy approaches, the cows react with interest; when she lays down, the cows crowd in for a close inspection by sight and smell. In this case, the skeptics respond with, oh well, cows eye and sniff their own calves too! But one cow is clearly apprehensive at first, not certain what sort of creature has appeared before her. Again, we see cows who are highly curious about their surroundings. In each clip, something new and intriguing is happening—new and intriguing to the cows themselves, not just to us who watch them on video. What the cows are thinking about during their close encounters with a boxer puppy and with American jazz musicians, I can't know, but I'm convinced they are thinking about *something*.

The days are coming when we'll be treated to more hard science on the questions I have taken up in this chapter, questions about cow personality, intelligence, and sentience and how these factors intersect with each other. Lorraine Lewandrowski, the New York state dairy farmer, touched on this intersectionality when she talked with me about her cows:

> Here is how I believe they are sentient. They experience pain, they experience happiness. I don't know the extent that they think about or remember these feelings. Some of them can solve problems. Example: Gate left open, whole herd escapes. Some of them are able to figure out how to get back to the barn while others wander around aimlessly. So perhaps there are different degrees of cow smartness. Same thing with learning. Open the barn doors for the first time in spring and send the cows to summer pastures down lanes that may differ depending on if grass is ready. Some cows figure it out right away and repeat the process the next day. Others just don't seem to remember that a particular lane led them to nice food. Same goes for water. The entire herd could be thirsty from a hot day in the sun. I walk out to pump fresh water from a nice spring. Certain cows (more often the leader cows) see me doing this and run for the water tub and get the water first . . . filling up with a cool drink themselves and pushing other cows out of the way till they are done.

What word first jumps into your mind when you see or hear the word "cow"? Exhibiting a bit of curiosity myself, if not rigorous scientific methodology, I posted that question on my Facebook page. Ninety-one people answered my query. Their diverse replies offered me intriguing glimpses into my friends' minds: "owl" and "synapse" were the most fascinating responses, entirely opaque to me then and now in terms of any association with "cow." "Moo" and "milk" led as the two most frequent responses, offered by nine people each. "Moon" came in third, with seven responses; probably my use of the verb "jump" acted as an unintended prompt in that direction. "Boy," "girl," "hand," and "poke" made up a further six answers in total. (If we allow that sort of clustering by meaning, though, the unsavory winner by a nose would be "pie/patty/chip/dung/shit," with ten responses.)

In the results of this just-for-fun word test, we see a mix of associations, ranging from cows as cows, to cows as animals requiring human control, to cows as food and cultural symbols. "Moo" is an especially fun response, because it's about the cows themselves—as we have seen, moo vocalizations may convey a good deal of the emotion that cows may feel day to day, as when two cows with ties to each other are forced apart. Circling back to this chapter's beginning with ribs, hamburgers, and ice cream, it's no surprise that cows may lodge in our minds primarily or exclusively as producers of our food—an observation that assumes the "milk" response in my little survey alludes to milk produced for *us*, just as the two "beef" responses surely refer to meat for us.

For now, "personality," "sentience," and "intelligence" may not be the first words that come to mind when someone says "cow." One friend did reply with the word "sentient." I like that reply best. In July of every year, the American fast-food chain Chik-Fil-A sponsors what it calls Cow Appreciation Day: every customer who appears at one of its restaurants dressed like a cow wins a free meal. Any push away from cow consumption is good news for bovines, no doubt. And it *could* be good news for the environment. The carbon footprint of beef cattle is about twenty-seven pounds of carbon dioxide per pound; a single pound of burger meat amounts to twenty-five pounds of carbon dioxide emission. These are staggering figures, higher than for other foods, including chicken.

But of course, Chik-Fil-A isn't about kindness to cows or about environmental protection: it's about selling chickens, instead of cows, as food. If we save some cows from slaughter but eat (and thus slaughter) more chickens, where does that leave us?

7. Pigs

Are pigs really smarter than three-year-old children? No one poses this question about the animals we have so far considered in this book, but they do ask it about pigs.

At Penn State University, pigs have distinguished themselves on their exams, enough so to make it into the scientific literature. Then–graduate student Candace Croney and her co-researchers carried blocks of wood shaped like Xs or Os to the PSU pigs, but only the O-carrying humans fed the animals. The pigs soon began to rush up to the food-bearing O carriers, ignoring the foodless X carriers. This result is unsurprising. The "wow" factor comes in when the experimenters switched from wood forms to T-shirts printed with X or O symbols, and the pigs ventured only toward the O-wearing humans. The animals had transferred their three-dimensional knowledge about real-world objects to the realm of two-dimensional symbols, a considerable brain-powered feat of perception and comprehension.

Croney tested the pigs on their computer skills, too, using a machine with a video monitor and a joystick modified for animals who use their porcine snout and lips rather than primate digits. (A metal rod with a large gear-shift knob did the trick.) The pigs' task was to move the cursor to hit a target. At one of PSU's yearly Ag Field Days events, a pig would demonstrate the task, then Croney would invite a child to try it. "It became highly entertaining for us," Croney told *Pig Tales* author Barry Estabrook. "But not so amusing for some of the parents. When their children couldn't perform the task, you'd hear the parents saying, 'Come on! A pig can do it.'"

Strictly speaking, the pig-child comparison is a misguided one. As we have seen throughout this book, evolution pushes each species in its own, well-adapted direction in terms of behavior and cognition as much as of anatomy and physiology. Human intelligence shouldn't be seen as a gold standard. Comparing pigs and human kids is about as sensible as comparing chimpanzees and goats. Yet the claim that pigs and preschoolers might be pretty well equivalent in the cerebral department pops up again, even in animal behaviorists' commentary.

Donald Broom of Cambridge University's veterinary school says flatly that pigs "have the cognitive ability to be quite sophisticated. Even more so than dogs and certainly three-year-olds." Broom's pigs succeed at what ethologists call the "mirror-mediated spatial localization" task: they were able to find food hidden from their direct gaze behind a barrier, but visible in a mirror. At least, seven of eight pigs tested by Broom solved the problem in a mean time of twenty-three seconds, once they had been exposed to the mirror for five hours. Pig number eight in Broom's group looked behind the mirror for food (as did the experimental pigs who had no mirror exposure), and a follow-up study elsewhere reported more failure than success on the part of another pig cohort tested. Results, then, are suggestive but not conclusive that pigs use mirrors in smart ways. It's notable that some of Broom's pigs seemed to watch themselves in the mirror as they moved over and over again in front of it, apparently gazing at their own bodies or movements from different angles. Do pigs recognize themselves in the mirror the way chimpanzees, gorillas, orangutans, elephants, dolphins, and magpies do? Carl Safina, in his book *Beyond Words*, has persuaded me that this is the wrong question because the mirror test—when an animal's body is marked in some way such that the individual would then use the mirror to examine the mark only if it possesses self-awareness or a self-concept—doesn't succeed in measuring what it is supposed to measure. Here's Safina to explain: "When a bird, say, *attacks* the mirror, it does so precisely because it believes the reflection is *another* individual—*not itself*. This proves that it understands that it is distinct from others. It demonstrates self-concept. It doesn't 'fail' the mirror test. . . . It just doesn't understand reflection." That interpretation may also apply to pigs, or maybe pigs grasp reflection as well. In any case, the hints we have about pigs' mirror smarts may, I hope, motivate researchers to create more pig-oriented ways of testing the question.

A pig celebrity named Esther (formally, if playfully, known as "Esther the wonder pig") lives not in a laboratory but in the home of Derek Walter and Steve Jenkins in Ontario, Canada. The pair bought Esther in 2012 when she weighed four pounds and was touted by the seller as a micro-pig, predicted to top out at about seventy pounds. Esther wasn't a micro-pig then, and she certainly isn't now at 650 pounds. As the British newspaper *Daily Mail*, not known for nuance, shouted in its headline, "The giant porker is now the size of a polar bear!" Esther nonetheless fits comfortably into the Walter-Jenkins family, where she can be seen in photographs and videos sleeping in her own bed or joining the family's two dogs in the kitchen for treats.

When I show these images to friends, inevitably they are startled by Esther's size. Dogs who bed down in our living rooms or rush to the kitchen with us for a snack, even quite large dogs, make for fabulous but familiar moments; the sight of Esther doing the same produces a jolt. Based my friends' responses, I would predict Jenkins and Walter are asked more often than they care to count, Is it *normal* for a pig to grow that large? And by the way, how and where does Esther go to the bathroom?

Esther has no control over her growing girth, the men note, and they vow to keep her with them as long as she lives. Esther makes it relatively easy on them. When toilet needs arise, she simply opens the back door on her own, trots outside, and relieves herself. (She can close the door too.) And yes, domestic pigs do run large: over six hundred pounds is far from unusual. Wild European boars may reach seven hundred pounds, but generally, it's pigs specifically bred for size who achieve this heft.

Esther's daily routine gives us a window on the nature of animal sentience much like those provided by glimpsing Mr. Henry Joy's days as a therapy chicken, looking over Sy Montgomery's shoulder at the watery intelligence of octopuses, or spending hours observing and playing with a loved dog or cat. Jenkins and Walter note Esther's quickness in learning how to unlock doors throughout their house — including the freezer door. Given a "treat ball," a mini mental puzzle that challenges the receiver to extract peanut butter, Esther succeeds more rapidly than do her dog companions. Esther could, I imagine, also distinguish X versus O symbols like the Penn State pigs did or use mirrors to find hidden food like the Cambridge pigs did. More than formal problem-solving, though, it's Esther's vivid presentation of self that clues us in to her mental life. She's keenly attentive to people and events around her; often she makes direct eye contact with the camera when being photographed. She loves frozen mango smoothies, bagpipe music, trotting around the spacious orchard outside her house, and cuddling with her dog and human companions.

Bob Comis, once a pig farmer, wants Esther's thousands of fans to note a central fact:

> Esther is not cute, lovable and loving, smart, playful, mischievous, gentle, well-mannered, mirthful, gregariously snuggly and fastidious because she is special. She is all of those things, so powerfully all of those things, because she is a pig. That string of adjectives does not describe Esther alone. It describes the very heart and soul of every pig on the planet.

Comis's sentiment, published in *Salon*, is well intentioned, but not grounded in a good grasp of intraspecific (within a species) variation in animal behavior. Not every pig is gentle and smart, just as there's no essential "cat" nature expressed by each of the six indoor cats with whom we live. Two of our rescued cats, Jenna and Marie, can be downright obnoxious in their delight of chasing and harassing their feline housemates, while Flame, Nicholas Longtail, Diana, and Bootsie tend toward a more laid-back approach—though they too have their moments. Likewise, we observe a continuum of responses in the sharp-witted, quick-to-learn department. This same variation was evident among the free-ranging baboons I came to know well in Kenya. In the high-ranking matriline, one alpha female wielded her dominant status against less powerful companions in anything but a gentle way, and some monkeys were cleverer than others. (Echoes of what we experience with human companions in our daily lives may be obvious here.) No need to discard Comis's central point, though, because it conveys a vital truth: the pig destined to become bacon or barbecue might, with the right rearing conditions, have lived a life as thoughtful and sweet as Esther does now.

Esther's life is enriched, a term that echoes the behavioral regimes ("enrichment") designed to stimulate animals at good sanctuaries and sometimes at zoos. Videos of orangutans operating iPADs or big cats playing with Halloween pumpkins convey the idea. In sanctuary settings, caregivers who wish to envelop a pig in a habitat that's both safe and stimulating may face major hurdles because a fresh arrival often comes directly from a sterile environment—or worse. Newly rescued pigs may be traumatized psychologically.

At Pigs Peace Sanctuary in the Pacific Northwest, about an hour north of Seattle, 190 pigs live in enriched conditions. They roam fields of grass and clover with other pigs, one or two of whom may become special companions; enjoy good food to eat; and slowly recover from what very clearly are disturbing memories of their previous lives. When the pig Betsy first came to Pigs Peace, she was depressed and indifferent to her surroundings. Judy Woods, the sanctuary's founder and director, described for me just how bad off Betsy was. "She was like a war bomb victim. She was unresponsive, with a blank, staring face. She would just walk slowly, almost like a robot; she would go any place you told her to go."

I first read about Betsy, a Hampshire cross ("the black and white standard pig," as Judy puts it) on the Pigs Peace website, where Judy described the filthy enclosure Betsy had endured on a farm in eastern Washington state. She dwelled in feces, surrounded by corpses. "The only way to sleep without drowning in the sludge," Woods wrote, "was to rest her head on the body of a dead pig." Finally, Betsy was confiscated by the local sheriff's department, and Woods brought her to Pigs Peace.

With this kind of trauma, physical as well as psychological in that Betsy was lame and in pain, you can't just introduce the newcomer pig to the others and hope for the best. At first, Woods placed Betsy in a private area, on several acres of grass with her own pond, hay-bed, and stall. Betsy had undergone medical quarantine elsewhere, after her rescue, and now she was free to move about as she pleased. Most important, she could see pigs all around her in the next field: calm, pleased pigs. "The biggest healing comes from just watching," Woods told me. With depressed pigs like Betsy, "you can almost feel their sigh of relief when they see that other pigs are here."

Betsy slowly came back to herself and joined the large sanctuary "sounder," a 150-pig-strong group of animals, in roaming the fields. She selected as her closest friend a younger pig named Tony. A "grandma" pig now around age thirteen, Betsy moves more slowly than Tony, but the two nap together every day and sleep together every night. Woods was surprised at Betsy's choice because from a human point of view the two friends are mismatched, but that's the beauty of a sanctuary like Pigs Peace: it's all up to the pigs.

Woods rattled off a short list of horrors experienced by her residents when, before they came to her, they had no control over their own lives: pigs thrown from vehicles, a pig burned with a blowtorch, a pig with paralyzed legs who had been made to live in the floorboards of a man's vehicle. Most of the pigs, though, were victims of straightforward neglect—a type of abuse in itself. Isabelle and Ramona, Yorkshire ("big white") pigs who were sisters, had been housed in an eight-foot-square concrete room at Sea World in San Diego. Sea World is best known (or I might say infamous) for its marine-mammal shows, but smaller animals like cats, dogs, and pigs may be part of the entertainment too. The problem was that Ramona and Isabelle no longer cooperated with attempts to make them perform, and so they had been living in that small, boring room for over a year by the time Woods was flown to San Diego to meet them.

In situations like these, Woods deploys her secret weapon to charm pigs: peanut-butter sandwiches. "It's rare that pigs will have had one," she explained. "Peanut butter is such a lovely sensation to a pig, and it stays in their mouth." (No wonder Esther the wonder pig learned so rapidly to master her peanut-butter-laced treat ball.) When Woods agreed to take in Isabelle and Ramona, Sea World drove them north to Pigs Peace, where they were met by Woods—and more peanut-butter sandwiches. Unlike Betsy, these two sisters were not depressed; Woods describes them as "gleeful!" A photograph of the pair's first encounter with snow (and another one of porcine peanut-butter delight) can be found on the sanctuary's website.

Ramona and Isabelle had had each other through their times of trouble and transition, which no doubt helped them cope. That kind of love, as each of us may come to know in our own lives, often exacts a price. Years after their rescue, when Isabelle fell ill, her sister hovered over her. When Isabelle died, Ramona grieved deeply. She lay on the ground, refused food, and simply didn't care to move. Woods believes the best way to acknowledge a survivor pig's grief is to share her own. When she buried Isabelle, Ramona could see Judy's sadness. Just as it took Betsy time to adjust to life at Pigs Peace, it took

Ramona time to adjust to life without her sister. When she bonded with another pig called Lucy, her recovery was cemented.

Time spent with social companions, especially in play, or even play with objects, boosts healthy physical and emotional states in pigs no matter where they live. Commercially raised piglets respond positively from a very young age to a more challenging environment. Edinburgh veterinary scientists Jessica Martin, Sarah Ison, and Emma Baxter showed this by dividing 117 piglets, the offspring of cross-bred (Large White × Landrace) dams and Pietrain boars, into two groups, each with different rearing conditions. Those in the "neonatal environment crate" (NEC) group were born into the standard farrowing crate, a barren environment that curtails both the physical and mental development of pigs. The pigs live on a solid, uninsulated concrete floor (except for in the small slatted "dunging area"), with only two handfuls of hay provided each day. While the piglets could move freely, including to a heated area at the front of the crate, the sow was confined to a central area by parallel bars. NEC pigs had no contact whatsoever with other sow-piglet groups.

By contrast, piglets in a second group (termed NEP to distinguish it from the NEC group) were born into what's called PIG-SAFE, the Piglet and Sow Alternative Farrowing Environment. In this larger enclosure, more straw is given to the sow before farrowing, and the floor is insulated concrete with a slatted dunging area. The key improvement in PIGSAFE, though, is in the social realm: it allows for substantially enriched interactions after farrowing. Because the sow is not confined, she and her piglets can play together, and both sow and youngsters have visual and some physical contact with neighboring mothers and piglets. Sloped walls are designed to shield piglets from the risk of crushing (presumably by the sow).

All piglets in the study were taken from their mothers at twenty-seven days of age, which therefore marked the time of weaning. They were housed (already sorted into NEC and NEP groupings) in weaner pens of identical design.

During the preweaning phase, the NEP youngsters not only played more, including with their mothers, but exhibited a more diverse play repertoire. After weaning, no doubt because the two groups now inhabited identical environments, any differences in play vanished. That the enriched environment made a difference for playfulness only in the short-term doesn't negate its importance: as Martin and her coauthors point out, pigs (like most animals) play only when they are relaxed and in a positive emotional state, surely a situation worth furthering in these animals.

One outcome at first glance seems to place the NEP piglets in a negative light: these youngsters behaved more aggressively. Could the enriched-environment piglets, counterintuitively, have experienced more stress? In fact, it turns out to be the opposite when we take into account not just the *amount* but also the *nature* and *timing* of the observed aggression. The NEP piglets' aggression, the researchers write, "was acute and sharply decreased by day seven, while NEC piglets remained aggressive for the entire seven days." It may well be, then, that piglets from more complex environments who can interact in some way with neighboring litters may "resolve social hierarchy disputes quicker," as the authors put it, than those reared in less challenging environments. Stress physiology measurements, they caution us, would help solidify or reject this interpretation.

In one way, the NEP piglets demonstrated a cognitive edge: they performed better in experimental tests at discriminating between a familiar object (a blue square device from which to drink) and a novel object (a small red and white traffic cone) following a fifteen-minute delay after exposure. An hour after exposure, though, they did no better than the NEC piglets in this object-discrimination ability. I'm not sure what to make of this mixed result, but it's clear that the NEP pigs approached the novel object more quickly in the fifteen-minute test. This outcome indicates a more open, less fearful attitude toward exploration at what is perhaps a critical young age.

Given the benefits regarding play, social behavior, and cognitive performance that accrued to the NEP group, we can see that enriched living does matter for pigs. Commercial pigs will never experience the freedom to roam, the cognitive challenges, and indeed the love that Esther does, but experimental results such as these argue for the offering of constant enrichment throughout a pig's life—"constant" because, as the authors take pains to specify, pigs' responses are highly dependent on their immediate environment.

If images of pig playfulness have put you in the mood for a porcine romp, consider the game developed collaboratively by Dutch animal welfare scientists and designers that allows willing pigophiles to help entertain livestock pigs. Pig Chase invites human players to send dancing balls of light to confined pigs to distract and amuse them. Here is how it works: using an iPad or similar device, a person moves the light images and is able to view the pigs' faces on the screen as the pigs respond to the balls' movement. And respond they do: one pig of a group, standing near a large screen, is shown briefly but avidly tracking the human-lobbed balls. It's a dynamic game too, because if certain conditions are met by the pig-person pair, a fireworks display explodes into the visual realm of both players. The pigs who would benefit most from this kind of "brain stim" are not pigs like Esther or the relatively few in sanctuaries, or even those on small farms, but instead the massive numbers of factory-farm pigs, who may endure significant boredom (as well as outright suffering). Interspecies gaming products are promising tools to combat this ennui, but it remains to be seen whether they will catch on where they would do the most good.

Pig Chase; the routines of Esther and sanctuary pigs; and the experiments with symbols, computers, mirrors, and challenging neonatal environments offer us distinct but overlapping views on pigs as much more than portable pork. There is no escaping the fact, though, that our framing of pig issues usually centers intently on pigs as food. The furor for pig products is arguably the most intense of any global food obsession.

BACON AND BARBECUE

Back when my daughter was in high school, I ordered from the Zingerman's food catalog a bacon chocolate bar as a Christmas present for the person she was then dating. Proud of myself for hunting down such a novelty product for someone who loved all things bacon, I presented it with a flourish. Not long after, the bacon craze hit the United States. Now, bacon chocolate is easy to find, along with other sweets like bacon ice cream. At Sunrise Donuts, my local shop that has deliciously heightened the donut-eating experience here in Gloucester County, Virginia, maple bacon donuts may sell out. Bacon nowadays is drinkable, in products like bacon milkshakes, bacon-flavored beer, and bacon vodka, and is found even in noningestible products like deodorant and shaving cream.

Even more so than bacon, barbecue is a study in anthropology, linguistics, and political economy all rolled into one. Where I grew up, in New Jersey, "barbecue" was something we *did* on weekends and holidays. Where I live now, in southeastern Virginia not far from the North Carolina line, it's something people *eat*. As Laura Dove puts it, "Northerners barbecue food on the backyard grill. In the South, however, barbecue is most definitely a noun," one almost always referring to pork. (That is the sense in which I use it here.)

Across the South, barbecue represents an avidly embraced form of cultural heritage. Anthropologist Brad Weiss, my colleague at William and Mary for many years, has carried out ethnographic research around pastured pork in the North Carolina Piedmont. He notes that Piedmont Carolina barbecue is almost invariably made from slowly smoked pork shoulders and adorned with a tangy ketchup-based sauce. Eastern Carolina barbecue is made from whole hogs, again slowly smoked, often over hickory. There's no ketchup—Weiss tartly adds "under any circumstances"—in this barbecue. The final stage of processing differs too between the regions: the barbecue may be pulled (shredded or pulled into strips) or sliced in the Piedmont but is chopped finely in Eastern Carolina. Pigs, as we will see, are big business in North Carolina: pigs matter and pig products matter and barbecue especially matters. People who indulge in barbecue remain as loyal to their region's preparation as sports fans do to their teams.

In a peculiar parallel to this excited consumption of bacon and barbecue (and other pig products too), pigs' learning abilities, intelligence, and variable personalities are exclaimed over in the media, far more so than those of other farmed animals. Popular pig-derived pejoratives point to gluttony ("you sure pigged out!") or to an unclean status ("son, your room is a pigsty"), but not to *birdbrains* or creatures *cowed* into submission or dim-witted barnyard creatures given over to goatly stubbornness or sexual excess. Honoring the view that, as Brent Mizelle writes in *Pig*, "pigs are more than just the 18 per cent ham, 16 per cent bacon, 15 per cent loin, 12 per cent fatback, 10 per cent lard and 3 per cent each of spare rib, plate, jowl, foot and trimmings that exit the modern packing plant," lists of "top ten smartest animals" often feature pigs—the only farmed animal I have seen included.

Domestic pigs differ in another way from chickens, goats, and cows: pigs yield no eggs, there's no such thing as a dairy pig, and no market exists for cheese fashioned from pig milk ("headcheese," prepared from pigs, is a jellied meat derived from parts of pigs' heads). Manure from pigs may be used as fertilizer on farms and in family gardens, yet that's a secondary consequence of the central fact that holds for no other farmed animal: we keep pigs only for their meat, a situation that requires their slaughter. (Breeder females may for some period be marked not for slaughter but only as the producers of other pigs for slaughter.)

As this bacon-and-barbecue lust hints, there's something terribly incomplete in our embrace of smart and sociable pigs. For one thing, as Lori Marino and Christina M. Colvin point out in a 2015 review paper on "thinking pigs," almost all that we know about domestic pig behavior, cognition, and emotion comes from behavioral research related in some way to industrial farming. A drive to comprehend what pigs—either domestic or wild—do under more natural conditions is still rare; the dominant agenda remains to *understand* pigs better so that we can *manage* them better and thus *eat* them better.

Pork is the most-consumed meat in the world. China now holds the alpha position in terms of global pig production. According to the *Economist*, half of all pigs raised and consumed live in China. Foods made from pigs have long been staples of the Chinese diet, a fact inscribed in Mandarin language: the words for "meat" and "pork" are the same, and the character for "family" is a pig under a roof. Through the 1970s, 95 percent of pigs were raised in groups of four or fewer on small farms. Now, three foreign breeds make up almost all (again, 95 percent) of the pigs raised in China. The steep increase in factory farming means that these pigs now routinely live, for their short allotted life spans, packed together by the thousands.

In the United States, of the more than a hundred million pigs raised annually, 97 percent live on factory farms. Among the most haunting images in Philip Lymbery's book *Farmageddon: The True Cost of Cheap Meat* are of the "huge lagoons of pig sewage, upwards of 3000 of them" that "dot the North Carolina landscape." These filthy pools are products of farms where the animals, confined indoors with no fresh air, are bred to stand on small patches of concrete and endure the wait to be turned into pork. The 134-page publication "Quick Facts: The Pork Industry at a Glance," issued in 2009 by the National Pork Board, nonetheless employs a lighthearted tone in discussing the animals who sustain the industry. Facts and figures cited include the world's heaviest hog, a Poland China hog named Big Bill from Tennessee who in 1933 weighed in at 2,552 pounds, and the single longest sausage, a 5,917-foot item cooked in Barcelona in 1986. In the "frequently asked questions" section, bits of information are offered in colorful patches on the page: "Where can I get a meat cut poster?" "Where can I purchase pig parts (ears, feet, intestines, tails or other non-meat)?" "How do I convert a carcass price to a live price?" Later, sections of the document address producers' "moral responsibility" to the pigs: "Producers realize that pigs are living beings and as such, they must receive a level of care that promotes their well-being." This last declaration by the National Pork Board may raise skeptical eyebrows.

Even as industrial conditions for pigs metastasize in China, public scrutiny of pigs' living conditions on factory farms is on the increase in North America, the UK, and Europe. Individual pigs who live on those farms remain largely anonymous to us, just as anonymous as the factory chickens and cows we have already met in this book. Yet even taking into account natural variation, these invisible pigs may be every bit as smart and sensitive as the pigs we know by name.

When confronted with the word "pig," it may well be an image of the iconic, pink, curly-tailed, squealing farm animal—portrayed with a jolly expression on barbecue restaurant signs—that pops into our mind. Esther herself is one of these curly-tailed pinks. A splendid diversity of pigs exists out there in the wider world, though: sixteen species of wild pigs and hogs exist, including the wild boar, the species from which all domestic pigs descended. Five of the sixteen— the bush pig, red river hog, forest hog, and two kinds of warthogs— live in Africa.

On my infrequent days off from baboon-watching in Kenya, I had no greater desire (once, that is, I had indulged in novel-reading and dipping into the chocolate stash under my bed) than to head into the bush and warthog-watch. No contribution to science was ever made by this activity, as my goal was merely to relax and have fun: these low-to-the-ground, fast-running pigs captivated me every bit as much as did the big tourist draws of lions, leopards, and elephants.

Hours sometimes elapsed without any sightings, then suddenly there they would be, a mother warthog followed by trotting babies (a sounder, just a smaller version of the one at Pigs Peace Sanctuary). With tails held high over the savannah, the warthogs were perhaps heading home to their subterranean burrow or out to a desirable food patch. Marvelous diggers, warthogs use both their snouts and feet to turn up the earth in a search for roots, bulbs, or insects; when worked up in a frenzy of digging, they scoot around on their wrists. If threatened, warthogs may shoot out at speed from their burrow. I was warned by my more experienced colleagues: if I veered too close to a burrow and unintentionally disturbed a resident mother, she might well explode in a charge outward and shatter my kneecaps.

Fortunately, the feared patella fracture never happened. Observing these skilled omnivores gave me some insight into the behavior of that force of nature otherwise known as the feral pig. Pigs are considered feral instead of wild if at one time they had been domestic. Perhaps they escaped from a pig farm of some sort or had mixed ancestry, as when an escaped sow mates with a boar (making the offspring feral). It's no joke when I refer to feral pigs as a force of nature, because they ferociously consume pretty much anything in their path. Here's a short list of the feral pig menu compiled by Barry Estabrook: wheat, barley, and corn crops; other cultivated foods such as potatoes, squash, beans, pumpkins, and grapes; crabs and toads; eggs of endangered sea turtles, turkeys, quail, and grouse; young goats, calves, and lambs; carrion of deer; and human corpses.

The "porcine underground," made up of feral pigs who "abide by their own rules, go wherever their curiosity takes them, and flaunt their essential piggyness" entrances Estabrook. As a pig-loving person, I enjoy this picaresque portrayal. In *Pig*, Mizelle takes things a step further by hinting that we might cheer on free-ranging pigs, including feral ones, for taking their just due, given how much these animals suffer in human company. Sighting wild pigs, he states, should be "an encouraging sign, a reminder that these highly adaptable, intelligent and social animals will never be fully controlled by humans."

Yet admiration for feral pigs' wayward ways is a hard sell to anyone, even pig fans, who must cope with the aftermath of their rampages. When these pigs blast through an area, massive damage to crops and forests may result. (Estabrook and Mizelle do explain this.) The pigs are winning the battle because their huge population numbers combine with their formidable learning capacities, which allow them to figure out counterstrategies to some of methods designed for their slaughter. Feral pigs who escape traps not only live on to breed more, but also notice and recall which areas to avoid in the future. Somewhere between four and eight million feral pigs now range across forty-eight of the United States. Inhabiting all continents except Antarctica, the pigs have invaded Australia to a spectacularly successful degree: they delight in decimating sugar cane and banana crops, and exceed in population their *Homo sapiens* adversaries.

In Italy, the problem isn't feral pigs but wild boars, who increasingly approach the outskirts of cities. In 2015 a wild boar was photographed walking past a bus stop outside Rome, and in Umbria a man was taken to the hospital with injuries sustained when a boar attacked him outside his grandson's kindergarten. *Cinghiale* has long been a favorite Italian dish, but now the prey animals are strolling right into the predators' core territory.

If wild boar is considered fine eating, and domestic pork a worldwide favorite, it seems to me counterintuitive that the vast majority of feral pigs are not consumed. Most go entirely to waste, at least by us; once shot or trapped, the pigs almost always remain where they fall, though nonhuman predators do sometimes feed on their carcasses. *Some* feral pigs are human-consumed: according to Estabrook, a hundred thousand of the animals a year taken from Texas alone wind up on diners' tables in high-end restaurants. The Centers for Disease Control and Prevention warns feral-pig hunters of the risk of brucellosis, a disease that may be passed to humans who kill, field-dress, or consume infected pigs. But wild boar too may suffer from brucellosis. The aversion to eating feral pigs is a peculiar situation, driven as always by cultural traditions.

EATING URSULA

Pigs in the popular imagination seem to be equal parts tasty, trouble-some, and terrifically fascinating. These divergent ways of looking at and thinking about pigs do not just coexist in uneasy tension: they are entangled in intricate ways, and we might even say they co-create each other.

Anthropologist Weiss notes that increasingly within the American food system, it's not *a pig* people want to eat but a *particular* pig. "Many farmers and their customers alike no longer want to deny the reality of the animal in question," he writes. "They want to have relationships with the animals they eat, and explicitly acknowledge that the meat they eat was once an animal." In North Carolina's Piedmont region, where he lived, Weiss helped care for pigs at Cane Creek Farm, a farm owned and operated by Eliza MacLean where pastured pigs are raised, and he sold pastured pork at the Carrboro Farmers' Market. This sort of profound engagement in an ongoing process or situation they wish to understand is what anthropologists often do, and in Weiss's case it brought him into encounters with animals he would later consume.

Weiss tells of eating barbecued pork belly with two friends, one an aspiring farmer and food entrepreneur and the other a chef, at a North Carolina restaurant called Saxapahaw General Store. One of his companions commented that the pork belly they were enjoying came from Ursula—a Farmer's Hybrid pig Weiss had known at the farm. "Known" doesn't really do it justice: as a greenhorn on the farm, Weiss had picked up by the hind leg one of Ursula's piglets, thinking to help restrain the infant from escaping a fenced-in area. Well-intended intervention of this sort was not looked upon favorably by Ursula; a hefty sow in an ornery mood, she charged, sending Weiss straight up a fence. "She [could] easily have clamped her jaws around my knee and snapped my leg in half," Weiss writes, and goes on to note wryly, "She was well within her rights to do so for my hav-

Pigs at Cane Creek Farm, North Carolina. Photos courtesy of Ezra Weiss.

ing been so careless in handling her pigs—and right in the vicinity of her teeth."

Across the board, Ursula was a challenging pig to keep on a farm like Cane Creek; readying her piglets first for independence from her and later for the market became impossible in the face of her intensity. And that's how the Saxapahaw General Store came to serve up Ursula:

> Ursula was taken off to slaughter, not, as was the case with other sows I knew, because she proved incapable of further "farrowing" (that is, of reproducing), but rather because she was *such* a good mother that she was far too ornery to keep on the farm without doing damage to the staff, to other farrowing pigs, and so to the farm as a whole.

This picture of Ursula trying to protect her babies from becoming just what Mizelle says pigs are not—just 18 per cent ham, 16 per cent bacon, and so on—tugs at the heart. I can't know where she fell along the dull- or sharp-witted continuum of pig intelligence, but whatever her mental acuity, Ursula stands out as a distinct personality. Weiss certainly saw Ursula this way, even as he ate Ursula: as a distinct pig individual who capably sized up risks in order to protect her family. For centuries, farmers and their families around the world have been eating animals they knew well and may have loved. Of course, the customers who ate pork belly at the General Store or bought it at Carrboro Farmers' Market, where the meat was also sold, did not know their meat had once been Ursula. Consumers of pork products may inquire about farm conditions, and how the pigs live generally, but for them there's no linkage between parcels of meat sold and individual pigs. If the day ever arrives when meat is sold stamped with animals' names (or even details about their personalities), it might come about first with pigs.

Ursula connects for us a pig's life on a small farm with the act of consuming a known pig, but other pigs push the issue in a different direction. Coming to see a pig as an individual leads some people to take pork off their menus. In an interview with the Humane Society's *All Animals Magazine*, Steve Jenkins tells about Esther the pig's impact:

> A 76-year-old vegetarian woman sent us a message that for the first time ever her husband picked up a pack of bacon at the grocery store and then put it down. She asked him why, and he said, "Because of Esther." This man is just a standard, Middle America, meat-and-potatoes kind of a guy who's worked hard his whole life. And here he is changing his diet because of Esther. I cried when I read that. We've had hundreds and hundreds of those kinds of messages.

It only took Jenkins and his partner Derek Walter a few weeks after living with Esther to question their own food habits. Cooking up some bacon together in the kitchen, they looked at each other and realized they couldn't proceed. They were done with eating pigs.

Let's imagine a vegans' utopia where pigs are no longer consumed at a society-wide level. What would happen? One consequence would surely be a loss of genetic diversity in our food system, because the remaining types of pigs bred would narrow considerably, and some would go extinct altogether. The Livestock Conservancy argues that rare breeds of livestock and poultry are key to healthy biodiversity and significant aspects of cultural heritage as well. "The loss of these breeds," the group's website declares, "would impoverish agriculture and diminish the human spirit." On its list of pig conservation priorities are first and foremost (in the "critical" subcategory) Choctaw, Mulefoot, and Ossabaw Island pigs, followed by the "threatened" breeds Gloucestershire Old Spots, Guinea Hogs, Large Black, Red Wattle, and Tamworth.

My first thought in reflecting upon this conservation initiative fell on the cynical side. Would the human spirit *really* be diminished if there were no more Mulefoot or Red Wattle pigs? Yet if someone made a churlish remark of that nature about advocacy for critically endangered or threatened wild species—ranging from black spider monkeys and Sumatran rhinos to bluefin tuna and Yangtze finless porpoises—I would bristle. The question is how equivalent are these two instances. The Livestock Conservancy believes that maintaining heritage breeds is critical for agriculture for all the reasons we could guess: genetic variety is a good thing for disease resistance and for breeding schemes related to sustainability. If the idea is to *save* the pigs so we can *eat* the pigs, though, isn't that a conundrum?

Saving heritage breeds gains traction in the context of small, comparatively humane farms like Cane Creek, where Brad Weiss worked in North Carolina, where, as he puts it in *Real Pigs: Shifting Values in the Field of Local Pork*, farmers must adjust their activities "to accommodate the particularities of individual hog lives." Places like this are somewhat parallel to small chicken farms in Uganda like the one (see chapter 4) where Chance Christine makes a good living for her family selling eggs and where chickens roam freely. In *Real Pigs*, Weiss's goal is to explore the idea of "authenticity" embraced by farmers, breeders, chefs, and consumers in the food networks set up around Piedmont pigs. Second only to the state of Iowa, North Carolina is riddled by large-scale industrial pig farms. Living in towns located near these factories, which house anonymous pigs in their millions, are people who value pasture-raised pork as a local (Piedmont) heritage. Ossabaw Island pigs—one of the breeds considered in need of urgent conservation by the Livestock Conservancy—and others are seen in Weiss's food networks as both sentient animals with their own needs and, more prominently, as a central node in the connection of farmer, meat seller, restaurant chef, and consumer. I would take pains to underscore the imbalance in these two factors; pigs are, like Ursula, known as individuals to be sure, but Weiss puts it plainly: they "lead lives that [are], with a very few exceptions, directed towards their transition into meat."

This chapter kicked off with smart pigs, pigs who recognize symbols, master computer programs, and use mirrors to find hidden food. It closes with endangered pigs, symbols of campaigns to save distinctive pig flavors and pig-based cultural heritages. In between are pigs confined to factory farms, but also pigs who, astonishingly enough, aren't used by us for anything at all—not for university-based animal-behavior science or for Sea World–type performances or for pork products. In one form or another, these pigs live in sanctuary. In the words of Judy Woods, before the Pigs Peace pigs were rescued "they could never imagine that such a place existed on the planet for a pig—and that they could get there." How many millions of pigs alive today won't get there, or anywhere remotely like it?

8. Chimpanzees

Besar lived in Taï National Park in the West African nation of Cote d'Ivoire. His life hadn't always been easy. At age seven, his mother died. Besar had no older siblings, and along with two younger male orphans, he trailed after the dominant male called Zyon for adult company. By the time he was in his teens, as a result of his resilience, Besar exhibited formidable skills in two activities prized in the culture of his chimpanzee community: cracking open hard-shelled nuts with hammers made of wood or stone, and collaborating with other males to bring down prey, usually colobus monkeys, to eat.

Meant to be havens for wildlife, African national parks like Taï remain keenly vulnerable to poachers because so few resources exist for wildlife guards to patrol their borders consistently and effectively. On September 1, 2004, when Besar was fifteen years old, two poachers named Ferdinand and Lucien, under contract to a third man named Leon who sought monkey meat for a party, slipped into the forest. Seeing Besar—not a monkey at all but an ape, a meatier animal—sitting in a tree, Ferdinand took aim, fired, and shot him in the head. Gone in that instant were Besar's fifteen years of life—and with it all his skillful prowess. Long-term Taï researcher and biologist

Christophe Boesch responded in this way to Besar's death: "What an absurd, criminal waste of a life for just one meal!"

We may recoil at the thought of any chimpanzee becoming a meal for our own kind; chimpanzees, together with bonobos, are humans' closest living relatives in the animal kingdom. Chimpanzees live in intensely social, tradition-based communities, balanced between compassion and cooperation on the one hand, and lethal aggression on the other. They make and use sophisticated tools in a variety of contexts; every community of chimpanzees across a wide swath of Africa is bound up in solving practical daily problems through the making and use of technology. They express emotions visibly, ranging from joy to grief. In his book *Ape*, John Sorenson puts the matter aptly: "Apes fascinate us because they seem to transgress the human-animal border." No insect, fish, octopus, chicken, goat, cow, or pig transgresses that border in quite the same way that a chimpanzee does, and I believe it's fitting that *Personalities on the Plate* should conclude with a chapter on these nonhuman primates.

Working from Sorenson's perspective, it's fair to say that human consumption of chimpanzees is a practice not all that far removed from the cannibalism that we humans occasionally practice on each other. When we eat apes, though, we refer to them as "bushmeat," an umbrella term meant to indicate free-ranging forest and savanna animals who are killed for food. Jane Goodall flatly states, "The bushmeat crisis is the most significant and immediate threat to wildlife populations in Africa today." The Jane Goodall Institute (JGI) reports that in the Congo Basin alone, five million tons of bushmeat are taken (that is, the animals are slaughtered) annually. The vast majority of this meat comes not from apes but from other animals, ranging from antelopes and pangolins to rats and fruit bats, sold in various contexts including local markets.

Unsurprisingly, given the illegality of the transactions, it's a challenge to determine reliable numbers for the chimpanzees affected by the bushmeat trade. In Cote d'Ivoire where Besar lived, for instance, hunting and trade in bushmeat was outlawed in 1974, yet in 2012 conservation researchers reported that the trade had gone *up* in the last decade. In the face of political and social instability during that period, the conservation policy on the books had been poorly enforced. In the case of Besar, consequences did accrue to two of the three poachers, through a combination of law enforcement and bad luck (or what we might be tempted to call bad karma). After Ferdinand killed Besar, Lucien hoisted the chimpanzee on his back and walked ahead of Ferdinand as the two made their way back to the village. After a short distance, a snake bit Ferdinand and he fell over in a faint. Lucien, still up ahead, failed to notice. When he did realize his companion was nowhere to be seen, he nevertheless continued on to the village.

After a drawn-out series of events, Ferdinand was eventually rescued—in fact, Besar was consumed at a party organized to celebrate Ferdinand's survival. Ferdinand soon fled to Liberia to avoid the law. Leon, the hunter's patron, did not flee, and for masterminding the killing of a chimpanzee within a national park, he was sentenced to eighteen months in jail.

Cote d'Ivoire is of course not the only hot spot for chimpanzee poaching. The Goodall Institute estimates that in a single year in the Republic of Congo, 295 chimpanzees were slaughtered for bushmeat: that's 295 Besars lost in twelve months. In many African communities, the eating of bushmeat represents a cultural tradition. The protein gained from this practice may be a critical resource for poor families who struggle to provide their children with adequate nourishment. The bushmeat trade cannot be understood without factoring in poverty; it takes no special anthropological knowledge to grasp that when people are hungry, issues of wildlife conservation will be low on their list of priorities. Poverty and inequality are among the driving factors for acts of poaching: bushmeat hunting brings in as much as a thousand dollars per year and certainly at least three hundred dollars, far exceeding the average household income in rural Africa.

Yet we shouldn't make the mistake of seeing the bushmeat slaughter of chimpanzees as a sad but economically necessary practice. In the first place, tradition plays a substantive role. Even when alternative foods are available, chimpanzee meat may be sought for rituals and celebrations, as Boesch explains: in some forest regions of Africa,

> people believe that chimpanzees have some special force or talent that can be acquired by eating their bones, hands, or parts of their heads in special traditional ways. They may attribute some magical therapeutic properties to chimpanzees; for example that young babies will grow strong and healthy if they have a bath in chimpanzee bone powder. As a result, chimpanzee meat is considered a special treat to local human populations in many regions in Africa.

Here is where local educational programs, together with law enforcement, may effect change—or fail utterly. Traditions, by definition, are closely entwined with long-cherished community habits, and their adherents may resist change. (Just ask wildlife conservationists in the United States who try to talk hunters out of poaching endangered black bears, or grapple unsuccessfully with the clamor for shark-fin soup, which causes shark slaughter.)

Further, meat of apes and monkeys is sold in venues far beyond the local market. In 2011 the German publication *DW* interviewed a man preparing to eat his dinner of bushmeat at an African restaurant in Paris. Identified in the article as "Roger, a Congolese thirty-something," the man had called ahead to the restaurant and ordered porcupine in black sauce. At other times, Roger had chosen for his meals there snake, pangolin, crocodile, or monkey. While Roger didn't mention chimpanzee as one of his favorite foods, chimpanzee meat is indeed smuggled into Europe and the UK for the restaurant trade. In London, the *Telegraph* noted in 2014 that "monkeys, gorillas and chimpanzees" brought illegally into the UK from Africa are considered a delicacy for African immigrants nostalgic for bushmeat.

For Westerners, it tends to be an acquired taste. Food critic Charles Campion told the newspaper, "It's stew—you've got a boiling pot and put things in it. It doesn't taste like chicken, that I can tell you."

The lives of chimpanzees born in forests or on the savannahs of African can end abruptly and violently, as Besar's did, for "just one meal." The trajectory of these lives and deaths tells three distinct but interwoven stories. One is about the chimpanzees themselves, and the complex behavioral and cultural patterns they exhibit. Another takes up the extent of loss and devastation in chimpanzee communities even as it illustrates the ways individual ape survivors may gradually recover physically and emotionally. The third returns us to thinking about the cultural context of eating animals. The tragedy of Besar's story is only deepened by the knowledge that the bushmeat trade threatens unique chimpanzee cultures and their networks of intergenerational social learning. At the same time, his story pushes us to think about the fact that *many* of us have choices to make about the animals we consume.

CULTURAL CHIMPANZEES

Wild chimpanzees display cooperation and violence toward each other reminiscent, in its blend of kindness and brutal horror, of the best and worst of human ways. Male chimpanzees work together in hunting parties and sometimes share with others the meat of the monkeys they seize from the tree canopy. They also systematically hunt down and slaughter their chimpanzee neighbors in acts of lethal aggression. Infants may be wrenched from their mothers by adult males and killed in acts of infanticide or, if orphaned at a young age, adopted and cared for tenderly by other adults of the community.

Female chimpanzees have it rough. Males stay in the community into which they are born; females transfer to another community when, at puberty, they develop swollen, pink perineal areas ("sexual swellings") that serve to advertise their fertility. Welcomed by eager-to-mate resident males who are of higher status and power than they, the females enter the new community, with all its unfamiliar social drama, and try to carve out a niche for themselves surrounded by strangers. The males, who may act aggressively toward the females, by contrast, live out their lives among their kin, including their mothers.

While the community is intensely social, it isn't a cohesive social unit of the type that moves as a group through the forest, woodland, or savannah, feeding, resting, and socializing together, as may happen with gorillas and many species of monkeys. The chimpanzee pattern, which we've also seen among goats, is called *fission-fusion*: small parties of individuals continually form and re-form, with ever-changing membership. A pair of chimpanzees may depart from a group of five and join up with another of seven, only to have three apes leave that unit and go off on their own. In combination with long life histories that put a premium on childhood and intense social learning, factors noted by biologist Carel van Schaik and his colleagues, it's this fission-fusion organization that pushes the development of acute chimpanzee intelligence. Hour by hour, chimpanzees interact with other apes of different social ranks, alliance loyalties, and personalities; they must continuously track these social variables and try to position themselves to their own best advantage.

Chimpanzees' intelligence is arguably most visible in contexts where they use technology. In Taï National Park, chimpanzees fashion and deploy tools in complex and sophisticated ways. In one of my favorite field monographs, *The Chimpanzees of Taï Forest*, Christophe Boesch and Hedwige Boesch-Achermann report that Taï chimpanzees use twenty-six different tool types, 83 percent of which are modified in some way to suit the task at hand.

During the annual nut season, chimpanzees on average spend two hours and fifteen minutes a day using hammers to crack open hard-shelled nuts, which make for dynamite little packages of protein once processed. To place a nut just so on an anvil, and hit it just so with a hammer of wood or stone of the appropriate size and shape, takes years of practice. A video of chimpanzees nut-cracking recorded at Taï was always a hit with my anthropology students because it depicts in humorous ways the infants' trial-and-error learning, with heavy emphasis on error. The youngsters struggle to lift ridiculously cumbersome, heavy pieces of wood that they can't effectively control, or bang two nuts together directly and ineffectively, without either a hammer or an anvil. It's not that the little ones haven't been paying attention to their nut-cracking elders; they do watch closely. It's not so different from what happens when we teach our children how to build a treehouse or follow a recipe to make chocolate chip cookies. When inexperienced apprentices first try out new skills, what looked easy at first soon enough becomes a challenge in the doing, and mistakes occur.

At Taï, four sequential phases of this learning process occur, a trajectory that underscores the degree to which observation and practice intersect with the infants' physical maturation. Only gradually do the youngsters gain enough strength to power through the tasks that they are coming to understand cognitively. Until age three, silly-looking mistakes in putting together the anvil, the nut, and the hammer predominate. Around age three, the infants evidently grasp what needs to be done but still lack the muscle power to do it. Eventually the juveniles gain enough strength and enter a period where they can manage the task pretty effectively, if not very efficiently; their young bodies still expend more energy than can be recouped by consuming the nuts they crack. The lengthy fourth and final stage, during which the balance tips decisively if gradually toward a net gain of calories for the nut-crackers, ends only when the chimpanzees gain full mastery of the technology as mature adults. "This slow progress," Boesch and Boesch-Achermann write, "reflects the fact that subadult individuals have problems in gaining access to good hammers and must often content themselves with less than optimal tools."

The old saying "practice makes perfect" is too simple, then, when applied to the perfecting of nut-cracking skills, because access to good hammers in the forest is constrained for some chimpanzees by social realities within the community. Age and dominance status matter in this context, as in most other aspects of chimpanzees' lives. Why then do the little ones persist in their clumsy attempts to crack nuts, when their success in obtaining nutrition and calories is severely limited? The data from Taï point to one of the most elegant systems in all the animal kingdom of coordination and cooperation across generations: mothers share their own nuts in strategic and thoughtful ways with their offspring, sometimes in response to the infants' begging, at other times spontaneously. The calories transferred in this way from master nut-cracker to apprentice mean that the young tool-users can afford, from a nutritional point of view, the time and effort required to keep on with the learning process. As Boesch and Boesch-Achermann put it, "Without this sort of permanent incentive, they might give up the struggle."

When I say that mothers share strategically and thoughtfully, I refer to data that show Taï chimpanzee mothers tailor their sharing behavior to the youngsters' skill levels; maternal nut giveaways taper off as the youngsters' efficiency increases. In addition, the amount of sharing varies according to the difficulty of the cracking task. *Coula* nuts are easier to force open than are *Panda* nuts, and mothers stop sharing them on average four years earlier (at youngster age eight) than they do with the more challenging *Panda* variety (shared through youngster age twelve).

Mothers also "scaffold" the learning behavior of their offspring by intervening in specifically patterned ways to enhance the apprentices' chances of success. There's next to no outright demonstration of good nut-cracking techniques by the mothers: Boesch saw this happen only twice. But the mothers engage in *stimulation*, when they leave suitable hammers or nuts around the anvil for infants at about age three to discover and work with, and *facilitation*, when they present nuts or excellent hammers directly to youngsters who, at age four or five, are seriously getting the hang of things. These ape students consistently accept offers of maternal facilitation, and their nut-cracking improves as a result.

Limits to this ideal of warm cooperation between mom and child do exist: infants may push their mothers to share more nuts than the mothers want to give, and maternal refusal or turning away from a begging youngster is common. (Maternal sharing is energetically costly, and in any case, maternal-offspring conflict is predicted by evolutionary theory, whether the resource in question is mother's milk or the forest's nuts, because the mom's and child's interests never completely coincide.) On the whole, though, this system speaks to the capacity for intense attunement between chimpanzee mothers and their children, and to adult chimpanzees' abilities to understand another's mental perspective. The mothers' actions of stimulation and facilitation indicate, because they are tailored to the specifics of the nut-cracker and the nut, that the moms understand what their infants do and don't know or can and cannot accomplish at a certain age. Then they offer help accordingly. That's not so different a basic principle from the one that teachers put to use in the classroom when they continuously assess and reassess each student's mastery of the material at hand, then intervene appropriately.

I mentioned that Boesch twice saw outright teaching on the part of the mothers. On February 18, 1987, a stunning scene unfolded between chimpanzee mom Ricci and her daughter Nina (unfortunately, Boesch does not cite Nina's age) as Nina struggled to crack *Coula* nuts on her own. Although these nuts are comparatively easy to crack, Nina held an inadequate, irregularly shaped hammer and was having little luck. As she worked the problem, she tried out different approaches, shifting her grip on the hammer about forty times. Finally, Ricci joined her daughter. Immediately Nina handed the hammer over to her mother.

What happened next, once again, points to chimpanzees' "theory of mind"—that mental perspective-taking capacity where one chimpanzee intuits how to fill a gap in another's knowledge:

Ricci, in a very deliberate manner, slowly rotated the hammer into the best position for pounding the nut efficiently. As if to emphasize the meaning of this movement, it took her a full minute to perform this simple rotation. . . . With Nina watching her, she then cracked ten nuts (of which Nina ate 6 entire kernels and portions of the 4 others).

At this point, Ricci stopped what she was doing, retreated to her previous location, and observed as Nina resumed cracking. Now Nina held the hammer exactly in the position her mother had, and opened four nuts in fifteen minutes. She still had some trouble, but progress had been achieved; a one-to-one teaching bout brought about a young learner's forward leap in skill mastery.

The Boesches' long-term research at Taï, and Jane Goodall's years of observation at Gombe, across the content in Tanzania, provide a comparative base to understand chimpanzee culture. At Gombe, hard nuts, anvils, and hammers are present, but the chimpanzees there do not nut-crack. Gombe chimpanzees are highly tool-capable in other ways; they expertly fashion termite-fishing sticks and ant-dipping wands to extract protein snacks from insects' homes. After nearly sixty years of field work on wild chimpanzees, it's clear that *every* known chimpanzee community uses and makes tools. The variation observed is cultural rather than ecological or genetic in nature.

At Fongoli, Senegal, primatologist Jill Pruetz discovered that chimpanzees use tools to hunt, which they aren't seen to do in the cooperative pursuits of prey by males at Taï or Gombe. The Fongoli chimpanzees—females, usually, in a fascinating twist on the usual pattern—make wooden spears from tree branches and deploy them to impale bushbabies in the tree cavities where they may often be found. Highly distinctive, this community's use of technology is cultural in origin—and so it goes right across Africa. In the Goualougo Triangle area of the Republic of Congo's Nouabale-Ndoki National Park, primatologists Crickette Sanz and David Morgan watched as a chimpanzee they named Dorothy used a series of three different tools to obtain honey from a beehive constructed high in the tree canopy. Dorothy first picked up a club and struck the hive entrance repeatedly (perhaps fortunately, the bees in question were of the stingless variety). Next, she modified a tree branch into a smaller club by shortening it and stripping it of twigs and leaves, then used the two tools in alternation as a hammer and a lever. After an hour's work, and with the hive now successfully opened, she paused to rest in the canopy, having eaten no honey whatsoever. "We were quite impressed," Sanz and Morgan write, "when she returned less than a minute later with a slender twig that was deftly fashioned into a dipping tool to extract the honey. Dorothy spent the rest of the afternoon enjoying the bounty of her tool-using skills."

Dorothy had used a tool set: multiple tools deployed in succession to solve a problem. She had recently transferred into that chimpanzee community from the one in which she had been born, and it's probable that she had brought her technological skills with her. By 2013, seven years after their observation of Dorothy's impressive honey-gathering behavior, Sanz and Morgan were able to report that among chimpanzees in the Goualougo Triangle, the use of tool sets is anything but a rarity. The chimpanzees routinely use them in gathering termites and driver ants as well as honey.

Just as applied technology is culture-specific, so are some aspects of hunting behavior, as we have seen with the spear-hunting at Fongoli. At Taï, hunting behavior is cultural and collaborative, with a specialization in taking red colobus monkeys as prey. Learning to hunt, say Boesch and Boesch-Achermann, may be an astonishingly slow process for the chimpanzees, slower even than the mastery of cracking *Panda* nuts. Just as there's a nut season at Taï, there's a hunting season also, a two-month period that corresponds to the monkeys' birth season. During this period, chimpanzees hunt every day, sometimes more than once a day, compared to a weekly frequency throughout the rest of the year.

Males at Taï begin to hunt when they are perhaps nine or ten. Two decades later they may finally excel at the most cognitively demanding techniques. Those twenty years represent almost half of a wild chimpanzee's maximum life span, a situation that may be resonate with those of us—athletes, artists, and anthropologists alike—who work to perfect our skills for decades and *do* measurably improve over that period.

At Taï it is the older males who take on the more challenging roles in the cooperative hunt, that of the blocker who cuts off a monkey's attempted escape and of the ambusher who anticipates the monkey's flight path and tries to disrupt it, sending the monkey toward other waiting chimpanzees. My favorite Taï chimpanzee of all, Brutus, was the alpha hunter of the community during the period of hunting assessed by Boesch and Boesch-Achermann in *The Chimpanzees of Taï Forest*. In Brutus's story we find another beautiful intersection (as we did with Besar, and Nina and Ricci, and Dorothy in the Congo) of culture and the individual. The single most cerebral feat of chimpanzee hunting at Taï is called *double anticipation*, when chimpanzees are able to predict not only the moves of their fellow hunters, but also the moves of the prey animal. The chimpanzee hunter, as Boesch and Boesch-Achermann put it, "does not anticipate what he sees (the escaping colobus), but how a future chimpanzee tactic will further influence the escaping monkeys." This is a substantive cognitive feat because so many contingencies are involved, resulting in a moment-by-moment shifting choreography that unfolds in the forest's three dimensions. Of the eight instances of double anticipation the Boesches witnessed, five were performed by Brutus. Brutus could reasonably be termed the genius of the Taï male hunters. Hands down, he was the best meat provider, often seen at the center of excited sharing bouts, during which ten males and females would eat from Brutus's prize of meat.

In the hunting behavior at Taï, we have more evidence that chimpanzees can think themselves into the perspective of others. Based on what we know of his hunting prowess, Brutus was, I believe, an exceptional chimpanzee. I credit him also with piquing my interest in animals' responses to death, a topic I ended up researching in depth for my book *How Animals Grieve*. At the time I "met" Brutus by reading about him, I simply had not thought much about whether animals mourn the losses of family members and friends who have died.

On March 8, 1989, a leopard killed a juvenile female of the Taï community named Tina. Tina's mother had died four months earlier, and together with her brother, five-year-old Tarzan, she had spent much time with the community's then-dominant male, Brutus. The community response to Tina's death spanned the gamut from aggression toward the body to inspection and grooming of it. For a continuous period of four hours and fifty minutes (broken only for seven minutes), Brutus attended Tina's still form. During this time, Tarzan came close to his sister and Brutus allowed him, but no other infant, to smell her and inspect her genitals. And then, the Boesches report, "Tarzan groomed her for a few seconds and pulled her hand gently many times, looking at her." We cannot know for sure what was going through the mind of Tarzan, suddenly finding himself without his big sister, so soon after the death of his mother. What is surer is that Brutus understood Tarzan's special relationship with Tina, and for him relaxed his gate-keeping behavior around the body. Here is yet another example of Brutus's ability to alter his own behavior based on his intuition about the perspective of another.

We shouldn't take too far my conclusion that Brutus had a special presence in his community. Perspective-taking abilities are widespread in chimpanzees, judging from reports from captivity as well as other free-ranging communities—even if those capacities may be expressed variably according to the apes' personalities. I cannot know for sure, but I like to imagine that Besar was just as good at mental perspective-taking as he was at the other skills needed for successful nut-cracking and cooperative hunting at Taï. I doubt, though, that Besar could have projected himself into the minds of two humans in order to understand how they could walk into the forest and take deadly aim at him as he sat peacefully in a tree.

COMMUNITY LOSS

Just as the social dynamics in their communities shaped the life histories of Besar and Brutus at Taï in Cote d'Ivoire, so did Besar's and Brutus's choices shape their communities. As is always the case, individuals matter, and we can only attempt to document the extent to which practices of the bushmeat trade, the killing of some chimpanzees and the orphaning of others, reverberate through ape communities in long-lasting ways.

The *Washington Post* reported a vivid scene from summer 2014, when reporters from the *Cameroon Tribune* (CT) visited an outdoor bushmeat market in a neighborhood of Cameroon's capital city, Yaounde. Here *Post* reporter Abby Phillip quotes from the *Tribune's* account:

> In spite of the current ban in the hunting of all species of animals due to their reproduction period, traders in bush meat do not seem bothered by the fact that they are into a forbidden trade. . . . Besides the enormous display of smoked bush meat of all sorts, the number of fresh meat available outweighs that which has been smoked. While CT reporters went round the market showing interest in buying fresh pangolin, over 10 traders in pangolin, mostly women rushed forward with newly killed or life [sic] pangolin at different cost.

Chimpanzees aren't as abundantly available on Cameroon's open market as other mammals such as pangolins, sometimes called scaly anteaters. But at Limbe Wildlife Centre (LWC) in southwestern Cameroon, we find the visible, and traumatic, evidence of how abundantly affected chimpanzees are by poaching. Founded in 1993, the sanctuary practices the three Rs: rescue, rehabilitation, and release/

reintroduction of wildlife. LWC's emphasis is on primates, including chimpanzees, gorillas (both western lowland and Cross River), mangabeys, drills, and guenons, but it takes in individuals from a swath of other species, including turtles and African gray parrots. With chimpanzees, the emphasis has been on rescue, and, as is the case with animals ranging from elephants to pigs who have suffered trauma, the result is a gradual, two-steps-forward-one-step-back rehabilitation of body and mind.

Jennifer Draiss, an American who began working at LWC immediately after graduating from college in Iowa, sent me a census sheet of the fifty chimpanzees living at the sanctuary as of spring 2015. (Draiss now works in Indonesia with rescued orangutans.) The apes' names—Mokolo, Akwaya Jean, Bernadette, Garoua-Papa, Yabien, Bazou—are as lyrical as their histories are searing. "All of the chimpanzees here, with the exception of two who were accidental births, are orphans of the bushmeat trade," Draiss told me. "Even those who had previously been kept as pets were originally captured after their mothers were killed, being 'worth' more money on the market alive than dead due to their small sizes."

Draiss points to a principle that complicates the search for bushmeat statistics and carries ominous implications for chimpanzees: it's not just the animals served up as meat who become the poachers' victims. Infant Yabien, now at LWC, is a case in point. When Yabien's mother was killed by poachers, the youngster was too tiny to be considered to amount to a decent meal. She ended up in the village of Yabien (for which LWC caregivers named her), almost certainly sold by poachers to someone who thought it a cute idea to adopt a baby chimpanzee. Whoever that someone was, he or she ended up tying Yabien's waist with a rope and chaining her to a wall. When she arrived at LWC in July 2011, Draiss told me, Yabien was estimated to be three years old:

> Upon arrival, Yabien's cries could be heard through the impossibly small wooden box she had been forced into, her knees pressed tightly

against her chest in fetal position. As soon as Yabien was taken out of the crate, it was clear that she needed immediate medical attention; the rope that had been tied around her waist as a young infant had never been loosened or removed, which had left extremely deep, rotting wounds that were crawling with hundreds of maggots.

LWC's veterinarian anesthetized Yabien, removed the rope, and put the little ape on an intensive regimen of treatment for malnourishment and dehydration. From the size of the rope and the degree to which it was cutting into her flesh, Yabien looked to have been captured by the poachers at about six months of age. Events of the two and a half years between that capture and her rescue by authorities from the Ministry of Forest and Wildlife, the arm of the Cameroon government that arranged her transport to LWC, will probably never be known.

At LWC, Yabien needed for reasons of physical health to be quarantined from the other chimpanzees, but it was in her psyche that the most intractable wounds lay. For weeks Yabien would not—or *could not*, due to the intensity of her psychological trauma—respond to Draiss or other members of the sanctuary care team. Often, she ate or drank nothing, and only rocked back and forth and stared blankly. Like the animal survivors I have written about in *How Animals Grieve*, Yabien was mourning her separation from her mother (and perhaps other family members). And like countless other animals (including dogs, monkeys, and humans) known to emerge from grief when presented with someone younger to care about and care for, Yabien improved noticeably when she was healthy enough to be introduced to Lolo, a six-month-old chimpanzee who had arrived at LWC a few months before. LWC caregivers' gentle ministrations throughout the quarantine period, and the new presence of Lolo, combined to make all the difference: "Yabien's personality began to emerge," Draiss says. "She was extremely patient and welcoming, and loved watching someone [Lolo] who looked like herself."

Before long, Yabien joined the sanctuary's nursery group, where she grew into an active, playful youngster. The changes in Yabien are striking, and she is now a symbol of hope at the sanctuary. "During the day," Draiss told me, "Yabien's extremely loud laughter can always be heard (although sometimes she enjoys quiet time to groom, too!), and when she goes inside at night, she's often too busy playing to eat her dinner!"

The chimpanzee Bazou's life history is similar in some ways to Yabien's. He too had been roped and chained, kept as a pet in isolation from other chimpanzees, and he too arrived at LWC malnourished and dehydrated. Unlike Yabien, though, Bazou at age sixteen was a full-grown adult when, in 2009, he arrived at LWC, physically mature but with no evident knowledge of how to act appropriately as a chimpanzee. For four years, Bazou's screaming and rocking behaviors so put off the other chimpanzees that only two of them, Marc and Jacob, tolerated him. During that period, though he had the option to go out into the sun, Bazou never ventured beyond his indoor cage.

Finally, in 2013, the LWC team decided to coax Bazou into a new family. Given that thirty-six chimpanzees were involved, this was no small undertaking. First, Bazou was introduced to the group's dominant male, TKC, a step not without risk given male chimpanzees' capacity for violence, especially in the presence of stranger males. Fortunately, TKC adopted a protective stance toward Bazou, and most of the other dominant males followed his lead. What trouble there was came not from the adults but from males whom Draiss affectionately calls "rowdy juveniles" who, in testing their limits with the adults, caused Bazou some small wounds. On the whole, however, this phase went extraordinarily well, better than I would have expected given Bazou's awkwardness.

As happened with Yabien and the infant Lolo, social companionship caused Bazou's personality to blossom. "After not having been outdoors for twenty years," Draiss told me, "Bazou finally was able to

Yabien, one of the many chimpanzees rescued from the bushmeat trade and now living at the Limbe Wildlife Centre in southwestern Cameroon. Photo courtesy of Jennifer Draiss/Limbe Wildlife Centre.

take his first step onto the grass, bathing in the sunlight, being as free as he could be in the enclosure. As we watched, there was not a dry eye in the Centre. As Bazou screamed, he was comforted by the entire group, with many of the males taking turns hugging him." From that point forward, life took a decidedly positive turn for Bazou: he now plays contentedly with the younger chimpanzees and grooms with the older ones.

Bazou and Yabien are just two of the chimpanzees at chimpanzee-dense LWC, and the LWC is just one sanctuary. The latest statistics known to me show that over eight hundred chimpanzees live in thirteen sanctuaries across twelve African countries, most of them, as at Limbe, orphaned by the bushmeat trade (plus the exotic pet trade). The Republic of Congo's Tchimpounga Chimpanzee Rehabilitation Center, operated by the Jane Goodall Institute, is the largest in Africa, caring for more than 150 orphans. These numbers are daunting, especially because chimpanzees in captivity may live into their sixties: a commitment to care for abandoned youngsters like Yabien is also a commitment to care for a strong-willed adult ape who attempts to make his or her way amid the complex and ever-changing dynamics of a chimpanzee group.

In the United States, Canada, and Europe, chimpanzee residents of sanctuaries are refugees mostly from biomedical laboratories, circuses, roadside zoos, and the film industry. Their life histories, while typically not associated with the bushmeat trade, may too be full of suffering. Since first reading about the chimpanzee Tom, who ended up at Gloria Grow's Fauna Foundation, the only chimpanzee sanctuary in Canada, I have not been able to forget him. Housed for fifteen years at New York University's Laboratory for Experimental Medicine and Surgery and before that sixteen years at the Alamagordo Primate Facility in New Mexico—both notorious biomedical laboratories—Tom endured what no individual being should endure. In *The Chimps of Fauna Sanctuary*, Andrew Westoll sums up Tom's life before he went to sanctuary:

For more than thirty years, he was repeatedly infected with increasingly virulent strains of HIV, went through numerous hepatitis-B studies, and survived at least sixty-three liver, bone marrow, and lymph-node biopsies. By Gloria's estimate, he was knocked unconscious at least 369 times, but this number is based on incomplete medical records and is certainly an underestimate.

A poignant aspect of Tom's trauma is rooted not in his own suffering but in his empathy for the suffering of others with the same terrible plight. Year after year, between his own "knock downs," he saw other chimpanzees going through the same cycle: shot with a dart gun, screaming and thudding unconscious to the cage floor, then taken away for invasive procedures, some done within Tom's line of sight and others carried out in a surgical suite. Gloria Grow believes that Tom's role as witness to these constant traumas took an extra toll on him. Given chimpanzees' capacity for theory of mind, I see no reason to doubt that belief.

When Tom finally reached safety at Fauna Foundation, in the Quebec pasturelands, he bore a foot injury sustained in a fight with another male. Antibiotics gave him severe diarrhea, so a new plan was needed. Knowing chimpanzees' capacity for reasoning, Grow, together with Tom's most trusted human friend, a man named Pat Ring, on whose land the sanctuary was built, requested (I imagine through a combination of spoken English and pantomime) that Tom participate in his own wound care. Tom complied, first bathing his foot in water then pushing it toward the caregivers so they could pat it dry and apply antibiotic cream. From there, events took an even more intriguing turn. Sanctuary staff made up a tray for Tom with the necessary equipment—a little cup of ointment, a spatula, paper towels and tissues—and Tom took over his *own* wound care. Later, his neighbor chimpanzee Regis sustained a bad bite wound. At first, Grow treated him, but once Regis's strength returned, that option was no longer safe for her. She then left all the medical materials out for Tom on a trolley, and Tom cleaned and treated Regis's wound for a week.

That Tom could do all this might sound incredible, yet it rings true to me and meshes well with knowledge that field primatologists have gained about chimpanzee cognition. I can easily envision Brutus, Taï National Park's consummate hunter of monkeys and protector of Tina's little brother Tarzan, carrying out similar actions were he to find himself in Tom's situation in captivity. Even while grieving for Tom's hard life in biomedical laboratories, it brings some comfort to know that he was encouraged to be himself, to express his own personality, at the Fauna sanctuary, where he died surrounded by those who loved him.

In accounts of chimpanzees sent to sanctuary after traumatic experiences, one theme that recurs is their capacity for forgiveness. Here it is necessary to walk a careful line between reasonable anthropomorphism and the too-fanciful variety. Some caregiver accounts of chimpanzees take on a near-mystical tinge, attributing literally incredible powers to the apes. (A similar phenomenon occurs with dolphins, whales, and elephants.) I have lost count of the number of times the chimpanzee Washoe, famous for communicating with humans using American Sign Language (ASL), has been credited in print with being "the first nonhuman to acquire a human language." Though well-intentioned, this statement is misguided. ASL speakers tell intricately woven stories of the past and future, recite poetry, and use their language in other thrillingly complex ways; a chimpanzee can no more "acquire" ASL than he or she can acquire German or Mandarin. That this is true in no way diminishes Washoe's considerable communicatory prowess, which I admire and celebrate. (The sole time I was asked to write an obituary for *Anthropology News*, my discipline's flagship newsletter, it was for Washoe upon her death in 2007, and I was happy to comply.)

I would be skeptical if anyone tried to convince me that chimpanzees understand and wield "forgiveness" in the conceptual way we humans may do. Yet it is straightforwardly clear that when they feel safe, chimpanzees who have to some degree recovered from trauma in sanctuary will reveal to selected humans the sparkle, or the quiet dignity, of their personalities. Many, if not all, seem able and willing to forge a connection with select people, despite having suffering *because* of people. Perhaps chimpanzees excel at distinguishing among individual humans according to our degree of visible kindness and compassion—as Tom distinguished Gloria Grow and Pat Ring from the biomedical researchers—just as their fission-fusion social organization in the wild requires them to distinguish among individual chimpanzees.

Sometimes, it must be said, the toll is too great; not every chimpanzee hurt because of human actions recovers emotionally, no matter how skilled and loving the care he or she receives in sanctuary. But at a minimum even these chimpanzees are rescued from the battering of continued stress and given a chance at peace. They are no longer made to perform through coercion at circuses or in films, their bodies are not invaded by biomedical tests, and they are not consumed for just one meal.

Globally speaking, most of us do not eat chimpanzees. The reason isn't only that many of us live far from regions where chimpanzees naturally dwell. Should seasoned carnivores find themselves buying food at an African outdoor market, or in a restaurant in a world capital where exotic meat is available, many, I think, would simply refuse to purchase or eat chimpanzee meat. Yet many of those same consumers do not think twice about eating fish, octopus, chickens, goats, pigs, or cows—and maybe even insects—all of the animals discussed in earlier chapters of this book.

When we humans eat a chimpanzee for food, we choose to consume an individual who thinks, who feels, who expresses his or her own personality even while embedded in a social network. This point may be intuitively sensible when made about our closest living relatives, because we so readily *recognize* the nature of their higher cognition, deep emotions, and variable ways of being in the world. But my claim doesn't stop with chimpanzees. As we work toward a world of empathy for other creatures, our gaze must take in not only the primates closest to us but also other mammals, birds, fish, and invertebrates. Only then will we see whom we are eating.

Afterword

Many, perhaps most, current discussions of what we owe animals fail
to attend to the particularity of individual animal lives and the very
different sorts of relationships we are in with them.

Lori Gruen, *Entangled Empathy*

Esther the wonder pig, who lives with her two human friends; Mr.
Henry Joy, the chicken who brought the emotion for which he is
named to nursing home residents; and Olive, the giant Pacific octopus whose curating of her eggs delighted Puget Sound divers, are
three of the animals profiled in this book whose lives entangled with
human lives. Besar the forest-dwelling chimpanzee, who was shot
by poachers and became party meat, is another. The groupers in
the ocean who signal to their hunting partners about the location of
hidden prey, and the goats, cows, pigs, and chickens who are forced
into anonymity on farms are among the many other animals who
may be thought to touch our lives less directly. The message here,
though, is that we owe it to all of these animals to become aware of
their sentience and to use our intelligence to acknowledge and act
on behalf of theirs.

Two questions leap right out from that paragraph. Why do I omit
insects from the list of deserving animals? While I don't want to re-

peat mistakes of the past, in which animals like octopus and fish were claimed to be too insensate to feel pain, much less to think or feel emotions, my interpretation of the evidence is that there's a qualitative gulf in intelligence and sentience between insects and the other animals I consider. Protein needs are great for the world's hungry, and as a supplement to plants, insects may fill those needs in ways that make economic sense and may improve the overall calculus of animal suffering. It goes without saying that cruelty to insects *can occur* and *must be avoided*, which will require not just the requisite "further study" but an a priori willingness to give insects the benefit of the doubt and treat them humanely.

Next, to whom do I refer in saying that "we" owe careful consideration to animals? Lisa Kemmerer offers an answer that I have woven implicitly through each of my chapters. Kemmerer wrote her book *Eating Earth: Environmental Ethics and Dietary Choice* for "those who have access to a variety of foods and who choose what they will bring to the table." She aims to wield her judgment with targeted precision: "*This book*," she declares in italics, "*is not intended as a criticism of those who have little or no choice in what they consume.*" Kemmerer strides into the provocative moral territory of oughts and shoulds to prescribe a vegan diet for all people with the luxury of options in what they choose to eat: "Not only environmentalists," she writes, "but anyone who cares about human beings—health and the world's poor—or is concerned about the sufferings of pigs and fish and pheasants, or who is committed to one of the world's great religions, ought to choose a vegan diet."

I can join Kemmerer's path here only partway. Her invocation of the acronym AMORE to summarize the global benefits of plant-based diets makes for a lovely mnemonic, as it points us toward concern for *animal suffering*; for our own *medical health*; for the welfare of *oppressed people*; for the values espoused by the world's *religions* (but of course not exclusive to the religious); and for our *environment*. I firmly believe, though, that all people, not only vegans, who take steps toward plant-based diets deserve encouragement and accolades. Progress toward the central goals set out in AMORE requires collective will and energy that can best be harnessed through an attitude of inclusion rather than exclusion.

That makes me a reducetarian and not an abolitionist. In a 2015 essay titled "Compromise Isn't Complicity," vegan activist Hillary Rettig links the vegan movement to earlier human-centered social justice movements, including opposition to slavery, and describes people who reject a partial commitment to veganism as abolitionists. Rettig makes it clear that she respects this hard-core commitment to *eliminating* all meat, fish, dairy, eggs, and other animal products from the diet, yet after a hard look at the realities of our food system, she backs the movement aimed at significantly *reducing* consumption of those foods.

"The barriers to veganism," Rettig writes, "are substantial and include not just the pervasiveness of animal exploitation in our culture and economy, and the resilience of animal agriculture as a capitalist system, but the central and intimate role that food plays in our lives." These factors in no way doom efforts to work on behalf of animals exploited for food, but I think they bolster the conclusion of Rettig's historical analysis, that compromise is fundamental to social change. Rettig makes beautifully clear just how much change can emerge from reducetarianism: by her calculations, if each person in the United States alone reduced his or her meat consumption by one meal a week, 450 million cows and other animals would be spared each year. (I assume she means spared from being born to lives of suffering, because supply and demand would reduce livestock breeding.)

I'm not suggesting that the goal of reducing meat intake by one meal a week is good enough when it comes to addressing animal suffering: it isn't. I think most of us can do better than that. Vegan activism supplies an important wake-up call about the role each of us plays in farmed animals' short, sad lives when we choose to eat not only meat but also eggs and dairy products. A reducetarian approach can take these nonmeat foods into account as well. Yet the mantra I hear from some vegans—"Either you're vegan or you're no friend to animals; there's no middle ground"—is not just off-putting, it's also wrong. Many paths exist to helping animals and a reducetarian approach to eating is one of them.

All of us who eat have to find ways to listen to each other across our breakfast, lunch, and dinner tables. This goal isn't as modest as it might first sound. I've lost count of the number of times I've written a blog post about pigs, cows, or chickens who suffer in the food industry only to run up against gleeful, mocking responses in comments section, along the lines of "Can't wait for my barbecue tonight!" Online interaction isn't the same, though, as one-to-one conversation carried out in person and mediated by mutual gaze; in direct personal encounters, most human beings are just well-enough-socialized primates to rein in any knee-jerk or "gotcha" tendencies most of the time. Again, I'm no idealist: I've heard both vegans castigating, and sometimes threatening, small farmers who truly work hard to give their animals good lives that end in deaths as free of pain and fear as possible, and omnivores hurling scorn at the substantive ethical principles at the heart of veganism; the rancor in both are painful to witness. I've also heard, and participated in, dialogues that focus reasonably, if testily at times, on common concern for animal lives.

Inevitably, eye-rolling moments of sincere disbelief will occur. In a 2015 *New York Times* article, "Blessed Be My Freshly Slaughtered Dinner," Kate Murphy talks to John Samecki, a scholar of philosophy and religious studies, who notes that he eats lobsters because lobster consciousness is not as highly developed as mammalian consciousness. Then he adds, "I draw the line at lobsters because they are delicious." I struggle, I will admit, in this instance to refrain from sarcasm given the evidence of an ethical system—espoused by a person who devotes his life to philosophy and religious studies—that places deliciousness of animal bodies at its center. But let's be fair. Samecki's honesty about what he eats reflects the bottom line for many people, doesn't it? Don't millions—well, billions—of people just plainly and simply find that animals taste good?

People do get to say that animals taste good to them: that's a completely subjective matter. (It's apparent to me at this point that I'll never lose my craving for chicken pot pie; at least so far, faux-chicken substitutes just don't do it for me.) But not everything that's relevant here is so subjective. Murphy concludes her *Times* piece by remarking that "we are all free to use our individual feelings, desires and experiences to shape eating ethos," and then adds, "There is no definitive scientific evidence that animals experience emotion as we do." Here she has veered right into trouble, because she's wrong about that claim, at least up to those last three little words, "as we do," and that phrase is a red herring.

The animals we have met in these pages demonstrate decisively that, to varying degrees, they think their way through their days and experience feelings about what they make happen and what happens to them. The "as we do" clause misses the point entirely. In the end, pain is pain: that species' sensory systems differ one from the other (and from ours) doesn't change that fact a bit, as is abundantly clear in the emerging consensus about the ability of fish to feel pain even though they lack the mammalian neocortex. No animal need be sentient *like us* to be sentient, just as no animal need be smart like us to be smart or feel emotions like ours to be known as a feeling being with a distinct and sometimes vivid personality.

Few of us are called upon in our daily lives to decide if we should cook and consume the animals with whom I concluded this book: chimpanzees. We are, though, faced every day with whether to eat chickens, pigs, cows, and other animals who are routinely labeled as food throughout much of the world. With a cross-cultural lens in place, I've come to think those daily decisions are not so qualitatively different from the decision whether or not to prepare an ape for dinner—or a dog.

Bringing into the mix our beloved canine companions is no red herring. Dogs in immense numbers are boiled alive or electrocuted as food animals in multiple regions of Asia. The organization In Defense of Animals reports that every year, about 2.5 million dogs are killed in South Korea for a meat meal or a popular dog broth. (A hundred thousand cats meet the same end in that country annually, made into soup or health tonics.) Humane Society International notes that in South Korea "any discarded or unwanted" dog is vulnerable for confinement in a dog-meat farm. South Korea is only an example, in the same way that the United States is only an example of a place where billions of chickens are confined and killed each year. In the Chinese city of Yulin in Guangxi province, the annual dog-meat festival draws headlines every summer solstice because during this ten-day festivity, at least ten thousand dogs are consumed.

Dogs are highly attuned problem solvers, they express joy and sorrow, and they differ one from the other in personality; we know these things primarily because we share our lives with and care for dogs, and the on-fire-popular field of dog cognition backs that knowledge up through ingenious experiments. This branch of ethology broke wide open in 2002 when Brian Hare, now of the Duke University Canine Cognition Center, and his colleagues published in *Science* the results of the first direct comparison of chimpanzee and dog social cognition. In an elegant series of experiments in which both species were tested to see if they could follow human "conspicuous" communicative cues—including pointing cues, gazes, and the marking of containers—to find hidden food items, dogs outperformed chimpanzees. This feat is, on the one hand, pretty remarkable given everything we know about the incisive minds of chimpanzees. On the other hand, it's a strong testament to the power of side-by-side living through domestication. Hare and colleagues, in fact, took pains to test—in addition to adult dogs and chimpanzees—wolves and puppies. The wolves didn't match adult dogs' capacities in decoding human communicative cues, but the puppies did very well.

It's not, in other words, general canid capabilities or prolonged exposure to humans during dogs' lives that explains why dogs can do what they do in "reading" us.

Writing together with Hare in *Science* in 2015, Evan L. MacLean notes anew the "remarkable case of evolutionary convergence" in cognitive capacities and behaviors of dogs and primates. They emphasize again that at least ten thousand years of domestication has shaped dogs and humans to make sense of each other: dogs do understand our gestures and our eye movements. MacLean and Hare conclude:

> Incredibly, dogs' attention to social information leads not only to skillful problem solving, but also to the same socially mediated errors that young children make. For example, both dogs and children are likely to interpret eye contact as communicative, even in contexts when it is not. Thus, dogs exhibit many of the same cognitive flexibilities and biases that characterize our own species.

Our huge popular appetite for the science of how dogs think and communicate—books and articles on these topics now appear in a veritable flood—surely rests on the experiences many of us have had growing up around or interacting with dogs. As Raymond Coppinger and Mark Feinstein put it in *How Dogs Work*, "Every hunter, every sled-dog racer, every shepherd, every dog trainer uses hand signals that are no different than a point." In other words, we know from experience what the experiments show—but as it turns out, with a twist.

Ironically, it may be a specific challenge to our perceptions of dogs that resonates most with the theme of this book. Hare based his research, and thus his conclusions, Coppinger and Feinstein say, on Fido and Spot: dogs who are family pets. Furthermore, he compared one species (dogs) whose representatives were free to move around much as they do at home, with familiar people and food nearby, with another (chimpanzees) who were captive, reaching through a hole in a glass enclosure to participate in the test. Reviewing the literature, including a key paper by Monique Udell, Nicole Corey, and Clive Wynne that shows shelter dogs not raised with humans can't use pointing information from humans, but hand-reared wolves can, Coppinger and Feinstein end up cautious about some of the more popular claims about dogs' social cognition versus that of other species.

These debates over comparative context are fascinating, but it's a single take-home message that I see and want to underscore: dogs make for desirable meals in some regions of the world, whereas in others they are shielded from human consumption by our own perspectives on who they are—and who they are to us. To some significant degree, most all the animals profiled in this book would come alive for us as smart, sentient personalities if we lived alongside them in acute mutuality in the ways we have done and continue to do with dogs. Here's where Mr. Joy the chicken, Esther the wonder pig, and those playful fish come back in.

I don't presume that we will ever warm up to fish the way we do to dogs, and I know that we shouldn't make wild animals our pets or endeavor to domesticate the octopus. Instead I want to foreground how critically important it is to remember, when we decide who to eat, that we have trained our minds to notice certain animals and not others, and to value the emerging scientific news about certain animals and not others. In North America and Europe, we like our dogs and chimpanzees smart and our chickens, cows, goats, pigs, octopuses, and fish stupid.

When our perception shifts, and we recognize that these so-called food animals think, feel, and express their individual personalities, do our eating patterns shift too? I could find no data that address the matter framed in this precise "before and after" way, but a 2014 review article by Steve Loughnan, Brock Bastian, and Nick Haslam shows that our view of animals' intelligence plays a significant role in our dining decisions. One study from 2012 found a strong negative relationship between perceived edibility of thirty-two animals and those animals' perceived mental capacities. Another project aimed to discover if animals are viewed as less mentally capable *because* they are eaten. American study participants judged tree kangaroos to be less capable of suffering and less deserving of moral concern when they were told that tree kangaroos are consumed as food in Papua New Guinea than when they were told only that the animal lived in that region. All it takes to change people's perception of the intelligence of animals (at least some animals) is to label them as food.

Loughnan and his colleagues conclude that "attributing [to] animals lesser minds and reducing their perceived capacity to suffer is a powerful means of resolving the meat paradox"—that is, the paradox that most people who say they care about harm to animals still eat meat. In her 2015 essay "Eating Apes, Eating Cows," Erin McKenna puts her finger on a key irony that relates to this conclusion. We don't breed and slaughter chimpanzees for food, McKenna says, because we know that apes are intelligent beings with complex social relations. Yet the very characteristics that made cows good candidates for domestication invite us to inscribe intelligence to them as well, and to see that their social relationships also matter to them. It's just that we don't. Given what can be gleaned from the studies I describe above and from anecdotes showing that familiarity with Esther the pig causes some people to swear off pork and bacon, it's reasonable to figure that people who are open to learning about and reflecting on cow intelligence may choose to eat fewer or no cows, or food products from their bodies. There's no question that our omnivorous tendencies have played a central role in our evolution on this planet, in the sense that meat-eating by first scavenging and later hunting helped fuel the development of large brains in our ancestral lineage. We *Homo sapiens* today are not locked in by evolution to be predators of other animals, however. As Marta Zaraska has shown in *Meathooked: The History and Science of Our 2.5-Million-Year-Obsession with Meat,* eating plants or mostly plants can give us the nutrients we need for robust health with a single exception: Vitamin B12, which is found only in meat, dairy products, and eggs (and nowadays, the easy-to-take dietary supplements that we use in my house). Evolutionary science tells us that meat-eating spurred the trajectory of human evolution: that's a plain fact. But it's a fact that does not determine our future.

If anything, it's these highly developed brains of ours that enable us uniquely to look at the world with fresh understanding of and heightened empathy for other sentient beings. All animals—how they live naturally and how we force them to live and die when we make them into food animals—deserve our full attention when we decide who to eat.

Acknowledgments

For talking with or writing me about their work with or perspectives on animals, thank you to Robert Nathan Allen, Jonathan Balcombe, Giacomo Bernadi, Jean Boal, Susie Coston, Katherine Harmon Courage, Katie Cox, Evan Culbertson, Jen Draiss, Beth Firchau, Lorraine Lewandrowski, Abby Alison McClain, Susan Riechert, Carl Safina, Paul Shapiro, Sunny Shacher, Alisha Tomlinson, Brad Weiss, and Judy Woods.

For contributing their wonderful photographs, thank you to Jen Draiss, Charles Hogg, Norman Fashing, Tianne Strombeck, and Ezra Weiss.

For conversations that have forever changed the way I view animals, thank you to Alka Chandna, Jen Draiss, Bruce Friedrich, Justin Goodman, Charles Hogg, Lori Marino, and Joanne Tanner. To these individuals and to others who work tirelessly in animal sanctuaries or as part of rescue groups or animal activist organizations, or who care compassionately for animals in other ways, my infinite respect.

Gratitude and good memories to Charles Hogg, Sarah Elizabeth Hogg, Charles Ernest, Joanne Tanner, and Stephen Wood for accompanying me in the field on animal explorations.

Michael Lemonick of *Scientific American* asked me a key question just in the nick of time. Thank you.

For saying "no" when it mattered and "yes" when it mattered more, thank you to Jill Kneerim, whose literary-agent eye is as sharp as her heart is kind.

With each year I appreciate even more profoundly my good fortune in working closely with Christie Henry and Levi Stahl at the University of Chicago Press, whose excellence in publishing is matched by their warmth, kindness, and humor. Also at the Press I thank Joel Score for considerably improving this book page by page, and Amy Krynak and Gina Wadas for making every interaction a pleasure.

The fact that I completed this book during some challenging months and am now cancer-free at its publication means that I owe thanks to those who, in 2013 and 2014, saved my life, literally and metaphorically. Oncology professionals Dr. William Irvin and Dr. Magi Khalil, and all the chemotherapy and radiation nurses (especially Sherry) and technicians at Peninsula Cancer Institute in Gloucester, Virginia, are the best. My cancer team, as I reckon it, includes also the friends and family who always made time for me— Sally DiSpirito, Heather MacDonald, Toni Deetz Rock, Ginny and Stuart Shanker, Carolyn Treyz and Mary Voigt, and those who one way or another never left my side: Marsha Autilio, Karen Flowe, Ron Flowe, Danielle Moretti-Langholtz, Linda Mundy, Sarah Hogg, Joanne Tanner, and Stephen Wood. To Pilar and Jonah, the closest of my cherished cat companions, who stayed so attuned and provided comfort during that period, I will miss you always.

To adequately thank Charles Hogg, who, with hard labor and easy love, made every single day better is impossible, but I look forward to trying, way into the future.

To Charlie and Sarah, my thanks and my love in abundance as we continue our adventures!

References

Sources are listed roughly in order of their mention in the text.

PREFACE

Safina, Carl. *Beyond Words: What Animals Think and Feel*. New York: Henry Holt, 2015. Epigraph, p. 29; quoted definitions, p. 21 (except definition of emotion, which came via personal communication with Safina, August 16, 2015).

Herzog, Hal. *Some We Love, Some We Hate, Some We Eat: Why It's So Hard to Think Straight about Animals*. New York: Harper, 2010. Quoted material, p. 265.

Pollan, Michael. *The Omnivore's Dilemma: A Natural History of Four Meals*. New York: Penguin, 2006. Quoted material, p. 10.

United Nations Environmental Program. 2010. *Assessing the Environmental Impacts of Consumption and Production: Priority Products and Materials*. A Report of the Working Group on the Environmental Impacts of Products and Materials to the International Panel for Sustainable Resource Management (E. Hertwich, E. van der Voet, S. Suh A. Tukker, M. Huijbregts, P. Kazmierczyk, M. Lenzen, J. McNeely, Y. Moriguchi). http://www.greeningtheblue.org/sites/default/files/Assessing%20the%20environmental%20impacts%20of%20consumption%20and%20production.pdf

US dietary guidelines: O'Connor, Anahad. "Nutrition Panel Calls for Less Sugar and Eases Cholesterol and Fat Restrictions." *New York Times*, February 19, 2015. http://well.blogs.nytimes.com/2015/02/19/nutrition-panel-calls-for-less-sugar-and-eases-cholesterol-and-fat-restrictions/

Pollan's recommendation "Eat food. Not too much. Mostly plants," in "Unhappy Meals." *New York Times Magazine*, January 28, 2007. http://www.nytimes.com/2007/01/28/magazine/28nutritionism.t.html

Morell, Virgina. *Animal Wise: The Thoughts and Emotions of Our Fellow Creatures.* New York: Crown Publishing, 2013.

CHAPTER 1

Jardin, Xeni. "This Ohio Cricket Farm Is First in US to Raise 'Chirps' for Human Consumption." http://boingboing.net/2014/05/23/this-ohio-cricket-farm-is-firs.html

FDA statistics: Goodyear, Dana. *Anything That Moves: Renegade Chefs, Fearless Eaters, and the Making of a New American Food Culture.* New York: Riverhead, 2013. Pp. 59–60.

North Carolina bug survey: Brill, Nancy L. "The Bugs in Our Homes." *New York Times*, March 20, 2014.

Raubenheimer, David, and Jessica M. Rothman. "Nutritional Ecology of Entomophagy in Humans and Other Primates." *Annual Review of Entomology* 58 (2013): 141–60. Quoted material, pp. 143, 147

VIDEO Bug Nomster, "Eating Giant Water Bugs." http://www.youtube.com/watch?v=xCTiNSXmLXQ

Entomophagy Wiki. http://entomophagy.wikia.com/wiki/Entomophagy_Wiki

Quenioux and *escamoles*: Goodyear, *Anything that Moves*, p. 66

Quenioux and *escamoles*: Snyder, Garrett. "Laurent Quenioux Pops Up at Good Girl Dinette with Escamoles." *LA Weekly*, April 27, 2012. http://www.laweekly.com/squidink/2012/04/27/laurent-quenioux-pops-up-at-good-girl-dinette-with-escamoles

FAO report: van Huis, Arnold, Joost Van Itterbeeck, et al. *Edible Insects: Future Prospects for Food and Feed Security.* FAO Forestry Paper 171. United Nations Food and Agriculture Organization, 2013. http://www.fao.org/docrep/018/i3253e/i3253e.pdf

Boesch on the chimpanzee Besar: Robbins, Martha M., and Christophe Boesch, eds. *Among African Apes.* Berkeley: University of California Press, 2011.

Yasmin Cardozo on insects as toys: Shipman, Matt. "This Is What Science Looks Like at NC State: Yasmin Cardoza," May 12, 2014. https://news.ncsu.edu/2014/05/science-looks-like-yasmin-cardoza/

Paper wasps' face recognition: Tibbetts, Elizabeth A., and Adrian G. Dyer. "Good with Faces." *Scientific American* 309, no. 6 (December 2013).

Fruit fly decision-making: DasGupta, Shamik, Clara Howcroft Ferreira, and Gero Miesenböck. "FoxP Influences the Speed and Accuracy of a Perceptual Decision

in Drosophila." *Science* 344, no. 6186 (May 2014: 901–4. http://www.sciencemag
.org/content/344/6186/901

BBC article on fruit fly research: Jonathan Webb, "Flies Pause While 200 Neurons
Help with Tough Decisions." http://www.bbc.com/news/science-environment
-27518484

Honeybee waggle dance and learning in insects: Dukas, Reuven. "Evolutionary
Biology of Insect Learning." *Annual Review of Entomology* 53 (2008):
145–60.

BBC article on crickets: Bardo, Matt. "Young Cricket Characters Shaped by 'Song.'"
http://www.bbc.co.uk/nature/19248230

DiRienzo, Nicholas, Jonathan N. Pruitt, and Ann V. Hedrick. "Juvenile Exposure to
Acoustic Sexual Signals from Conspecifics Alters Growth Trajectory and an adult
Personality Trait." *Animal Behaviour* 84 (2012): 861–68. On crickets.

Martin, Daniella. *Edible: An Adventure into the World of Eating Insects and the Last
Great Hope to Save the Planet.* Boston: New Harvest, 2014. Pp. 220 (tarantulas),
206 (crickets).

Limits of tarantula cognition: Marshall, Samuel D. "Home Is Where the Hole Is."
Forum (American Tarantula Society) 6, no. 1 (1997). http://atshq.org/articles/
homehole.html

Interview with Samuel D. Marshall: Balog, James, and Sy Montgomery. "Stalking Spiders." *Discover Magazine*, February 2004. http://discovermagazine.com/2004/
feb/stalking-spiders

Riechert, Susan E., and Thomas C. Jones. "Phenotypic Variation in the Social
Behavior of the Spider *Anelosimus studiosus* along a Latitudinal Gradient." *Animal
Behaviour* 75 (2008): 1893–1902. Quoted material, p. 1898.

AAAS on Pruitt research on spider temperament: Maxmen, Amy. "For Spiders, It's
Cruel to Be Kind," *Science Now*, May 9, 2013. http://news.sciencemag.org/plants
-animals/2013/05/spiders-its-cruel-be-kind

Eating tarantula in Cambodia: Martin, *Edible*, p. 154.

Jandt, Jennifer J., Sarah Bengston, Noa Pinter-Wollman, Jonathan N. Pruitt, Nigel E.
Raine, Anna Dornhaus, and Andrew Sih. "Behavioural Syndromes and Social
Insects: Personality at Multiple Levels." *Biological Reviews* 89, no. 1 (2014): 48–67.
http://www.ncbi.nlm.nih.gov/pubmed/23672739

Interview with Robert Nathan Allen: King, Barbara J. "The Joys and Ethics of Insect
Eating." NPR (blog), April 3, 2014. http://www.npr.org/blogs/13.7/2014/04/
03/297853835/the-joys-and-ethics-of-insect-eating

Deroy, Ophelia. "Eat Insects for Fun, Not to Help the Environment." *Nature* 521
(2014): 395.

Berry, Wendell. "In Distrust of Movements." *Orion*, Autumn 2001.

Sacks, Oliver. "The Mental Life of Plants and Worms, Among Others." *New York Review of Books*, April 24, 2014. http://www.nybooks.com/articles/archives/2014/apr/24/mental-life-plants-and-worms-among-others

Stone, Glen, and Jon Doyle. *The Awareness*. 2014. New York: Stone Press. Quoted material, p. 149.

CHAPTER 2

Finn, J. K., T. Tregenza, and M. D. Norman. "Defensive Tool Use in a Coconut-Carrying Octopus." *Current Biology* 19, no. 23 (2009): R1069–70.

VIDEO Museum Victoria, "Coconut-Carrying Octopus." https://www.youtube.com/watch?v=1DoWdHOtlrk

VIDEO National Geographic, "Eating Live Octopus." http://video.nationalgeographic.com/video/skorea-liveoctopus-pp

Johnstone, Michael. "Sannakji: Is Eating Live Octopus Cruel." *Asian Persuasion* (blog), May 22, 2012. http://theasianpersuasion.org/articles-about-korea/korean-food/sannakji

Courage, Katherine Harmon. *Octopus! The Most Mysterious Creature in the Sea*. New York: Current Books, 2013. Quoted material, pp. 118, 150, 151.

"Don't shy away from the eyes": "How to Eat Octopus." *eHow*. http://www.ehow.com/how_2121658_eat-octopus.html

VIDEO "Luiz Antonio—Why He Doesn't Want to Eat Octopus." https://www.youtube.com/watch?v=SrUo3da2arE

Octopus in Greece: "Just Hangin' Around 'Til Dinnertime." *My Greece Travel Blog*. http://mygreecetravelblog.com/2011/09/24/just-hanging-around-til-dinnertime/

Octopus Garden store: Wharton, Rachel. "Octopus Garden Prepares for Feast of Seven Fishes." *New York Times*, December 22, 2013. http://www.nytimes.com/2013/12/22/nyregion/octopus-garden-prepares-for-feast-of-seven-fishes.html

Mather, Jennifer A., Roland C. Anderson, and James B. Wood. *Octopus: The Ocean's Intelligent Vertebrate*. Portland, OR: Timber Press, 2010.

VIDEO Octopus squeezing through small opening: National Geographic. "Octopus Escape." http://www.youtube.com/watch?v=SCAIedFgdYo

"How Smart Is an Octopus?" *NOVA scienceNOW*. Roger Hanlon's camouflage video starts at around 3:50; cuttlefish experiment follows. http://video.pbs.org/video/1778564635/

Olive the octopus: Mather, Anderson, and Wood, *Octopus*, p. 33.

Gloomy octopus social signaling: Scheel, David, Peter Godfrey-Smith, and Matthew Lawrence. "Signal Use by Octopuses in Agonistic Interactions." *Current Biology* 26 (2016): 377–82. Quoted material, p. 377.

Octopus mating surprise: King, Barbara. "Attempting Sex, an Octopus Gets a Surprise." NPR (blog), November 16, 2014. Includes Huffard's video clip. http://www.npr.org/blogs/13.7/2014/11/16/364509158/attempting-sex-an-octopus-gets-a-surprise

Octopus cannibalism: Courage, Katherine Harmon. "First Common Octopus Cannibalism Filmed in the Wild." *Scientific American* blog, September 30, 2014. http://blogs.scientificamerican.com/octopus-chronicles/2014/09/30/first-common-octopus-cannibalism-filmed-in-the-wild/

Planning by rock-carrying octopus: Mather, Anderson, and Wood, *Octopus*, p. 124.

Truman: Montgomery, Sy. "Deep Intellect: Inside the Mind of the Octopus." *Orion Magazine*, November/December 2011.

Fiorito, Graziano, and Pietro Scotto. 1992. "Observational Learning in *Octopus vulgaris.*" *Science* 256 (1992): 545–47.

Seattle octopuses, octopus personality: Mather, Anderson, and Wood, *Octopus*, p. 113.

Blaszczak-Boxe, Agata. "How to Anesthetize an Octopus." *Science*, November 14, 2014. http://news.sciencemag.org/plants-animals/2014/11/video-how-anesthetize-octopus

Cambridge Declaration on Consciousness. http://fcmconference.org/img/CambridgeDeclarationOnConsciousness.pdf

Alupay, Jean S., Stavros P. Hadjisolomou, and Robyn J. Crook. "Arm Injury Produces Long-Term Behavioral and Neural Hypersensitivity in Octopus." *Neuroscience Letters* 558 (2014): 137–42. Quoted material, pp. 138, 139.

Boal and Beigel impoverished versus enriched experiment: Courage, *Octopus!*, pp. 125–26.

Virginia Aquarium: King, Barbara. "Viewing Octopus Choreography in Captivity." NPR (blog), May 28, 2015. http://www.npr.org/sections/13.7/2015/05/28/410209112/viewing-octopus-choreography-in-captivity

Montgomery, Sy. *The Soul of an Octopus: A Surprising Exploration into the Wonder of Consciousness.* New York: Simon and Schuster, 2015. Quoted material, pp. 241, 55–56, 114, 166, 221.

My review of Montgomery's book: King, Barbara. "The Watery World of Cephalopod Intelligence." *Times Literary Supplement*, June 17, 2015. http://www.staging-the-tls.co.uk/tls/public/article1569549.ece

VIDEO "Red Wings Fans Throw Octopus onto Ice, Get Thrown in Jail." *Huffington Post*, May 25, 2011. http://www.huffingtonpost.com/2010/04/26/red-wings-fans-throw-octo_n_552035.html

"Detroit Red Wings: Legend of the Octopus." http://redwings.nhl.com/club/page.htm?id=43781

Farmed octopus: Jensen, Chelsea. "Kanaloa Octopus Farm Looking to Rear Cephalopods Sustainably." *Hawaii Tribune-Herald*, December 29, 2015. http://hawaiitribune-herald.com/news/local-news/kanaloa-octopus-farm-looking-rear-cephalopods-sustainably

CHAPTER 3

Vail, Alexander L., Andrea Manica, and Bshary Redouan. "Referential Gestures in Fish Collaborative Hunting." *Nature Communications*, April 23, 2013.

Brown, Culum. "Fish Intelligence, Sentience and Ethics." *Animal Cognition* online, June 19, 2014.

Bshary, Redouan, and Manuela Würth. "Cleaner Fish *Labroides dimidiatus* Manipulate Client Reef Fish by Providing Tactile Stimulation." *Proceedings of the Royal London Society B* 268 (2001): 1495–1501. Quoted material, p. 1495.

Bernardi, Giacomo. "The Use of Tools by Wrasses (Labridae)." *Coral Reef* 31 (2012): 39.

VIDEO "The Use of Tools by Wrasses Labridae," https://www.youtube.com/watch?v=awHj5EiiXIg

Bernardi interview: Stephens, Tim. "Video Shows Tool Use by a Fish." *University of California Santa Cruz Newscenter.* http://news.ucsc.edu/2011/09/fish-tool-use.html

Bernardi quotes: personal communication (email), January 21, 2015.

World Wildlife Fund. "Humpback Wrasse." http://wwf.panda.org/what_we_do/endangered_species/humphead_wrasse/

VIDEO "Wally the Humphead Maori Wrasse," https://www.youtube.com/watch?v=sGNNBE659Ps

Diving and spearfishing discussion thread: "Eating Wrasse." *Deeper Blue.* https://forums.deeperblue.com/threads/eating-wrasse.101276/

World Bank report: *Fish to 2030: Prospects for Fisheries and Aquaculture.* World Bank Report no. 83177-GLB, December 2013. http://www-wds.worldbank.org/external/default/WDSContentServer/WDSP/IB/2014/01/31/000461832_2014 0131135525/Rendered/PDF/831770WP0P11260ES003000Fishto002030.pdf

Mercury levels: Carl H. Lamborg, et al. "A Global Ocean Inventory of Anthropogenic Mercury Based on Water Column Measurements." *Nature* 512 (2014): 65–68, 2914.

Mercury in fish: George Mateljan Foundation. "Should I Be Concerned about Mercury in Fish and What Fish Are Safe to Eat?" http://www.whfoods.com/genpage.php?tname=george&dbid=103

Florida Bay fish warning: Frommer's. "Everglades National Park: Planning a Trip." Subhead: "Would You Like Some More Mercury with Your Bass?" http://www.frommers.com/destinations/everglades-national-park/656967

Norway salmon production: Lien, Marianne Elisabeth. *Becoming Salmon: Aquaculture and the Domestication of a Fish*. Berkeley: University of California Press, 2015.

California salmon: Richtel, Matt. "To Save Its Salmon, California Calls in the Fish Matchmaker." *New York Times*, January 15, 2016. http://www.nytimes.com/2016/01/19/science/new-tactics-to-save-californias-decimated-salmon-population.html

Salmon migration distance: National Oceanic and Atmospheric Administration. http://www.nefsc.noaa.gov/faq/fishfaq2d.html

Coates, Peter. *Salmon*. London: Reaktion Books, 2006.

World Wildlife Fund. "Farmed Salmon: Overview." http://www.worldwildlife.org/industries/farmed-salmon

Lymbery, Philip, with Isabel Oakeshott. *Farmageddon: The True Cost of Cheap Meat*. London: Bloomsbury, 2014. Quoted material, p. 84.

Shubin, Neil. *Your Inner Fish: A Journey into the 3.5-Billion-Year History of the Human Body*. New York: Pantheon, 2008.

Review of *Your Inner Fish*: King, Barbara. "The Missing Link." *Washington Post*, February 17, 2008. http://www.washingtonpost.com/wp-dyn/content/article/2008/02/14/AR2008021403111.html

Shouting minnows: Holt, Daniel E., and Carol E. Johnston. "Evidence of the Lombard Effect in Fish." *Behavioral Ecology* (2014). http://beheco.oxfordjournals.org/content/early/2014/04/10/beheco.aru028.abstract?sid=85240ac5-ff60-448f-8bb5-57cb37997dc0

Antarctic fish: Fox, Douglas. "Discovery: Fish Live beneath Antarctica." *Scientific American*, January 21, 2015. http://www.scientificamerican.com/article/discovery-fish-live-beneath-antarctica/

Godin, J.-G. J. "Fish Social Learning." In *Encyclopedia of Animal Behavior*, edited by M. D. Breed and J. Moore, 1:725–29. Oxford: Academic Press, 2010. Quoted material, p. 726.

VIDEO "Orcas Cooperate to Catch Fish," http://www.animalplanet.com/tv-shows/animal-planet-presents/videos/the-ultimate-guide-to-dolphins-orcas-cooperate-to-catch-fish/

VIDEO "Sardine Tanks at Monterey Bay Aquarium," https://www.youtube.com/watch?v=cwDREqFJwPc

Fish schooling: Marras, Stefano, et al. "Fish Swimming in Schools Save Energy Regardless of Their Spatial Position." *Behavioral Ecology and Sociobology* 69 (2015): 219–26.

Guppy personality: Budaev, Sergey V. "'Personality' in the Guppy (*Poecilia reticulata*): A Correlational Study of Exploratory Behavior and Social Tendency." *Journal of Comparative Psychology* 111, no. 4 (1997): 399–411.

Rainbow fish personality: Brown, Culum, and Anne-Laurence Bibost. "Laterality Is Linked to Personality in the Black-Lined Rainbowfish, *Melanotaenia nigrans*." *Behavioral Ecolology and Sociobiology* 68 (2014): 999–1005.

Balcombe, Jonathan. 2016. *What a Fish Knows: The Inner Lives of Our Underwater Cousins*. Scientific American/Farrar, Straus and Giroux.

VIDEO "Man Playing with Fish," http://www.dailymotion.com/video/x2eibc9_man -playing-with-fish_animals

Burghardt, Gordon. "Play in Fishes, Frogs, and Reptiles." *Current Biology* 25, no. 1 (2015): R9–R10.

Lymbery, *Farmageddon*. Quoted material, p. 86.

Key, Brian. "Why Fish Do Not Feel Pain." *Animal Sentience* 2016.003. http:// animalstudiesrepository.org/cgi/viewcontent.cgi?article=1011&context= animsent. Responses from Jonathan Balcombe ("Cognitive Evidence of Fish Sentience," http://animalstudiesrepository.org/cgi/viewcontent.cgi?article=1059 &context=animsent), Culum Brown ("Comparative Evolutionary Approach to Pain Perception in Fishes," http://animalstudiesrepository.org/cgi/viewcontent .cgi?article=1029&context=animsent), Gordon Burghardt ("Mediating Claims through Critical Anthropomorphism," http://animalstudiesrepository.org/ cgi/viewcontent.cgi?article=1063&context=animsent), and Jennifer Mather ("An Invertebrate Perspective on Pain," http://animalstudiesrepository.org/cgi/ viewcontent.cgi?article=1046&context=animsent)

Almadraba tuna fishing: Minder, Raphael. "Spanish Tuna Fishing Melds to Japan's Taste, Reshaping a 3,000-Year-Old Technique." *New York Times*, June 6, 2015. http://www.nytimes.com/2015/06/07/world/europe/spanish-tuna-fishing -melds-to-japans-taste-endangering-a-3000-year-old-technique.html

Greenberg, Paul. "Three Simple Rules for Eating Seafood." *New York Times*, June 13, 2015. http://www.nytimes.com/2015/06/14/opinion/three-simple-rules-for -eating-seafood.html?_r=0

Safina Center. "Sustainable Seafood Program." http://safinacenter.org/programs/ sustainable-seafood-program/

CHAPTER 4

VIDEO "Mr. Joy, Therapy Chicken, Visits the Nursing Home," https://www.youtube .com/watch?v=qZ3T_El63mY

"My Life as a Turkey." *Nature* (PBS series), 2011. http://www.pbs.org/wnet/nature/ my-life-as-a-turkey-full-episode/7378/

Potts, Annie. *Chicken*. London: Reaktion Books, 2012.

"Avian Flu Confirmed in Nebraska." *New York Times*, May 12, 2015. http://www.nytimes .com/2015/05/13/business/avian-flu-virus-confirmed-in-nebraska.html?_r=0

Nicol, Christine J., and Stuart J. Pope. "The Maternal Feeding Display of Domestic Hens Is Sensitive to Perceived Chick Error." *Animal Behaviour* 52 (1996): 767–74.

Edgar, J. L., E. S. Paul, and C. J. Nicol. "Protective Mother Hens: Cognitive Influences on the Avian Maternal Response." *Animal Behaviour* 86 (2013): 223–29. Quoted material, p. 228.

Mary and Notorious Boy, Violet and Chickweed: Hatkoff, Amy. *The Inner World of Farm Animals*. New York: Stewart, Tabori & Chang, 2009. Pp. 26, 31.

Chase, Ellen. "What a Blind Chicken Can Teach Us about Humanity." *New York Times*, November 8, 2013: http://kristof.blogs.nytimes.com/2013/11/08/what-a-blind-chicken-can-teach-us-about-humanity/?_r=0

Potts, *Chicken*, p. 48.

King, Barbara J. *How Animals Grieve*. Chicago: University of Chicago Press, 2013.

Mike the Headless Chicken website: http://www.miketheheadlesschicken.org

VIDEO "Mike the Headless Chicken," https://www.youtube.com/watch?v=LqDjRCHyjTY

Rogers, Lesley J., Paolo Zucca, and Giorgio Vallortigara. "Advantages of Having a Lateralized Brain." *Proceedings of the Royal Society of London B (Suppl.)* 271 (2004): S420–22.

Rogers, Lesley J. "Development and Function of Lateralization in the Avian Brain." *Brain Research Bulletin* 76 (2008): 235–44.

Avian Brain Nomenclature Consortium. "Avian Brains and a New Understanding of Vertebrate Brain Evolution." *Nature Reviews Neuroscience* 6 (2005): 151–59. http://www.ncbi.nlm.nih.gov/pmc/articles/PMC2507884/

US chicken consumption: Spiegel, Alison. "Chicken More Popular Than Beef in U.S. for First Time in 100 Years." *Huffington Post*, January 2, 2014. http://www.huffingtonpost.com/2014/01/02/chicken-vs-beef_n_4525366.html

"Julia Child's Kitchen at the Smithsonian." http://amhistory.si.edu/juliachild/flash_home.asp

Julia Child's tonalities: Jacobs, Laura. "Our Lady of the Kitchen." *Vanity Fair*, August 2009. Quoted material, p. 131. http://www.vanityfair.com/culture/2009/08/julia-child200908

VIDEO "Julia Child, *The French Chef*—To Roast a Chicken," https://www.youtube.com/watch?v=fRZxaUuFA1Y

Diana Henry's chicken cookbook reviewed: Rosenstrach, Jenny. "Cooking." *New York Times Book Review*, May 31, 2005, p. 24. http://www.nytimes.com/2015/05/31/books/review/cooking.html

Nonboring recipe: Tranell, Kim. "An Easy Chicken Recipe That Won't Bore You to Death." *Men's Fitness*. http://www.mensfitness.com/nutrition/what-to-eat/an-easy-chicken-recipe-that-wont-bore-you-to-death

"Americans to Eat 1.25 Billion Chicken Wings for Super Bowl." National Chicken Council, January 22, 2015. http://www.nationalchickencouncil.org/americans-eat-1-25-billion-chicken-wings-super-bowl-2/

Harris, Jenn. "First Look: Chocolate Fried Chicken, Bacon Biscuits and More at Chocochicken."*Los Angeles Times*, May 23, 2014. http://www.latimes.com/food/dailydish/la-dd-first-look-chocochicken-chocolate-fried-chicken-20140523-story.html

Live-bird pie: Lee, Paula Young. *Game: A Global History*. London: Reaktion Books, 2013. P. 93.

Ortolan: Wallop, Harry. "Why French Chefs Want Us to Eat This Bird—Head, Bones, Beak and All." *Independent*, September 18, 2014. http://www.telegraph.co.uk/foodanddrink/11102100/Why-French-chefs-want-us-to-eat-this-bird-head-bones-beak-and-all.html

Balut: Goodyear, Dana. *Anything That Moves: Renegade Chefs, Fearless Eaters, and the Making of a New American Food Culture*. New York: Riverhead Books, 2013. Quoted material, p. 186.

UK chickens: "Food Poisoning Bug 'Found in 73% of Shop-Bought Chickens.'" BBC, May 28, 2015. http://www.bbc.com/news/uk-32911228

US chickens: "Dangerous Contaminated Chickens: 97% of the Breasts We Tested . . ." *Consumer Reports*, January 2014. http://www.consumerreports.org/cro/magazine/2014/02/the-high-cost-of-cheap-chicken/index.htm

Potts, *Chicken*. Quoted material, pp. 159, 139.

Kristof, Nicholas. "To Kill a Chicken." *New York Times*, March 14, 2015. http://www.nytimes.com/2015/03/15/opinion/sunday/nicholas-kristof-to-kill-a-chicken.html?_r=0

Barber, Dan. *The Third Plate: Field Notes on the Future of Food*. New York: Penguin, 2014. Quoted material, pp. 158, 289.

McWilliams, James. "Why Free-Range Meat Isn't Much Better Than Factory-Farmed." *Atlantic*: http://www.theatlantic.com/health/archive/2010/12/why-free-range-meat-isnt-much-better-than-factory-farmed/67569/

Interview with Alka Chandna: King, Barbara. "Does Being Vegan Really Help Animals." NPR, March 12, 2015. http://www.npr.org/sections/13.7/2015/03/12/392479865/does-being-vegan-really-help-animals

Safran Foer, Jonathan. *Eating Animals*. New York: Back Bay Books, 2009. Quoted material, pp. 66–67.

United Poultry Concerns. "International Respect for Chickens Day." http://www.upc-online.org/respect/

Krishnan, Deepna. "Ugandan Women Entrepreneurs: Chicken Farming as the Next Revolution." *Women's International Perspective*, July 2, 2010. http://thewip.net/

2010/07/02/ugandan-women-entrepreneurs-chicken-farming-as-the-next
-revolution/

Indigenous vegetables in Kenya: Cernansky, Rachel. "The Rise of Africa's Super Vegetables." *Nature*, June 9, 2015. http://www.nature.com/news/the-rise-of-africa-s
-super-vegetables-1.17712

CHAPTER 5

Spike in goats as pets: Hofmann, Michelle. "Forget Potbellied Pigs—Raising Goats Is
All the Rage." *Los Angeles Times*, July 25, 2015. http://www.latimes.com/home/
la-hm-hobby-goats-20150725-story.html

Callner quote, Goat Simulator: Gummer, Chase, and Sven Grundberg. "The World
of Internet Memes Embraces the Year of the Goat." *Wall Street Journal*, January 15,
2015. http://www.wsj.com/articles/the-world-of-internet-memes-embraces-the
-year-of-the-goat-1421277268

VIDEO "2013 Super Bowl XLVII Doritos Goat 4 Sale Commercial," https://www
.youtube.com/watch?v=DoM6IhfY8No

VIDEO "Goats Yelling Like Humans," http://knowyourmeme.com/videos/59495
-animals

Goats in Pliny: *The Natural History of Pliny*. London: George Bell & Sons, 1890. Vol.
2, p. 341. http://books.google.com/books?id=v4BiAAAAMAAJ&pg=PA341

Jesus, Pan, and goats: Brad Kessler, *Goat Song: A Seasonal Life, A Short History of
Herding, and the Art of Making Cheese*. New York: Scribner, 2009. Pp. 29–30.

Baphomet statue: Jenkins, Nash. "Hundreds Gather for Unveiling of Satanic Statue
in Detroit." *Time*, July 27, 2015. http://time.com/3972713/detroit-satanic-statue
-baphomet/

Goats as satanic: Alford, Henry. "How I Learned to Love Goat Meat." *New York
Times*, March 31, 2009. http://www.nytimes.com/2009/04/01/dining/01goat
.html?pagewanted=all

Heavy-metal goats: "A Condensed History of Goat Worship through the Ages." http://
www.invisibleoranges.com/2011/11/a-condensed-history-of-goat-worship/

Weinstein, Bruce, and Mark Scarbrough. "Goat Meat, the Final Frontier." *Washington
Post*, April 5, 2011. http://www.washingtonpost.com/lifestyle/food/goat-meat
-the-final-frontier/2011/03/28/AFop2OjC_story.html

Rich, Nathaniel. "Los Angeles: Goat-Stew City, U.S.A." *New York Times Magazine*
October 20, 2013. http://www.nytimes.com/2013/10/20/magazine/los-angeles
-goat-stew-city-usa.html?pagewanted=all&_r=0

Goat cheese and Alice Waters: Severson, Kim. "For American Chèvre, an Era Ends."
New York Times, October 18, 2006. http://www.nytimes.com/2006/10/18/
dining/18chenel.html?pagewanted=all&_r=0

VIDEO "16 Goats in a Tree [in Morocco]," http://youtu.be/oQev3UoGp2M

International Fainting Goat Association website: http://www.faintinggoat.com/

VIDEO National Geographic, "Fainting Goats," https://www.youtube.com/watch?v=f_3Utmj4RPU

VIDEO *The Men Who Stare at Goats* trailer, http://www.youtube.com/watch?v=TXV8iBfMocU

Goats Music and More Festival website: http://www.goatsmusicandmore.com/

NPR. "Buzkashi." http://apps.npr.org/buzkashi/

Animal Place. "Mr. G and Jellybean." http://animalplace.org/?s=jellybean

Harley Farms website: http://harleyfarms.com/

Wilder Ranch State Park website: http://www.parks.ca.gov/?page_id=549

"The Passing of a Prince." Farm Sanctuary (blog). http://blog.farmsanctuary.org/2015/07/rip-prince-goat/

VIDEO "Farewell to Prince Goat, Friend to All at Farm Sanctuary," https://www.youtube.com/watch?v=WWZ9Dhk8R-4

Goat map: USDA Census of Agriculture. "All Goats—Inventory: 2012." http://www.agcensus.usda.gov/Publications/2012/Online_Resources/Ag_Atlas_Maps/Livestock_and_Animals/Livestock,_Poultry_and_Other_Animals/12-M154.php (see other animal maps at http://www.agcensus.usda.gov/Publications/2012/Online_Resources/Ag_Atlas_Maps/Livestock_and_Animals/)

Ingraham, Christopher. "Map: Literally Every Goat in the United States." *Washington Post*, January 12, 2015. http://www.washingtonpost.com/blogs/wonkblog/wp/2015/01/12/map-literally-every-goat-in-the-united-states/

Goat domestication: Zeder, Melinda A., and Brian Hesse. "The Initial Domestication of Goats (*Capra hircus*) in the Zagros Mountains 10,000 Years Ago." *Science* 287 (2000): 2254–57. https://www.researchgate.net/profile/Melinda_Zeder/publication/200033774_The_initial_domestication_of_goats_%28textit Capra_hircus%29_in_the_Zagros_mountains_10000_years_ago/links/54f4dd270cf2eed5d735a55f.pdf

Fruit box: Elodie F. Briefer, Samaah Haque, Luigi Baciadonna, and Alan G. McElligott. "Goats Excel at Learning and Remembering a Highly Novel Cognitive Task." *Frontiers in Zoology* 11 (2014): 20.

Object permanence: Christian Nawroth, Eberhard von Borella, and Jan Langbein. "Object Permanence in the Dwarf Goat (*Capra aegagrus hircus*): Perseveration Errors and the Tracking of Complex Movements of Hidden Objects." *Applied Animal Behavior Science* 167 (2015): 20–26. Quoted material, pp. 25, 24.

"Sally-Anne test." *Wikipedia*. https://en.wikipedia.org/wiki/Sally%E2%80%93Anne_test

Categorization: Meyer, Susann, Gerd Nurnberg, Birger Puppe, and Jan Langbein. "The Cognitive Capabilities of Farm Animals: Categorization Learning in Dwarf Goats (*Capra hircus*)." *Animal Cognition* 15 (2012): 567–76.

Vocal memory: Briefer, Elodie F., Monica Padilla de la Torre, and Alan G. McElligott. "Mother Goats Do Not Forget Their Kids' Calls." *Proceedings of Royal Society B* 279 (2012): 3749–55. Quoted material, p. 3753.

Buttercups Sanctuary for Goats website: http://www.buttercups.org.uk/

Lizzie the goat; boy goats eaten: Kessler, *Goat Song*, pp. 143, 155, 153–54.

Experiment on goat mood: Briefer, Elodie F., and Alan G. McElligott. "Rescued Goats at a Sanctuary Display Positive Mood after Former Neglect." *Applied Animal Behaviour Science* (2013). Quoted material, p. 5.

CHAPTER 6

Mighty Quinn's restaurant review: Wells, Pete. "Big League BBQ Arrives." *New York Times*, March 5, 2013. http://www.nytimes.com/2013/03/06/dining/reviews/restaurant-review-mighty-quinns-barbeque-in-the-east-village.html?ref=dining &_r=1&

"Zen of Beef Ribs." http://amazingribs.com/recipes/beef/zen_of_beef_ribs.html

16 billion burgers: Bittman, Mark. "The True Cost of a Burger." *New York Times*, July 15, 2014. http://www.nytimes.com/2014/07/16/opinion/the-true-cost-of-a-burger.html?_r=0

Cheese consumption: Laskow, Sarah. "We Eat Three Times as Much Cheese Now as We Did in 1970." *Grist*, September 23, 2013. http://grist.org/list/we-eat-three-times-as-much-cheese-now-as-we-did-in-1970/

Milk consumption: Tuttle, Brad. "Got Milk? Increasingly, the Answer Is No." *Time*, September 7, 2012. http://business.time.com/2012/09/07/got-milk-increasingly-the-answer-is-no/

Ice cream consumption: "The Straight Scoop on Ice Cream." http://www.icecream.com/funfacts/funfacts.asp?b=105

Steak-eating challenges: "Largest Steaks in America." *Wikitravel*. http://wikitravel.org/en/USA_Biggest_Steaks

Fears, Danika. " Mesmerizing! Mom Downs 72-Ounce Steak in under 3 Minutes." *Today*, January 10, 2014. http://www.today.com/food/mesmerizing-mom-downs-72-ounce-steak-under-3-minutes-2D11890243

Ozersky, Josh. "The Problem with the American Steakhouse." *Time*, April 11, 2012. http://ideas.time.com/2012/04/11/the-problem-with-the-american-steakhouse/

Bowman, Angela. "Cows Produce Milk? 40% of British Young Adults Unaware." *Drovers*, June 15, 2012. http://www.dairyherd.com/dairy-resources/retail/Cows-produce-milk-50-of-British-teens-unaware-159200065.html

Van der Veer, Judy. *November Grass.* California Legacy Book, 2001 (original 1940).

Van der Veer, Judy. *A Few Happy Ones.* 1st ed. D. Appleton–Century Company, 1943.

Lorraine Lewandrowski interview: Ziehm, Jessica. "20 Questions with 'NYFarmer.'" New York Animal Agriculture Coalition, May 23, 2014. http://www.nyanimalag.org/20-questions-with-nyfarmer/

The Moo Man film: http://trufflepigfilms.com/the-mooman/

Longleys Farm: "Hook & Son." http://www.hookandson.co.uk/TheFarm/index.html

Lymbery, Philip, with Isabel Oakeshott. *Farmageddon: The True Cost of Cheap Meat.* London: Bloomsburg, 2014. Quoted material, pp. 14, 15.

Pollan, Michael. *The Omnivore's Dilemma: A Natural History of Four Meals.* New York: Penguin, 2006. Quoted material, pp. 68, 71.

Bulls and horses at Lascaux: "Lascaux Cave Paintings—an Introduction." http://www.bradshawfoundation.com/lascaux/

Aurochs: Hannah Velten, *Cow.* London: Reaktion Books, 2007. Quoted material, p. 22.

Cows recognize us: Peter Rybarczyk, et al. "Can Cows Discriminate People by Their Faces?" *Applied Animal Behaviour Science* 74 (2001): 175–89.

Gammell, Caroline. "Cows with Names Produce More Milk, Scientists Say." *Telegraph,* January 28, 2009. http://www.telegraph.co.uk/earth/agriculture/farming/4358115/Cows-with-names-produce-more-milk-scientists-say.html

Gaillard, Charlotte, et al. "Social Housing Improves Dairy Calves' Performance in Two Cognitive Tests." *PLoS One,* February 26, 2014. DOI: 10.1371/journal.pone.0090205. http://www.plosone.org/article/info%3Adoi%2F10.1371%2Fjournal.pone.0090205

Daros, Rolnei R., et al. "Separation from the Dam Causes Negative Judgment Bias in Dairy Calves." *PLoS One,* May 21, 2014. DOI: 10.1371/journal.pone.0098429. http://www.plosone.org/article/info%3Adoi%2F10.1371%2Fjournal.pone.0098429

Proctor, Helen S., and Gemma Carter. "Measuring Positive Emotion in Cows: Do Visible Eye Whites Tell Us Anything?" *Physiology & Behavior* 147 (2015): 1–6. Quoted material, p. 6.

Curious cow videos: King, Barbara. "The Cows Did What?" NPR (blog), May 22, 2014. http://www.npr.org/blogs/13.7/2014/05/22/314871620/the-cows-did-what

Chik-Fil-A Cow Appreciation Day: http://www.chick-fil-a.com/Cows/Appreciation-Day

Carbon footprints re cows: Bittman, "True Cost of a Burger."

CHAPTER 7

Croney's symbol-distinguishing pigs: Estabrook, Barry. 2015. *Pig Tales: An Omnivore's Quest for Sustainable Meat.* New York: W.W. Norton, 2015. Cited material, p. 34.

Broom on pigs smarter than kids: Friedrich, Bruce. "New Slant on Chump Chops." May 17, 2003. http://lists.envirolink.org/pipermail/ar-news/2003/000713.html

Broom's mirror experiment: Marino, Lori, and Christina M. Colvin. "Thinking Pigs: A Comparative Review of Cognition, Emotion, and Personality in *Sus domesticus.*" *International Journal of Comparative Psychology* 28 (2015).

Carl Safina on mirrors: *Beyond Words: What Animals Think and Feel.* New York: Henry Holt, 2015. Quoted material, p. 277.

Esther the Wonder Pig website: http://www.estherthewonderpig.com/

Esther: Metcalfe, Luisa. "The Little Piggy Got Massive: Meet Esther, the 48 Stone 'Micro-Pig'!" *Daily Mail*, January 11, 2015. http://www.dailymail.co.uk/femail/article-2905353/Meet-Esther-48-stone-micro-pig-Ten-times-larger-predicted-giant-porker-size-POLAR-BEAR-forced-owners-buy-bigger-house.html

Esther's intelligence: "Some Kind of Wonder-Pig." *All Animals* magazine (Humane Society of the US), September–October 2014. http://www.humanesociety.org/news/magazines/2014/09-10/some-kind-wonder-pig.html#.U-71_JjAm8M.facebook

Comis, Bob. "Esther the Wonder Pig Is Wondrous Indeed—but So Are All Pigs." *Salon*, May 3, 2015. http://www.salon.com/2015/05/03/esther_the_wonder_pig_is_wondrous_indeed_special_but_so_are_all_pigs/

VIDEO National Zoo, "Apps for Apes: Smithsonian Orangutans using iPads for Enrichment," https://www.youtube.com/watch?v=ZsSIKj5ULp4

VIDEO Big Cat Rescue, "Big Cat Halloween—Tigers Lions vs. Pumpkins," https://www.youtube.com/watch?v=F_lBqWM7LXA

Judy Woods, personal communication (telephone call), July 7, 2015.

Pigs Peace Sanctuary website: http://www.pigspeace.org (see the pages "Betsy," http://www.pigspeace.org/stories/betsy.html, and "Isabelle & Ramona," http://www.pigspeace.org/stories/ramona.html)

Martin, Jessica E., Sarah H. Ison, and Emma M. Baxter. "The Influence of Neonatal Environment on Piglet Play Behavior and Post-Weaning Social and Cognitive Development." *Applied Animal Behaviour Science* 163 (2014): 69–79. Quoted material, p. 76.

"Pig Chase" designers' website: http://www.playingwithpigs.nl/

Dove, Laura. "BBQ: A Southern Cultural Icon." http://xroads.virginia.edu/~ma95/dove/bbq.html

Weiss on barbecue: personal communication.

Mizelle, Brett. *Pig.* London: Reaktion Books, 2011. Quoted material, p. 7.

"The 10 Smartest Animals." NBC News, n.d. http://www.nbcnews.com/id/24628983/ns/technology_and_science-science/t/smartest-animals/#.U-ofIBC5KMo

Review of thinking pigs: Marino and Colvin, "Thinking Pigs."

Pigs in China: "Empire of the Pig." *Economist,* December 20, 2014. http://www
.economist.com/news/christmas-specials/21636507-chinas-insatiable-appetite
-pork-symbol-countrys-rise-it-also

97 percent US pigs on factory farms: Estabrook, *Pig Tales,* p. 19.

Lymbery, Philip, with Isabel Oakeshott. *Farmageddon: The True Cost of Cheap Meat.*
London: Bloomsbury, 2014. Quoted material, p. 183.

National Pork Board. "Quick Facts: The Pork Industry at a Glance." http://
porkgateway.org/wp-content/uploads/2015/07/quick-facts-book1.pdf

Feral pigs: Estabrook, *Pig Tales,* p. 46; Mizelle, *Pig,* pp. 179–80.

Squires, Nick. "Italy Fears Growth in Wild Boar Numbers." *Telegraph,* February 5,
2015. http://www.telegraph.co.uk/news/worldnews/europe/italy/11393007/
Italy-fears-growth-in-wild-boar-numbers.html

CDC on brucellosis: "Wild Hog Hunting: Stay Healthy on Your Hunt!" http://www
.cdc.gov/brucellosis/pdf/brucellosis_and_hoghunters.pdf

Weiss, Brad. 2014. Eating Ursula: ethical connections and an authentic taste for real
pork. *Gastronomica* 14, no. 4 (2014): 17–25. Quoted material, pp. 21, 18–19.

Humane Society interview with Esther's owners: "Some Kind of Wonder-Pig." *All
Animals,* September–October 2014.

Livestock Conservancy website: http://www.livestockconservancy.org/

Weiss, Brad. *Real Pigs: Shifting Values in the Field of Pastured Pork.* Durham, NC:
Duke University Press, 2016.

CHAPTER 8

Christophe Boesch on Besar: "Our Cousins in the Forest—or Bushmeat?" In C.
Boesch and M. M. Robbins, *The African Apes: Stories and Photos from the Field.*
Berkeley: University of California Press, 2011. Quoted material, p. 85.

Sorenson, John. *Ape.* London: Reaktion Books, 2009. Quoted material, p. 128.

Jane Goodall Institute. "Bushmeat Crisis." http://www.janegoodall.ca/chimps-issues
-bushmeat-crisis.php

Bi, Sery Gonedele, et al. "Distribution and Conservation Status of Catarrhine
Primates in Cote d'Ivoire (West Africa)." *Folia primatologica* 83 (2012): 11–23.
Quoted material, p. 12.

Boesch, "Our Cousins?," p. 80.

"Illegal Bushmeat Served Up in Parisian Restaurant." *DW* magazine, February 23,
2011. http://www.dw.de/illegal-bushmeat-served-up-in-parisian-restaurant/
a-14870602

Bushmeat in London: Goldhill, Olivia. "Ebola Crisis: Why Is There Bush Meat in
the UK?" *Telegraph,* August 2, 2014. http://www.telegraph.co.uk/news/health/
news/11006343/Ebola-crisis-why-is-there-bush-meat-in-the-UK.html

Van Schaik, Carel P., Signe Preuschoft, and David P. Watts. "Great Ape Social Systems." In *The Evolution of Thought*, edited by Anne P. Russon and David R. Begun, pp. 190–207. Cambridge: Cambridge University Press, 2004.

Taï nut-cracking data: Boesch, Christophe, and Hedwige Boesch-Achermann. *Chimpanzees of the Taï Forest*. Oxford: Oxford University Press, 2000. Quoted material, pp. 207, 208, 215, 245.

Fongoli spear hunters: Pruetz, Jill D., and Paco Bertolani. "Savanna Chimpanzees, *Pan troglodytes verus*, Hunt with Tools." *Current Biology* 17, no. 5 (2007): 412–17.

Dorothy's three tools: Sanz, Crickette, and David Morgan. 2011. "Discovering Chimpanzee Traditions." In *Among African Apes*, edited by Martha M. Robbins and Christophe Boesch, pp. 88–100. Berkeley: University of California Press, 2011. Quoted material, pp. 97–98.

Habitual use of tool sets: Sanz, Crickette M., and David B. Morgan. "The Social Context of Chimpanzee Tool Use." In *Tool Use in Animals: Cognition and Ecology*, edited by Crickette M. Sanz, Josep Call and Christophe Boesch, pp. 161–75. Cambridge: Cambridge University Press, 2013.

Brutus hunting behavior: Boesch and Boesch-Achermann, *Chimpanzees of the Taï Forest*, p. 182.

Animal grief: Barbara J. King *How Animals Grieve*. Chicago: University of Chicago Press, 2013.

Phillip, Abby. "Why West Africans Keep Hunting and Eating Bush Meat despite Ebola Concerns." *Washington Post*, August 5, 2014. Account of Cameroon bush-meat market. http://www.washingtonpost.com/news/morning-mix/wp/2014/08/05/why-west-africans-keep-hunting-and-eating-bush-meat-despite-ebola-concerns/

Limbe Wildlife Centre website: http://www.limbewildlife.org/

Westoll, Andrew. *The Chimps of Fauna Sanctuary*. Houghton Mifflin Harcourt, 2011.

Tom's empathy for suffering chimpanzees: Fauna Foundation. "Tom, 1965–2009." http://www.faunafoundation.org/chimps/chimps-in-remembrance/tom/

AFTERWORD

Lori Gruen, *Entangled Empathy: An Alternative Ethic for Our Relationships with Animals*. New York: Lantern Books, 2015.

Kemmerer, Lisa. 2015. *Eating Earth: Environmental Ethics and Dietary Choice*. Oxford: Oxford University Press. Quoted material from pp. 3, 142.

Rettig, Hillary. 2015. "Compromise Isn't Complicity." *Vegan Strategist* November 6, 2015. http://veganstrategist.org/2015/11/06/compromise-isnt-complicity-four-reasons-vegan-activists-should-welcome-reducetarianism-and-one-big-reason-reducetarians-should-go-vegan/

Murphy, Kate. "Blessed Be My Freshly Slaughtered Dinner." *New York Times*, September 5, 2015. http://www.nytimes.com/2015/09/06/sunday-review/blessed-be-my-freshly-slaughtered-dinner.html?_r=0

Dogs as meat in South Korea: In Defense of Animals. http://www.idausa.org/campaigns/dogs-cats/dogs-and-cats-of-south-korea/

Humane Society International. "Dog Meat Trade." http://www.hsi.org/issues/dog_meat/

Hare, Brian, Michelle Brown, Christina Williamson, and Michael Tomasello. "The Domestication of Social Cognition in Dogs." *Science* 298 (2002): 1634–36.

MacLean, Evan L., and Brian Hare. "Dogs Hijack the Human Bonding Pathway." *Science* 348 (2015): 280–81. Quoted material, pp. 280, 281.

Coppinger, Raymond, and Mark Feinstein. *How Dogs Work*. Chicago: University of Chicago Press, 2015. Quoted material, p. 207.

Udell, cited in Coppinger and Feinstein: Udell, M. A. R., N. R. Dorey, and C. D. L. Wynne. "Wolves Outperform Dogs in Following Human Social Cues." *Animal Behaviour* 76 (2008): 1767–73.

Loughnan, Steve, Brock Bastian, and Nick Haslam. "The Psychology of Eating Animals." *Current Directions in Psychological Science* 23, no. 2 (2014): 104–8. Quoted material, p. 106.

McKenna, Erin. "Eating Apes, Eating Cows." *Pluralist* 10, no. 2 (2015): 133–49.

Zaraska, Marta. *Meathooked: The History and Science of Our 2.5-Million-Year Obsession with Meat*. New York: Basic Books, 2016.

Index

Page numbers in italics indicate figures.